Etiquette FOR DUMMIES® 2ND EDITION

by Sue Fox

WILEY

John Wiley & Sons, Inc.

Etiquette For Dummies®, 2nd Edition

Published by
John Wiley & Sons, Inc.
111 River St.
Hoboken, NJ 07030-5774
www.wiley.com

WILEY

About the Author

Sue Fox has provided etiquette products, group training, and private consultations to business professionals, celebrities, corporations, and educational institutions since 1994 with her company, The Etiquette Survival Group. Prior to that, she was employed in the high-tech industry with ten years of experience in sales and marketing and event planning at Apple Inc.

Sue has traveled extensively, is well-acquainted with various international cultures, and has provided train-the-trainer programs in India, Singapore, Malaysia, Hong Kong, China, Central America, East Africa, and Europe. She has developed teaching curricula and set up many Etiquette Survival Consultants nationally and internationally.

She is a Member of the International Association of Protocol Consultants (IAPC) and has an additional background in image consulting and makeup artistry, with 20 years of fashion-modeling experience in television and print.

Sue is also the author of *Business Etiquette For Dummies*, published by John Wiley & Sons, Inc. She is the Executive Producer of *The Etiquette Survival Kit*, a series of educational videos and DVDs featuring dining and social etiquette and proper table settings for adults and teens.

The Etiquette Survival Group and its affiliates, MCE International in Los Angeles, California and Global Adjustments in Chennai, India, have formed strategic alliances and are currently developing etiquette and diversity products and programs. They are working together to create a better understanding of people in diverse business and social environments by emphasizing the importance of respect, diplomacy, and civility in every aspect of life.

Sue and her businesses have been featured in many national and international publications, including *Woman's Day*, *Vogue*, *Ladies' Home Journal*, *Real Simple*, *American Baby*, *Newsweek*, *Fortune*, *New York Magazine*, *US Weekly*, *People*, *Los Angeles Times*, *New York Times*, *Wall Street Journal*, *New York Post*, *Chicago Tribune*, *Washington Times*, *San Francisco Examiner*, *Boston Globe*, *USA Today*, *Sunday London Times*, *Australian Financial News*, *Folha de S. Paulo*, *Brazilian Daily News*, *Nikkei Business Journal*, *Times of India*, and *The Hindu Businessline*.

Media credits include radio interviews and feature stories on CNBC TV, KRON-TV San Francisco, Knowledge TV, San Francisco Mornings On 2, KOVR Sacramento, ABC World News, ABC News with Sam Donaldson, KQED San Francisco, CNET News.com, and KABC Los Angeles.

Etiquette Survival has offices in Northern and Southern California. Sue is the mother of two grown sons, Stephen and Nathan, and two grandsons, Joseph and Michael Fox.

Dedication

In memory of my parents, Ray and Betty Swanson.

Author's Acknowledgments

Etiquette For Dummies could not have come about without the contribution and participation of many talented and generous people.

First and foremost, I'd like to express my sincere appreciation to the wonderful team at John Wiley & Sons, Inc., especially to my Acquisitions Editor, Tracy Boggier; her guidance and expertise were essential in the preparation of this second revision. My deepest gratitude and thanks to my Project Editor, Georgette Beatty. Georgette's amazing talent, creativity, advice, professionalism, and patience were truly invaluable.

My continued gratitude goes to my Copy Editor, Sarah Westfall, for her editing genius, and special thanks goes to the additional talent at John Wiley & Sons, Illustrator Liz Kurtzman and fabulous cartoonist Rich Tennant, who all helped shape this book. Thank you to my Technical Editor and colleague, Roxanne Steffens, for her expert knowledge and contribution. I would also like to acknowledge Holly McGuire, my first Acquisitions Editor; without you, Holly, I wouldn't have had this opportunity. It has been a privilege to work with all of you.

To my *always gracious* friend and business partner, Linda Cain. My gratitude for your continued support, beautiful spirit, and faith in me is beyond words. And a special thank you for keeping the business afloat when I was unavailable!

My appreciation and gratitude to all my colleagues, clients, students, and The Etiquette Survival Group consultants who offer their encouragement and motivate me to continue on our quest to raise the awareness of treating ourselves and others respectfully.

I acknowledge gratefully the unfailing love and support of *all* my family and friends. To my sons, Stephen and Nathan; my sisters, Shirlee and Sandy; my brother Rick; my daughter-in-law Anne Fox; my niece Kelly Moynahan and her husband, Steve — your witty and clever input was much appreciated. And to my biggest fan, Robert Sibley, thank you for being a positive influence in my life and for always believing in me.

Finally, to my two adorable grandsons, Joseph and Michael, you'll never know the joy you have given me.

May we all strive for a more peaceful and civil society.

Publisher's Acknowledgments

We're proud of this book; please send us your comments through our Dummies online registration form located at www.dummies.com/register/.

Some of the people who helped bring this book to market include the following:

Acquisitions, Editorial, and Media Development

Project Editor: Georgette Beatty

(Previous Edition: Pamela Mourouzis)

Acquisitions Editor: Tracy Boggier

Copy Editor: Sarah Westfall

(Previous Edition: Billie A. Williams)

Technical Editor: Roxanne Steffens

Editorial Manager: Michelle Hacker

Editorial Assistants: Erin Calligan Mooney, Joe Niesen, Leeann Harney

Cover Photo: © Legacy Photography

Cartoons: Rich Tennant
(www.the5thwave.com)

Composition Services

Project Coordinator: Jennifer Theriot

Layout and Graphics: Joyce Haughey, Stephanie D. Jumper, Heather Ryan

Special Art: Elizabeth Kurtzman

Anniversary Logo Design: Richard Pacifico

Proofreaders: Aptara, Todd Lothery

Indexer: Aptara

Publishing and Editorial for Consumer Dummies

> **Kathleen Nebenhaus,** Vice President and Executive Publisher

> **Kristin Ferguson-Wagstaffe,** Product Development Director

> **Ensley Eikenburg,** Associate Publisher, Travel

> **Kelly Regan,** Editorial Director, Travel

Publishing for Technology Dummies

> **Andy Cummings,** Vice President and Publisher

Composition Services

> **Debbie Stailey,** Director of Composition Services

Contents at a Glance

Table of Contents

Introduction

❖❖

*Y*our time will come. When you least expect it, you'll receive an invitation to a banquet where each table setting involves more utensils than you have in your entire silverware drawer at home. Your company's annual holiday party will be designated semiformal, and you won't even have a clean tie. You'll buy exactly four steaks for Sunday dinner with your in-laws, and they'll bring along two cousins you never even knew existed. Life is full of moments when you don't know exactly what to do — but have no fear, a little bit of etiquette can help you through.

Yes, etiquette deals with which fork to use for the salad course and concerns your behavior at cocktail receptions. But etiquette is a much broader issue. Etiquette is your key to surviving every human contact with your sense of humor and your self-esteem intact, and your reputation enhanced. Etiquette works in supermarket checkout lines, at family picnics, at company holiday parties, on the phone, online, and yes, at wedding receptions.

Remember that there's no such thing as a vacation from good manners. Politeness works everywhere, all the time, and is all about taking the lead, making guests feel welcome, taking the time to evaluate the needs and intentions of others, and behaving in a way that ensures a pleasant outcome. At home, your polite behavior helps everyone in your family develop self-esteem. On the job, good manners encourage others to work well with you. As you go about your errands and chores, polite contacts with others earn you pleasant and helpful responses. As Ralph Waldo Emerson wrote, "Your manners are always under examination, and by committees little suspected, awarding or denying you very high prizes when you least expect it."

Unfortunately today, many people are exhibiting less civility toward one another, and children are following suit with teachers and peers in the classroom. The point is that everyone should do his best to set a good example and put others first. And that's a point that you hear again and again in this book. *Etiquette For Dummies,* 2nd Edition, can help you find a way to put others at ease in almost any situation.

About This Book

You certainly can't find a shortage of books loaded with the so-called rules of etiquette. This book contains rules, too, but I approach the subject from the perspective of an ordinary person faced with social situations that are just a bit challenging. If you have time to put up your feet and read this book from cover to cover, you can come away with a working knowledge of etiquette in all its aspects. On the other hand, if you just received an invitation to a party and you aren't sure how to dress or how to behave, you can turn to the appropriate section in this book, find the information you need, and head out to the party with confidence.

Conventions Used in This Book

I include the following conventions to help you navigate this book easily:

- *Italics* point out defined terms and emphasize certain words.
- **Boldface** text indicates the key words in bulleted and numbered lists.
- `Monofont` highlights Web addresses.

When this book was printed, some Web addresses may have needed to break across two lines of text. If that happened, rest assured that I haven't put in any extra characters (such as hyphens) to indicate the break. So, when using one of these Web addresses, just type in exactly what you see in this book, pretending as though the line break doesn't exist.

What You're Not to Read

Feel free to skip sidebars (the shaded gray boxes within chapters). They contain information that's definitely interesting (to me, at least!) but not crucial to understanding the fine points of etiquette.

Foolish Assumptions

As I wrote this book, I made the following assumptions about you, dear reader:

- ✔ You want to build better relationships with your family, friends, co-workers, and other important folks in your life through good etiquette.

- ✔ You seek information on how to behave with courtesy and consideration no matter the situation — whether you're addressing an in-law, answering your cell phone, opening a gift, or attending a special function.

- ✔ You may want to provide guidance to someone in your life who needs help with the finer points of etiquette.

- ✔ You may want to have a competitive advantage in a growing work environment, and good manners just might do the trick.

- ✔ You just want to refresh what you already know or clear up confusions about the complexities of contemporary etiquette — such as the etiquette rules for new technologies.

For whatever reason you're reading this book, remember to always trust your instincts, because your gut feeling can be quite powerful and can help you come out feeling better about yourself and those around you.

How This Book Is Organized

I've organized this book into parts and then chapters by specific topics and situations. You don't need to read any previous section to understand the one that interests you; just plunge in anywhere and get what you need. Following is a description of each part and what you can find in it.

Part 1: Starting Down the Road to Better Etiquette

In this part, I focus on *you!* I explain how to take pride in your own manners, give and receive compliments, and rise above rudeness. I also tell you all about how to keep yourself neatly groomed and how to send the right messages with your body language. And if you need to figure out what you should wear to a semiformal or formal event, or you need to get to the bottom of this business-casual thing, look no further than this part of the book.

Part II: Fostering Well-Mannered Relationships

Etiquette is all about putting others at ease. The result is that you build better relationships, whether it's with the members of your family, your friends, or your co-workers. This part walks you through each type of relationship, giving you advice about making all your relationships better. I also address the particulars of gender relations — an especially tricky area in modern times. Do you hold the door for her or don't you? Do you allow him to pay the tab or not? This part of the book has the answers.

Part III: Converse with Care: Saying Everything Right

Good communication is essential to good relationships, and thus an essential part of etiquette. This part explains how to handle yourself gracefully on paper, on the telephone, online, and in face-to-face conversations. I also include a chapter on business communication and the particular issues associated with communicating in the workplace.

Part IV: That's Entertainment! Meals, Parties, and Gifts

Many etiquette questions come up when you're planning to host a party or dinner. This part provides quite a bit of useful material for uncertain hosts who want to provide a good time for all guests. I also explain how to be a gracious guest who will definitely be invited back and how to both give and receive with the best of manners. You also receive a dose of proper table manners and discover the art of selecting, ordering, and tasting wine!

Part V: Making the Most of Special Situations

Special occasions are times that put many people into a panic, because "normal" behavior may no longer apply. The chapters in this part address those special situations, such as weddings, funerals, baptisms, and bar and bat mitzvahs. I also cover travel, both local and international, as well as the special etiquette that's required when you're interacting with someone who has a physical disability or illness.

Part VI: The Part of Tens

This part contains three quick chapters that give you small, easily digestible bits of information. Here, you can find hints on teaching etiquette to children and tips on tipping.

Icons Used in This Book

Every *For Dummies* book uses icons to help you navigate your way through the text and to point out particularly noteworthy information. Here's what the icons in this book look like and what they tell you:

This icon highlights important information that you need to bear in mind.

The Tip icon indicates etiquette pointers that can help you get through a particular situation with ease.

Pay special attention to this icon that alerts you of areas you can trip up on if you aren't careful.

If you see this icon, you can find out about faux pas to avoid at all costs.

Where to Go from Here

So what now? You may use this book as a reference guide, reading any section that interests you. But if you're new to this etiquette thing, I recommend starting off with the basics in Part I. There, you can get the info you need to set a solid foundation for future good manners. Even if you feel like you have basic manners down pat, a little review never hurt anyone.

If you have a specific situation or event in which you need some etiquette coaching, Parts IV and V offer chapters on a variety of topics. For example, if you've been invited to a wedding and you aren't sure what to wear or what to bring, check out Chapter 18. Or maybe you want to host a dinner party at your home; if so, Chapter 14 is where you want to start.

Part I
Starting Down the Road to Better Etiquette

The 5th Wave   By Rich Tennant

"Oh, quit looking so uncomfortable! It's a pool party! You can't wear a cape and formal wear to a pool party!"

In this part . . .

This part explores the basic questions of why *knowing how* to treat each other and behaving in a polite and considerate manner hasn't gone out of style. I touch on how good manners apply to your life and ways for you to extend courtesy to everyone. You'll be a model of good manners in no time! And, why knowing how to best present yourself can get you started down the road to better etiquette!

Chapter 1

Examining Etiquette Basics

Good manners are all about making people feel comfortable all the time. Believe me, being polite isn't just for high society, formal events, and the boardroom. Good manners are badly needed everywhere every day! This chapter provides an overview of etiquette basics; you discover guidelines on everything from presenting yourself positively to handling special occasions with ease. As you read, grade yourself on how you generally conduct yourself right now, noting where you can improve and bring some style and poise into your behavior. It won't go unnoticed or unrewarded for long.

 People have relaxed some rules of etiquette in this century, but you'll find that the ones you read about in this book will last you for the rest of your life. Being rude or unkind will never be in style. And remember: When in doubt, treat other people as you would want to be treated yourself.

Taking Pride in Your Own Manners

Everyone can greatly benefit by relearning and sometimes revising traditional *good manners* as they apply to their lives. The first order of any study is to examine how it affects you and how you can make a difference. Are you well versed in the ways of etiquette?

People are often confused by the complex combination of traditional etiquette and contemporary values. What once was considered a show of respect may now unintentionally offend. In fact, what many once considered acceptable isn't any longer. So, how do you know which rules apply?

Generally, you should always observe etiquette rules that both value human beings and show courtesy. And you should also behave respectfully to everyone, regardless of gender. Why? Because civility builds character and self-esteem. It creates a serene environment and shows regard for yourself and others. Here are a few common courtesies to start you off:

- Speak softly.
- Reply when someone speaks to you.
- Always say "Please," "Thank you," and "Excuse me."
- Give and receive compliments sincerely.
- Give people space — don't crowd!

For more on how to take pride in your manners, see Chapter 2.

Making Sure to Present Yourself Positively

People may try to avoid passing judgment too quickly, but at first meetings, they inevitably assess others by how they look. First impressions: You only get one chance! Psychologists say that most people form impressions of others in the first four minutes after their initial meeting and that 80 percent of the impression is based on nonverbal signs. In other words, what comes out of your mouth has very little to do with how people judge you. And, after a first impression is made, getting people to change that judgment is very hard.

How you dress, groom yourself, and handle yourself in public is all part of your *packaging*. Like product packaging, you can present yourself to be most appealing. And, you can present yourself differently according to the time and place. For example, your appearance should differ depending on your geographic area — how you dress and act in Yellowstone National Park, as opposed to Midtown Manhattan.

Here are a few important guidelines for an appropriate presentation:

- Being casual doesn't extend to poor grooming — *always* be clean and neat.
- Avoid clothing extremes, revealing clothing, and evening or party wear in the workplace.
- Don't sacrifice comfort for trends or fashion.
- Use good taste or get help figuring out what is tasteful.

You don't need a millionaire's budget to be perceived as confident and self-assured. As important as clothes and makeup are to your image, posture, and how you carry yourself are essential parts of the package. When you stand with a slouch or sit with a slump, you're telling others that you don't feel confident and you'd like to be left alone. On the other hand, when your head is erect, your gaze outward, and your backbone as straight as Mother Nature made possible, you're inviting others to meet with you on equal terms. For more on making a positive impression, see Chapter 3.

Extending Courtesy to Everyone in Your Life

You may feel like you have a lot of rules to follow in order to behave appropriately in all situations. Clearly, one of the most important aspects is getting along with those close to you and with those you interact with on a daily basis. In the following sections, I give you some guidance on being courteous to family, friends, dates, and business colleagues.

Family

Behaving like a polite adult all the time isn't easy, and unfortunately, as time passes, familiarity often leads to shortcuts in considerate communication. However, you can't find a better place to practice good manners than in your own home! Treating your family with respect and exhibiting polite behavior contributes to a peaceful environment and refuge from daily aggravations.

Remember a few of the following tips (for more in-depth advice, check out Chapter 4):

- **Go ahead and say those nice things.** Don't just enjoy a meal; say that you enjoyed it.
- **Be considerate of your better half and children by respecting their privacy.** Don't snoop, knock before you enter a room, and practice being a good listener.
- **Treat your family members as if they were honored guests.** Their responses may surprise you.

Friends and relationships

You have many reasons to figure out good manners and follow the rules of etiquette — especially in personal relationships. Treating others with respect, kindness, and consideration creates meaningful friendships and leads to self-fulfillment. I listed just a few important guidelines here (see Chapter 5 for the full scoop on the art of friendships and relationships):

- Create boundaries and set limits.
- Discover how to communicate clearly to avoid misunderstandings.
- Express delight in other people's accomplishments.
- Don't give advice unless asked.
- Figure out when you need to agree to disagree.
- Never break an appointment with friends in favor of a date.

Business colleagues

In business relationships today, you need to know how to conduct yourself properly in a variety of situations; your ability to respectfully respond to certain individuals and situations can not only put others at ease, but also build your self-confidence. Remember that your behavior is observed and judged daily by employers, clients, and co-workers, and your ability to establish effective working relationships with others can make or break your career.

Regardless of what your job is, you can count on the following do's and don'ts of making a positive impression in the business world:

- ✔ **Never keep people waiting.** If you can't avoid being late, call ahead, and after you arrive, remember to apologize.

- ✔ **Dress appropriately at all times.** When in doubt, always dress conservatively. Look at management for ideas and stay with well-made, tasteful clothes. If your company has a dress code, follow it.

- ✔ **Keep a cheerful, positive attitude.** Don't be a complainer, and always think before you speak. Stay away from gossip, offensive language, or off-color jokes.

Head to Chapter 6 for additional details about etiquette in the workplace.

Saying the Right Thing

Communication is an essential part of being courteous to others — whether you're conversing, writing a letter, talking on the phone, or chatting on the Internet. What you say reflects who you are, so you want your words to build others up, rather than tear them down in any way. And while not everyone is a natural communicator, you can figure out some simple communication tools so you don't come across rude or lacking confidence. In the following sections, I provide you etiquette know-how on various methods of communication.

Polite conversation

A *conversation* is when two or more people discuss different topics, exchange ideas, share information, and give each other an opportunity to contribute. Having a conversation is the best way to find out what other people like, think, and need. It's what people do to get to know one another.

During a chat, always think of the other person. Show your interest by asking questions about her. Asking questions that require more of an answer than yes or no graciously brings the other person into the conversation. For example, instead of asking, "Oh! Is that a new shirt?" you may want to say, "I really like your shirt; it looks great on you. Where did you find it?"

Another objective of polite conversation is to be aware of *how* you say something. The tone of your voice is just as important as what you say. Do your best not to ever use profanity or name call, and try to respond politely and with respect — even if you're angry. The old adage of "don't say anything if you can't say something nice" still applies.

A few additional key elements of a good conversation include the following:

- Good eye contact and body language
- Active listening
- Not interrupting
- Not monopolizing the conversation
- Responding and contributing to the conversation
- Using polite words such as "Please," "Thank you," and "Excuse me"
- Not talking where others can overhear and be put off
- Avoiding gossip

See Chapter 7 for more information on engaging in polite conversation.

Correspondence

Interested in writing a letter? Before you begin, you need a few essentials, such as proper stationery, a writing utensil, envelopes, and stamps. A letter also should have the following proper formatting:

- Address
- Date or dateline
- Salutation
- Main body with headings
- Closing phrase
- Signature

With the formatting down, it's time to write your letter with the right words. The basic rule of etiquette in any circumstance, including written communication, is to have and to show consideration for the other party. If you just stop and think how the other person is likely to receive your communication, you can go a long way in preventing misunderstandings and not giving offense. To find out more about correspondence, see Chapter 8.

The telephone

Hello! The telephone seems to bring out either the best or the worst in people. If someone is looking for an opportunity to be rude and unmannerly, the telephone provides the perfect avenue. On the other hand, you can bring out the very best in the person on the other end of the line by going the extra mile to be courteous. You can also bring out the best in yourself when using the telephone.

A few elements to keep in mind when speaking on the phone or leaving messages are:

- Always adjust your tone to be appropriate to the situation.

- Enunciate clearly, so the person on the other end can understand you.

- Consider whether you're calling at an appropriate or convenient time. Ask the person you've called whether the time is convenient or if they would like you to return the call at another time.

- When leaving messages on others' voice mails, speak clearly, slowly, and briefly and tell the person why you called and when she can call you back.

- Whether or not the person you're calling has your number, show courtesy by leaving it anyway. Say the number and area code at the beginning of your message and again at the end.

Even if the purpose of your call is unpleasant (such as to make a complaint to a store), sounding pleasant can get the conversation off on the right foot and make the recipient of your call more inclined to help you in an equally pleasant manner. Take the opportunity to reinforce your friendships and social and business contacts by exercising your very best manners when using the phone.

For more on using the phone, including cell phones, voice mail, answering machines, caller ID, and teaching telephone etiquette to children, see Chapter 9.

The World Wide Web

My grandfather always said to never put down in writing what you don't want someone else to read. This saying is a great one to remember when you write e-mails and send communications over the Net. Because you're putting your correspondence into the written word, anyone who receives it can copy, edit, change, store, or otherwise manipulate your message. What you send may be printed for future review. So make sure you never appear rude, intrusive, crass, arrogant, uneducated, or plain lazy.

Here are a few general tips for communicating on the Internet:

- ✔ Always use the subject line to state the purpose of your e-mail.
- ✔ Keep sentences short, clear, and to the point.
- ✔ Spell out words and don't use acronyms; otherwise, your reader may not understand what you're saying.
- ✔ Limit subject matters. People like to read short e-mails.
- ✔ Use words that are simple, clear, and concise.
- ✔ Always use a greeting and salutation.

The Internet is a wonderful source of information and, of course, presents a great ability to share information and have fun. Saying that, it can also be a terrible and frightening place especially for children and unaware users. I recommend that parents take control of their children's computers and place controls and security procedures in place.

For more details and guidelines for minding your cyberspace manners, see Chapter 10.

Business communication

Communication is essential in business, just as it is in personal life. Check out Chapter 11 for a crash course on the following essential tasks and more:

- ✔ Making introductions
- ✔ Addressing your staff, colleagues, and boss
- ✔ Communicating successfully at meetings
- ✔ Making the most of special business events
- ✔ Handling phone calls, voice mail, faxes, and e-mails
- ✔ Writing business letters

Will knowing the proper way to handle these challenges really make a difference in your career or help you get ahead? Absolutely!

A Big Deal: Entertaining (and Being Entertained) with Style

Entertaining plays an important role in your life, one that is universal to all types of people in every segment of society. Entertaining can do the following:

✔ Provide you with invaluable moments, the sharing of your time, home, food, and families.

✔ Provide you an avenue through which new relationships and memories are made, ideas are exchanged, and business alliances are formed.

✔ Lift your spirits by rescuing you from the same old routine. You just never know what may transpire! When you take time to enjoy the pleasure of another's company, the possibilities are endless!

In the following sections, I outline the important elements of entertaining and being entertained.

Dining and drinking

Polite dining at the table, whether formal or informal, has been one of the codes of behavior that has always set human beings apart from animals. Human beings may also be "animals," but they think and converse with each other — and this sets people apart from all other creatures. Nowhere else is a person's difference from beasts more evident than in his eating manners and social behavior.

Say the words *dining etiquette* and many people automatically conjure up images of old, stuffy rules of behavior at the dinner table. And long ago, those rigid rules were needed. Formal dining still reflects this level of etiquette, but today, dining has become simplified.

Table manners and dining etiquette are just a means to an end. Knowing how to enjoy the finer things in life — good company, good food, and good conversation — is the backbone of a great dining experience. Knowing proper etiquette simply gives you more confidence in embracing new dining experiences, whether it's dinner at the White House, job interviews over a meal, or brunch at your best friend's home. Dining etiquette today is more important than ever.

Don't eat your food like a vacuum cleaner picking up dust! Take time to talk with those around you and finish when everyone else finishes. Food was meant to be enjoyed, not merely ingested.

Behaving politely at the table, whether informal or not, hasn't disappeared or gone out of style! To find out what to do before dining begins, during the meal, and afterward, see Chapter 12. For details on the wonders of wine, head to Chapter 13.

Throwing a get-together

Being an outstanding host comes naturally for some, but this skill can be learned. What does it mean to be an outstanding host? Simply make sure your guests have a good time. Your guests take subconscious clues from you, so be comfortable. If you're laughing, talking to people, and having a good time, the chances are greater that they will as well.

Here a few specifics for hosting a memorable event:

- ✔ Select a dynamic blend of invitees and work out the seating before your guests arrive.
- ✔ Invitations should be specific and give guests enough details so they know what to expect.
- ✔ After you've decided on a menu, make sure that you know how to prepare everything.
- ✔ Greet your guests at the entrance with a welcoming smile.

A hostess never allows her guests to drink and then drive. If your guests have had too much to drink, call a taxi or take their car keys and put them up for the night. You can all sleep much more soundly knowing everyone is safe.

For more key strategies for successful entertaining, see Chapter 14.

Behaving when you're a guest

Whether you're a houseguest or attending a grand formal evening, your role as a guest is as important as that of the host. To be a well-mannered guest, you need to do more than be well-mannered. Keep the following tips in mind (and head to Chapter 15 to discover everything you need to know about being a gracious guests who always gets invited back):

- ✔ Respond to invitations promptly.

- ✔ Mingle! Introduce yourself to other guests, start a conversation, and be sure to participate.

- ✔ Use your table manners.

- ✔ When you're a houseguest, offer to pitch in with chores and clean up after yourself — never leave your belongings strewn around the house.

- ✔ Always follow up with a thank-you note, card, or letter of appreciation within a few days of the event (the sooner, the better!).

Giving and receiving gifts

One of the great pleasures in life is giving to others. Giving a gift isn't a simple matter of spending as much as you can afford on an item and just handing it over. Stay within your means when selecting a gift, and keep the recipient in mind.

As the recipient, you need to be mindful of the giver, and be sure to express your thanks for whatever you may have been given. Even if the gift isn't exactly what you were hoping for, you can still show great poise by making the giver feel appreciated.

For the basic responsibilities of the giver and the receiver of gifts, as well as certain etiquette rules to presenting, exchanging, returning, or refusing a gift altogether, check out Chapter 16.

Handling Special Situations

Special occasions such as weddings and funerals can put your manners to the test. Even though you encounter these situations less frequently, they often require you to be aware of a different set of etiquette rules. Travel, whether within your own country or in an entirely new culture, poses challenges as well. And interacting with people who have disabilities or illnesses may take you into a new realm of etiquette in which you're unsure of the proper behavior. I address how to handle these situations in the following sections.

Major life events

Celebrating life's big events are often a challenge: They call on you to stop what you're doing and give of yourself to others. Whether you're attending a christening, a funeral, or a graduation, what matters most is that you're there for your friends and family and that you care. For more information to help you make it through life's major events with grace and style — and your composure intact — see Chapter 17.

Engagements and weddings

One of the most important (and possibly most stressful) events in life is planning a wedding. And traditional wedding etiquette has evolved with time, which only adds to the confusion and uncertainty for the happy couple. You may be wondering who pays for what, what kind of a ceremony should you have, how to deal with blended families, and what you need to include on your invitations. You can find the answers to these and other questions on engagements and weddings in Chapter 18.

Above all, don't turn into bridezilla or the groom from the black lagoon. Try to remain gracious and keep other people's feelings in mind as you proceed with your wedding plans. The big day is yours, and the decisions are yours to make, but you don't need to bulldoze anyone in order to get what you want.

Travel near and far

Being a model of good manners means that when you leave home, your manners travel with you. A few key elements for having a safe and successful trip include the following:

- ✔ Select your travel companions with care.
- ✔ Get to know about the place you'll be traveling to beforehand.
- ✔ Dress appropriately.
- ✔ Behave with extra courtesy in a foreign country.
- ✔ Adapt to local customs of eating and drinking.

Make your way to Chapter 19 for full details for traveling anywhere with your manners intact.

Disabilities and illnesses

The misunderstandings, lack of awareness, and thoughtlessness toward a person with a disability, impairment, or serious illness not only creates barriers, but it also causes fear, hurt, and isolation. As with most equalities issues, use of appropriate language and correct use of terms is crucial for respectful and dignified communication. You need to educate yourself (and perhaps your children) and give considerate thought to remove any unnecessary discrimination and avoid misunderstandings.

For more information about interacting with people who have disabilities and illnesses, see Chapter 20.

Chapter 2

Becoming a Model of Good Manners

In This Chapter

▶ Knowing the benefits of practicing thoughtful behavior

▶ Mastering the art of compliments

▶ Handling rudeness

*P*eople constantly ask me questions like, "Is there really any need to know about old-fashioned etiquette?" or, "Does etiquette still matter in today's society?" My answer? Absolutely!

Today's world is fraught with everyday stresses about work, family, children, finances, and even homeland security. People are so entrenched with their own personal concerns and agendas that they tend to ignore others around them. That ignorance is what leads to bad behavior.

President George W. Bush has called the incivility, the lack of manners, and the mean-spiritedness in American schools "a national crisis." Recent surveys show that educators, politicians, and parents agree. Though many people may agree that a problem exists, they aren't asking themselves the important question: How much am I a part of this problem?

Everyone can greatly benefit by re-examining traditional good manners as they apply to contemporary life and the work environment. Taking stock of what really counts is important — like acknowledging someone with a proper introduction or treating family and friends with common respect and consideration.

Good manners are much like a roadmap, providing ways to improve how you feel about yourself and others. Simple skills and techniques of common courtesy that can improve all your relationships and your overall state of happiness can be incorporated into the way you live and work.

Yes, some elements of etiquette deal with which fork to use for the salad course and your behavior at cocktail receptions. But etiquette, in general, is a much broader issue. Being a model of good manners is your key to surviving every human contact with your sense of humor and your self-esteem intact and your reputation enhanced. In this chapter, I offer some guidelines with the hope that you're inspired to think about and practice good manners every waking hour.

Practicing and Benefiting from Thoughtful Behavior

Practice is a word with several meanings. The expression "practice makes perfect" implies that the mere repetition of an action makes it second nature. Saying that a routine is common practice means that it's habitual behavior. Music students know that practicing is a way to sharpen skills and prepare for public performances. Constantly applying good manners in your daily interactions, as I show you how to do in the following sections, rewards you and those around you.

Start by becoming aware! Try to grade yourself on how you generally conduct yourself socially and professionally right now, noting where you can improve. Begin by asking yourself how you feel after the fact. Do you later regret your comments or behavior? Did you overreact or respond in anger? Make a mental note where you can make positive changes. Make a list or keep a journal of the areas you would like to improve. Check it weekly or monthly to see whether you've made progress. This isn't rocket science — improving your conduct just takes a level of awareness and a little (here's that word again) practice!

You can have no such thing as a vacation from good manners or politeness. A well-mannered person behaves nicely toward everyone, all the time.

Building character and self-esteem

Webster's New World College Dictionary defines *civility* as 1) politeness, especially in a merely formal way 2) a civil, or polite, act or utterance.

You direct civility, or courtesy, outwardly to those around you rather than inwardly. In being civil, you make small sacrifices for the good of all and the sake of harmoniously living together on this earth. However, you can find personal benefits when you're respectful of others: a gift of superior character and heightened self-esteem. I cover these benefits in the following sections.

Character

"Character may be manifested in the great moments, but it is made in the small ones." What does this quote from preacher Phillips Brooks mean? The little acts of kindness are what really counts, such as going out of your way to help a friend; remembering to say "Please," "Thank you," and "Excuse me"; being a good listener; smiling often; and responding to other's rudeness with restraint.

Behave as if you care about others as a way of caring about yourself. Your behavior is an indicator of your character. If you work on building your character, your behavior never embarrasses you!

Here are a few specific tips for building character:

- ✔ **Develop thoughtfulness.** Thinking with your head and your heart can help you go a long way in putting other's needs before your own wants and desires. Look for ways you can help others at home or at work.

- ✔ **Watch what you say — and how you say it.** Your choice of words has an enormous impact on the way you interact with others, and try to be aware of your tone of voice when you speak to others.

- ✔ **Celebrate diversity; tolerate and accept differences.** Get to know people who are different than you. Enlighten yourself! Become a considerate human being and encourage your family to follow your lead. You'll be doing everyone a favor.

Self-esteem

The way you feel about yourself impacts the types of choices you make and also in how you treat others. Your self-esteem includes you accomplishments in life, also in the way others see you and how you think of yourself as a person.

Self-esteem develops largely through your experiences with successes and challenges as you grow up. If you've had experiences of being praised, loved unconditionally, trusted, and listened to, then you're likely to have healthy self-esteem.

If, on the other hand, your experiences have been those of being harshly criticized, ridiculed, ignored, abused, or made to feel inadequate, then you're likely to experience low self-esteem.

Fortunately, no matter what your experiences have been until now, you have the opportunity to improve your self-esteem, and the self-esteem of those around you, by applying good etiquette. Skills and tools to raise, or reinforce, your self-esteem include the following:

✔ Give and receive compliments with sincerity and grace. (I cover compliments later in this chapter.)

✔ Practice and use table manners at all times (see Chapter 12 for details).

✔ Always say "Please," "Thank you," and "Excuse Me."

✔ Make time to do things with those that care about you.

✔ Ignore or stay away from people who put you down or treat you badly.

✔ Do things that you enjoy and that you do well.

✔ Focus on and work to develop your special talents.

✔ Set short term and long term goals and reward yourself when you succeed.

✔ Make good choices for yourself, and take responsibility for yourself and your actions.

✔ If you've made a mistake, apologize immediately, and then move on.

✔ Always do what you believe is right.

✔ Write positive traits about yourself in a journal.

✔ List etiquette traits you would like to achieve and maintain.

Using common sense

Etiquette may be intimidating for most — but hey, relax! Common courtesy is nothing more or less than common sense. You can find nothing more common than those little magic words, *please* and *thank you*. Or are they that common? They certainly should be. Simply looking someone in the eye and saying "Thank you" can make all the difference in the world.

If you're feeling a little unsure about yourself in certain situations, just think about how you want others to treat you. If you treat others with dignity and respect, they will do the same. What goes around really does come around.

Manners must be sincere, so practice until it comes naturally and from the heart. Try to bring some consideration, grace, and style back into your life through your personal presence and demeanor. Be perceptive, aware, and mindful — and always use your best judgment. Here are a few basic tips:

✔ When in public, be discreet with your cell phone calls and keep the vibrate mode on. Avoid taking cell phone calls when you're having face-to-face time with other people, such as during meals.

✔ Always check behind you when entering or exiting a door. If someone is behind you, be sure to hold the door open no matter whether the person is a male or female.

✔ Being pushy and speaking loudly in public, especially in a small shop, in line at the post office, or in a restaurant, is unfortunately common nowadays. However, it's not the loudest person who impresses his dinner companions or strangers in public; it's the person with quiet confidence and good manners. Always try to use low, intimate tones, and if you're waiting in a long line, practice patience, don't complain out loud, or make a scene.

Making lasting impressions

Most people have heard the saying, "You only have one chance to make a first impression." Though you may not always admit it, most people do make character judgments within the first few seconds of meeting someone. Appearances and behavior leave a lasting impression about a person's overall abilities and character.

Good manners and thoughtful behavior do matter. They were important years ago at your mother's dinner table and are vital today if you're looking to close the deal or simply leave positive impressions at social gatherings. People are still watching, but the stakes may be higher for you. The judgments others make about you can affect your future.

You need to show that you understand what is appropriate and that you care about the impression you make. Often your behavior can make or break a relationship or a career. Here are a few tips to help you make a good first impression:

✔ **Dress for success.** While the saying may seem cliché, what you wear gives others an idea of who you are. So if you're going to meet a new client at your law firm, don't you dare pull out the sweat pants and flip flops. And remember that personal hygiene is just as important as what you wear. (For more on personal dress and hygiene, head to Chapter 3.)

- ✔ **Be punctual.** Arriving late for a first date makes a bad impression. If you're late, be sure to apologize. If it was your fault, admit it.

- ✔ **Present yourself with confidence.** Stand up straight, smile, shake hands, and make eye contact. By doing so, you come across as someone who has his act together.

- ✔ **Make sure what you say is courteous and positive.** Your words say a lot about who you are. You need to be sure to not use profanities, avoid off-color jokes, and stay away from gossip. Gossip can be entertaining when it passes along positive and interesting information, but is dangerous when it demeans or endangers another person's character.

Empowering yourself through good manners

Another way to think about civility is to associate it with the word *leadership.* When you take the lead in putting people at ease and making every situation pleasant, you exhibit poise. Poise comes from being self-confident.

In today's climate, etiquette and civility are sometimes seen as snobbery. Others view polite behavior as a sign of weakness, and some professionals actually believe that it's impossible to get to the top while being gracious and polite. None of this is true. Knowing how and when to ask for what you want in a polite manner means empowerment.

When you need to ask for something, be sure to remember the following:

- ✔ **Speak up.** Even if you feel intimidated or nervous, you can get around these roadblocks that undermine your efforts by speaking with confidence.

- ✔ **Invite reactions, making it easy for your allies to respond to your request or expectation.** Be open to constructive criticism.

- ✔ **Be specific, focus clearly on what you really want or need, and *ask* for it.** You may even want to jot down a few notes or rehearse mentally before making your request, especially if you're about to ask someone on a date.

- ✔ **Don't undermine yourself.** Adding on demeaning tag beginnings or endings — such as, "I know this is a stupid question, but. . ." or "I'm sorry to have to ask you this. . ." — makes you sound like you lack self-confidence.

Being assertive doesn't equal rudeness. Take responsibility for nurturing and maintaining your own self-esteem. When you're competent in using basic assertive skills, you can feel confident to handle most situations and can achieve the respect you deserve.

Creating a serene environment

You can find no better place to practice good manners than with people in your day-to-day life, those with whom you live and work. Treat your family, friends, and co-workers with respect and courtesy, and all the difficulties of the outside world are easier for them (and you) to bear.

Simple expressions of politeness at home contribute to an environment of refuge from daily aggravations. Don't be stingy when using courteous expressions like the following (and don't limit yourself to only these five):

- ✔ "Please pass the potatoes."
- ✔ "Thanks for the glass of water."
- ✔ "I really appreciate your help in folding the laundry."
- ✔ "You look nice this morning."
- ✔ "I'm proud of your grade in biology."

It looks a little corny on paper, but this approach can accomplish miracles at home. Do it. Say it. Be nice. Treat your family members as if they were honored guests, and their responses may surprise you. Courtesy is contagious!

Even in the professional setting, common courtesies and good etiquette improve your working environment. After all, you can spend approximately one-third of your day at the office, so a little effort can pay huge dividends in positive energy in your workplace.

For instance: On the job, a timely "Hello" or "Good morning" greeting and a sincere smile can humanize the office. After you've greeted a person, you've paved the way for a silent nod as you pass each other several more times that day.

Head to Part II for more information on fostering well-mannered relationships with everyone in your life.

Spreading civility to those who need it most

Your considerate behavior can have a magical effect on others in your life. If you succeed in surviving a good manners challenge, then others around you can feel more confident and empowered.

This ability to influence is especially true for parents of teenagers (teens often find themselves in difficult peer situations outside in the "real world"). Teenagers (and children) need more than lessons to figure out how to behave. They need assurances that they are valued, good people. By praising and complimenting your child when she exhibits good manners, you give the world much more than a well-mannered human being. You give the world a person who has self-respect and respects others.

If your child does things that don't meet with your approval, tell her why in a polite and courteous manner. Either way, you've communicated with her in terms that are supportive, which leads to growth and development. Check out Chapter 4 for additional information on developing good manners in your children.

 Treat everyone with courtesy, even co-workers who drive you crazy. Remember the morning affirmation of Marcus Aurelius, a former Emperor of Rome: "Today I will be surrounded by people who irritate me. I will not demonstrate my irritation."

Extending everyday courtesies when you're out and about

Etiquette is often regarded as something you can turn on and off for special occasions, like if you happen to have tea with the queen. But that just isn't so. Contrary to popular belief, etiquette is simply using common sense and making others feel comfortable — something you should be doing on a daily basis.

As you go about your errands and chores, polite contact with others can garner pleasant and helpful responses. Thoughtful behavior works in supermarket checkout lines, at family picnics, in restaurants, at the theater, and at your favorite coffee shop.

 Here are some simple, everyday uses of etiquette that you can use when you're out and about:

- ✔ Keep good eye contact.

- ✔ Smile. Even when you aren't in a good mood — a smile may just change your, and someone else's, demeanor!

- ✔ Greet those you come in contact with or even those just walking by on the street with "Hello" or "Good Afternoon."

- ✔ Use "Please" and "Thank you" when being waited on.

- ✔ Try to use a person's name, particularly when he dons a nametag.

- Reply when someone speaks to you.

- Give people space. Don't crowd!

- Don't make a mess with public spaces (such as coffee shops or condiment bars).

- Be discreet. You never know who may be within earshot if you're gossiping.

- Speak softly when you're in public

- Stay to the right when walking on a sidewalk or standing on a moving walkway or an escalator.

- Open doors for others.

- Refrain from using off-color language.

- Don't be a rude, obnoxious cell-phone user! (See Chapter 9 for the full scoop on telephone etiquette.)

- Properly dispose of your trash and pick up trash others leave behind.

- Drive with patience and yield to other drivers.

Giving and Receiving Compliments

In order to be a model of good manners, you need to be able to give and receive compliments. The goal of a compliment is to make others feel good about themselves, not just to make a shallow comment to start a conversation. And when someone else gives you a compliment, you should show courtesy by graciously accepting the kind word. However, giving and receiving praise doesn't always come easy.

To be successful, a compliment (or your response to one) should be sincere and specific. For example, a sincere compliment goes something like this:

> **Carl:** "You look great in that suit; I really admire your taste in clothes. Maybe you can help me shop for a couple business suits."
>
> **Jenny:** "Well, thank you! I'm flattered and would be happy to help."

Here are a few guidelines to remember about giving and receiving compliments:

- **Be sincere when complimenting someone.** It's usually obvious if you're not.

- **When you receive a compliment, always say "Thank you," and don't discount or dispute what the person said.** For example, when someone compliments your outfit, don't respond with, "This old thing?" Simply say something like, "Thank you. Yes, I love it, too!" or, "My mother bought this for me."

Working wonders with "Good morning!"

The world of courteous behavior reserves a special corner for actions that are *nice*. Etiquette doesn't require you to issue a friendly greeting to everyone you encounter, but most people, including perfect strangers, consider those greetings to be unexpected and, well, nice.

In a hotel, for example, as you make your way toward your room, you can certainly give a friendly nod and a "Good morning" to the people you pass on your way to the elevator. When you're inside the elevator, a cheerful "Good morning" is a lot nicer than a silent scowl. The hotel doorman may appreciate your greeting along with, perhaps, a comment on the weather.

And when you enter a taxi, saying "Good morning" sounds a lot nicer than just sliding into the back seat and barking out, "Grand Central Station!" Using consideration and everyday common courtesy can brighten everyone's day!

✔ **If you notice someone's accessory — earrings, eyeglasses, a button — admire it.** Here are three approaches you can try:

- "Those are lovely earrings — and so unique! Do they have a story?"

- "I've never seen eyeglass frames like that. Where did you find them?"

- "That's an interesting button on your lapel. What does it mean?"

The power of a question starts a conversation or keeps it moving. If you're the recipient of the compliment, accept it graciously and help continue the conversation with a question of your own, such as:

- "Why, thank you! I picked up these earrings while I was on vacation in Thailand. Have you ever been to Thailand?"

- "It's so nice that you noticed. I found a new optical store at the mall. I thought the frames were great when I picked them out, but now I wonder if they're too big. What do you think?"

- "It's kind of you to ask. I got the button for 15 years of service with the county. Can you imagine working at the same job for 15 years?"

See Chapter 7 for more handy tips on engaging in polite conversation.

✔ **Try giving more compliments.** You may be surprised at how good it makes you feel, especially if your compliments make people feel better by cheering them up.

✔ **Not accepting or giving compliments properly is usually a sign of low self-esteem or low self-confidence.** Liking yourself is okay! (See the section "Self-esteem," earlier in this chapter, for more information on building your confidence through etiquette.)

Rising Above Rudeness

Most people are rude because they're responding to others who have been rude to them. This domino effect can stop in your presence if you rise above rudeness, even if it's difficult for you. When you take the higher ground, you always come away feeling a lot better about the situation and yourself. By treating others with respect and dignity, you create a win-win situation for all parties, and it shows you have respect for yourself. In addition, you just may change someone's bad attitude and show them a few tricks of good behavior. Remember, the rude buck *can* stop here!

The following are a few examples of rude behavior and how to respond when you're faced with them:

- **Cutting in line:** Yes, waiting your turn and then having someone decide that waiting just isn't his thing is unpleasant. But in this case, don't yell, "No cuts, no buts, no coconuts!" Instead, just politely ask if that person has particular reason that he's unable to wait in the queue like everyone else.

- **Driving like a maniac:** On today's roads and highways, the prevalence of rudeness abounds. If someone cuts you off, tailgates, or ignores other road rules, you usually have two choices:

  - Exhibit bad behavior back by tailgating (or stomping on your brakes if he's tailgating you), honking your horn, or gesturing, which could most likely result in some shared road rage or who knows what may happen.

  - Let the person go, wave, and smile (even if you're truly annoyed). In fact, wave as if to say, "I assume you didn't see me, but have a nice day!" This choice is definitely the better of the two.

- **Handling interruptions:** If you're interrupted when working in your office, or if a co-worker is making too much noise in an adjacent area, calmly and respectfully inform him that you need quiet. Chances are he'll be happy to comply, and you'll have nipped the problem in the bud. You can be polite and firm at the same time. And always treat your co-workers with consideration and respect in all exchanges. No need to respond with loud noises of your own, lose your temper, or complain to someone else.

When you've been inadvertently rude, made a mistake, blundered, created an accident, or said the wrong thing, apologize immediately! The longer you wait to express your regrets, the less effective your gestures are.

If you need to apologize, you can say (without making a long list of excuses) that you were just not thinking, and say you're sorry for not being more sensitive to that person or the situation. Don't call further attention to the blunder or try to explain yourself (doing so may only make things worse). Instead, find something supportive to say and honestly show you have an interest in the person, such as in the following example:

> "I'm really sorry about forgetting about our dinner date — I completely forgot to mark it on my calendar. It's completely my fault. How about I treat you to dinner next week? Please pick the date, and I will be sure to mark it in my planner this time!"

The eyes don't lie. So, remember to look the person straight in the eyes when extending your apology and check your body language. Your body communicates as much about you as your words.

If you believe that the verbal apology wasn't enough, follow up with a hand-written apology or card. See Chapter 8 for tips on a written apology.

Chapter 3

Presenting Yourself Positively: Dress, Grooming, and More

In This Chapter

▶ Looking at your wardrobe and personal grooming practices

▶ Striking a pose with the correct body language

▶ Handling awkward or unexpected situations with grace

The word *etiquette* is so often used to describe the things you say to others that people tend to overlook some mighty important details that have nothing to do with words. If you haven't thought about the effects of your wardrobe and body language on others, you can come away from this chapter with a lot of new insights.

How you cope with little surprises and personal emergencies also can have a big affect on those around you. Do the sensible thing, smoothly, and nobody will think twice about the difficulty you may be facing. This chapter's second purpose is to help you plan ahead and cope with the unexpected.

Although dressing well and grooming yourself properly show that you respect yourself, those things alone don't ensure your success, either socially or professionally. You also need to demonstrate a positive attitude in everything you do.

Putting Together a Winning Wardrobe

What you wear and how you wear it can communicate just as clearly as the words you speak. The messages you provide through your wardrobe are an important part of the manners you display in public.

First, try to wear clothing that is appropriate, of the best quality you can afford, and in good taste. What counts isn't how many outfits you have or the labels you wear, but how you care for your clothing and put it together with style. Most important is that your clothing reflects your positive attitude toward yourself, your work, and others.

Begin by thinking about your profession, your place of work, and your leisure time. If your work life and your "play" life are very different, separate your work wardrobe from your leisure wardrobe. Does your work wardrobe present a confident, well-groomed image? Are the clothes suitable for the type of work you do? Do you have clothes that can take you from your work to a social engagement? Are your leisure clothes also neat, even if they're casual? Are they in good repair, without stains or tears?

After you've thought it through, venture into your closet. In the following sections, I provide some handy guidelines for assembling a great wardrobe.

Assessing your existing wardrobe

Every once in a while, closets need a spring cleaning — whatever the season. Follow these guidelines to determine what to keep and what to pitch:

- ✔ Each year, try on your clothes in front of a full-length mirror. If you've gained weight, make sure that your clothes aren't stretching or pulling. No matter how much you suck in your stomach in front of the mirror, in real life people tend to relax. If you've lost weight and your clothes are hanging on you, you can have them taken in.

  If you can't have your clothes altered properly to accommodate a weight gain or loss, donate them to charity.

- ✔ If pant legs or skirts are too wide, they can be altered to be narrower, if that is the style. Unfortunately, if they are narrow and the style is the opposite, that can't be easily changed. You can avoid some of these problems by never buying extremes in fashion trends for your basic wardrobe.

  Check your existing wardrobe (including ties) for large, bold patterns; checks; florals; and geometric patterns. These types of patterns generally don't wear well with time.

- ✔ Color is something you should also look at in a wardrobe review. Although that lime-green leisure suit may have been all the rage in the 1970s, it's probably not going to convey the same impression decades later. Save it for a 1970s theme party!

✔ Take a look at the type of fabrics you have in your closet. Wool, silk, and cotton are always in style, whereas blends and new fabrics that include Lycra are also coming into their own. Even polyester has made a comeback, although it shouldn't be your first choice for business clothing. Natural fabrics cost more and are expensive to maintain, but they make beautiful, high-quality garments. Combinations of cotton, wool, silk, and synthetics are a good compromise, because they combine a good appearance and fairly low-maintenance care.

A good test of fabric is to take the clothing in your hand and crumble it. When you let go, see whether there are wrinkles in the fabric. If not, buy it! The garment needs less care and is less likely to wrinkle by the middle of the day.

✔ While you're going through your closet, make sure that all your clothes are properly cleaned and pressed. Shine your shoes, brush your suede garments, and have any rundown shoes resoled. Then go through your clothes and hang them so that outfits are together and easy to reach.

If you haven't worn the item in the last eight months, most likely you will never wear it. Don't hesitate to give away clothes that don't make your cut. Admit your mistakes and move on!

Adding new items

Consider the following points when adding to your wardrobe:

✔ If you don't like to shop, simply shop twice a year — once for spring and summer and once for fall and winter. Purchase well-made classics that will last for several years and that you can mix and match with other items to create new outfits.

✔ Trendy clothing is fun to have, but make sure to balance it with long-lasting, classically styled items. Consider putting together a trendy shirt and a classic pair of wool pants, for example, for an updated and stylish look. You may want to spend more for the classics and less for the trendy items, which you won't be able to wear as long.

✔ Choose garments that suit you in style and color. For example, dark colors and simple lines are more flattering to heavier people.

✔ Be wary about purchasing something if you aren't sure where you'll wear it. Finding a bargain or an item that you just adore is great, but it's of no use to you if it sits in your closet untouched for years.

✔ Remember that new accessories, such as scarves and ties, can make old outfits seem new. If you don't have the money to purchase new garments, pick up a couple of accessories to freshen your look.

✔ At work, keep the trendiness to a minimum. You can alter the length of your skirt or sleeve or the style of your collar, for example, but you don't want to wear anything too out-there. If you yearn to express yourself with your clothing, purchase some trendy accessories that you can pair with your business basics.

✔ Know your company's dress code and the norms of attire in your industry. Even if your office is a casual one, make sure that you purchase neat, good-quality garments so that you present a professional image. If your office is more conservative and requires you to wear business suits, stick to more conservative clothing that isn't too flashy.

If you're unsure what professional clothes to wear, a good guide is to take note of what successful co-workers and your superiors are wearing and follow suit.

✔ Clothing services, professional shoppers, and image consultants are available to assist you in selecting a professional wardrobe. These personal shopping services are provided by many upscale department stores such as Nordstrom, Bloomingdale's, and Barneys.

Try meeting with a few different personal shoppers at a couple of different department stores. Remember that they make a living knowing what's in style, what's classic in design, what price ranges carry which styles, and so on, saving you a lot of time and energy. The more ideas and information they provide, the more comfortable you can feel when you make your purchase decisions.

Dressing tips for women

Appearance matters. With some discipline, you can create a wardrobe that stays current and looks smart without breaking the bank. The following guidelines give you a style advantage:

✔ **Make sure that your clothes fit you properly.** Clothing that is too big, too small, too short, or too long isn't flattering. If an item is too large for you, a tailor may be able to take it in.

✔ **Dress according to your body type.** As you've probably already figured out, certain styles complement your figure, and others don't flatter you at all. If you need help determining what styles are best for you, consult a salesperson at an upscale department store.

✔ **Find a color palette that suits you.** Although you can't find any strict rules about who can wear which colors, you should know which colors are most flattering to you. Also make sure to have a variety of neutral-colored items of clothing that you can mix and match with bright-colored garments.

✔ **Avoid loud colors at the office.** If you simply must wear bright colors, limit them to accessories, such as a bright scarf or a colored blouse under a neutral suit.

✔ **Dress tastefully.** Yes, you have the right to look like a woman, but please refrain from wearing very short skirts, low-cut blouses and dresses, sheer clothing, and the like, especially at work.

✔ **Make sure that your undergarments don't show through your clothing.** Purchase a variety of undergarments to suit your various outfits, such as strapless and convertible-strap bras and slips in a variety of lengths.

✔ **If you prefer to wear pantyhose with your outfit, make sure that they fit properly.** In business situations, stick to sheer, flesh-colored stockings or sheer, black stocking when you wear dark clothes — no fishnets or large-patterned stockings please!

✔ **Remember that shoes can tell people a lot about you.** For comfort and style reasons, spending a little extra on a good pair of shoes that go with a variety of outfits is better than purchasing several cheaper pairs that won't last. Keep the heel at a low or medium height. At work, make sure to wear shoes that cover your toes — simple flats or pumps are best.

✔ **Accessorize well, but in moderation.** Keep your jewelry simple and understated. Tasteful earrings and perhaps a necklace or lapel pin can really accentuate an outfit. A lovely scarf can add a splash of color. If you wear a watch, make sure that it is of good quality — sport watches and watches with worn-out bands are appropriate only for the most casual occasions.

✔ **Make sure that your purse is appropriate to the season and the dressiness of your outfit.** For example, if you're wearing a navy blue business suit with brown pumps, you shouldn't carry a black fabric handbag. Also discard any purses that are worn out or torn.

✔ **Don't carry several bags at once, such as a purse, a briefcase, and a tote bag.** Carry one bag that can accommodate all the items that you need to carry in it — or, at most, two bags.

Dressing tips for men

Not that long ago, men didn't have as many style or clothing options as women. Those days are long gone! Men's fashion today has as many choices in styles, colors, and fabrics as women's clothing. Dressing well today means making an investment in your professional or personal wardrobe. Check out the following guidelines:

✔ **Don't get into a rut and wear the same thing every day just because you're male.** You can vary your look by wearing different shades and fabrics, for example.

- ✔ **Choose separates, such as sport coats and pants, that you can mix and match easily.** That way, you can create several different outfits from just a few articles.

- ✔ **Find clothing in colors that are flattering to you.** White dress shirts may be the norm, for example, but you may look better in a subtle cream shade. The same goes for suits, which come in a wide range of neutral shades. You may be surprised at how much better you look in one shade of gray than in another.

- ✔ **Look first for fabric, fit, and comfort; look second for style.** Don't buy something if it doesn't fit quite right — if the pants are a little too snug around your waist, for example, or if the shirt collar doesn't lie quite right. Remember that too big is no better than too small.

- ✔ **Choose jacket and pant styles that are of good quality and that flatter you.** If you're thin, you may want to try a double-breasted jacket and flat-front pants to make yourself look broader. Conversely, if you're on the heavy side, you may opt for a vest and pants with pleats.

- ✔ **When you purchase dress shirts, make sure that the tails are long enough to be tucked in and stay there and that the shirt sleeves aren't too long or too short.** Take some time to find the right fit.

- ✔ **Select your ties carefully.** If you aren't confident in your taste in ties, go for subtle colors and conservative patterns. As a rule, novelty ties are not appropriate in a business setting.

- ✔ **Coordinate your belts and shoes with each other and with your outfit.** Belt and shoes should be the same color (unless you're wearing casual clothing with tennis shoes). Also, make sure that your belts and shoes are in good repair, and keep your shoes shined.

- ✔ **If you choose to wear jewelry, make sure that it's tasteful.** Flashy jewelry doesn't enhance your business image.

Dressing Appropriately for Any Occasion

Overdressing can be an accident. You may have been misinformed about the situation, or you may have misunderstood someone's advice. But if you wear a full business suit to a beach party, you're telling the others that you don't wish to participate in their idea of fun. And if you show up wearing a cocktail dress and a lot of fancy jewelry for an afternoon bridge party with neighbors, your friends may feel you're telling them that you're better than they are.

Underdressing sends just as strong a message. When you wear blue jeans and a sweatshirt to a symphony concert, you're telling everyone around you that you place a low value on the evening's entertainment and that you have little respect for the other members of the audience.

Here's a message for those people who say that they have "gotten beyond the artifice of clothing and personal grooming": You generally look terrible, and whenever a gathering is planned, you don't receive an invitation. Only best-selling authors, Nobel Prize–winning scientists, and movie stars can afford to ignore the situational dress code. On them, the inappropriate attire looks charmingly eccentric. On you, it will look like you have no respect for others. Proper clothing, clean and neatly pressed garments, well-matched accessories, and just the right touch in a necktie or some jewelry is a sign that you're in tune with whatever is going on.

The key is to ask about the proper attire. If you're going to a party, ask the host. If you're attending a theatrical performance, call the ticket office. By asking, you can feel more confident in your choice of attire.

In the following sections, I discuss different types of events and how to dress properly for them.

Never pretend to be anything you aren't. There's a huge difference between dressing appropriately for an occasion and being a fake. You shouldn't be uncomfortable or present an image that isn't you, but you should present the best you that you possibly can.

Sorting out the meaning of "casual"

Most companies allow casual attire at least once a week, but dress codes can vary, creating some confusion between the difference between casual and business casual. *Business casual* is a step below business formal. For example, if you normally wear a suit and tie to work, business casual would mean you could wear a pair of khaki slacks and button down shirt. *Casual* attire may allow for clothing other than a suit, but it doesn't mean jeans, a T-shirt, and tennis shoes. The following sections look at how to dress for both business casual and casual occasions.

Business casual

If you're used to the comforting rules of business suits, casual day at the office may strike terror in your heart. What on earth should you wear? You may find your answer lying with the professional term *business casual.* Business-casual wear is in its own category.

Business casual may allow for something other than a suit, but it doesn't mean that you should go to work in a tube top and Birkenstocks either (unless you work at a surf shop). Business casual isn't the same as other kinds of casual. No sandals, tennis shoes, or hiking boots.

Keep to the KISS principle even with business casual clothes: Keep It Simple and Sophisticated. Dark colors convey authority; bright colors convey friendliness. Light colors such as taupe and khaki are generally more casual than black, gray, or navy. Beyond that, you may want to consider a few subtleties that can affect your choice of outfit. For example, to impress the boss, wear an outfit that suits the projects at hand. You can work at your desk and computer in neat slacks, a well-pressed shirt or blouse and slacks, and sensible shoes. In other words, for the purposes of your career, treat casual day as if it were an ordinary day without a necktie or business suit.

Casual business attire for women requires some thought, because you have so many choices. Women can wear casual skirts, pants, and blouses. Skirts should be at knee length or slightly above, but never too short or with slits too high up your legs. Blouse fabrics can be cotton, silk, or blends. A sheer fabric can be appropriate with a sweater or jacket over them. The key is not to wear anything that fits too tight, shows cleavage, or calls attention to you. Save the extreme colors or shiny fabrics for evenings.

Business casual for men generally means khaki pants paired with a plain polo shirt; a long-sleeved, button-down shirt; a V-neck sweater; or sometimes a sports coat or blazer. Men usually choose to wear brown leather shoes. Loafers are a good choice, but be sure to wear socks.

For more on proper business attire, check out my book *Business Etiquette For Dummies* (Wiley).

Casual dress outside the office

Casual dress outside the office generally refers to social events and some fine dining. For men and women, the main rule in a conservative environment is usually no jeans and something slightly more conservative and similar to, or slightly dressier than, business casual. There are numerous options for casual clothing for both men and women. Depending on the occasion, time of year, and weather, women can wear a pair of sandals, a sleeveless blouse, and khaki pants. Men can wear cotton slacks, button-down shirts, and sweaters. Some occasions, such as a barbecue, allow for more casual clothes including jeans and a nice top — as long as the jeans are neat, have no holes, and aren't too faded.

Planning for after-work engagements

You don't need a lot of clothes strictly for business. Choose pieces you can mix and match and also wear for after-work engagements. For example, as a woman, if you look good in gray and black, keep your basic wardrobe in those colors and choose blouses, sweaters and accessories in complementary colors such as red and pink. Simply add a dressy accessory or two, such as a necklace, brooch, shawl, dressy scarf, or evening shoes. Many of the items and accessories you use to dress up a professional look for an evening look can be left at your office or brought along the day of the event.

A dress looks dressier than a suit and is easier to dress up with accessories for an after-work dinner or party.

Fortunately, men don't have to be as concerned about what they wear; most business suits are appropriate for after-work or evening functions.

Distinguishing between formal and semiformal occasions

An invitation stating *formal dress* normally means formal eveningwear, which is very dressy by American standards. Formal attire rules are similar to black tie for both men and women, although by not specifying black tie, the options today can be a little more creative if the setting is appropriate. Consider the following suggestions on formal attire:

- A long dress, a cocktail-length dress, or a dressy suit is acceptable for a woman. Colors and fabrics should vary with the season, location, and time of day of the event. In some settings, a woman can wear dressy separates rather than a dress.

- Formal for men commonly means wearing a tux, but a dark suit is also acceptable. Wearing a dark suit, a white shirt, and dark tie is recommended along with dark dress socks and well-polished dark dress shoes. A man can wear a tuxedo jacket minus a tie in some settings, such as a cocktail party in a large, metropolitan city such as New York or Los Angeles.

The term *semiformal* historically means just a cut under black tie and commonly refers to social gatherings and fine dining. Here are some semiformal dress tips:

- For women, semiformal attire means a nice cocktail-length dress, fancy pumps, and normally a more elegant hairstyle, and jewelry.

- For men, semiformal requires a dark suit either in navy, black, or dark gray with a tie, and in some cases, an invitation may call for dinner jackets, though this term is rarely used.

The fanciest types of occasions are *white tie*. Though it's more formal than black tie, white tie evening dress is generally worn only after 6 p.m. A white tie invitation requires women to wear long formal gowns, and men to wear full dress, which is a black tailcoat tuxedo, white tie, vest, and shirt.

Getting Spruced Up and Squeaky Clean

Although having appropriate clothing is important, being clean, well groomed, and well cared for is even more essential to a positive presentation of yourself. Some people dress in the latest styles and the right colors, yet they aren't socially successful or successful in business. Why? They may not be properly groomed: Their shoulders are dotted with dandruff, they have ring-around-the-collar, they have greasy hair, or their breath is bad.

If you use the following tips, you're sure to be in good stead grooming-wise:

- Make sure to daily bathe or shower and apply a deodorant/antiperspirant (be careful not to get it on your clothes!). Body order is a definite taboo.

- Brush your teeth after you eat — or if you can't, suck on a breath mint to freshen your breath. If you have yellowed or stained teeth, use whitening toothpaste or whitening strips (found at most drugstores), or talk to your dentist about further steps that you can take to get a whiter smile.

- Be subtle with scents — they should never precede your entrance or linger when you leave. Apply perfume, cologne, or aftershave sparingly, keeping in mind that you become accustomed to the scent, so it may be harder for you to detect on yourself. Remember, too, that hair-care products, deodorants, and so on also contain perfumes, so make sure that the products you use don't have clashing scents.

  The world is full of people who are allergic to many perfumes and colognes. If you know that you will be around someone with such allergies, do that person a favor and don't spray on the smelly. Being clean must suffice.

- Shampoo and condition your hair often to keep it looking fresh and grease free. Have your hair trimmed regularly and keep it neatly groomed. Use products that keep hair in place if you need to, but don't overdo it — if your hair doesn't move, you've probably used too much hairspray, mousse, or gel.

I provide additional grooming tips for both women and men in the following sections.

Grooming in public is never acceptable — your co-worker doesn't want to see you clipping your nails or applying lotion to your legs at the office. Putting yourself together should be done in the privacy of your home before you step out the door. If you happen to forget a step or are running late, wait until you can sneak into a private bathroom to finish your grooming ritual.

Grooming tips for women

Wearing the perfect clothes and having the right body language won't do any good if you aren't groomed properly. Unclean hair, dirty nails, or the wrong make up can ruin the most stylish of outfits and give a negative impression. To make personal grooming a priority, take heed of the following guidelines:

- ✔ Take good care of the skin on your face, keeping it clean and well moisturized. If you have problems with excess oil, use an oil-free powder to cut down on the shine.

- ✔ Use makeup to enhance your features and give yourself a finished look, but use it sparingly. Heavy makeup can look cheap and is certainly inappropriate in an office setting.

- ✔ Getting lipstick all over your cup or napkin is a big faux pas. To avoid this problem, make sure to blot your lipstick after you apply it. Also check your teeth to make sure that no lipstick has found its way onto them.

- ✔ Keep your fingernails trimmed to a reasonable length, and make sure to file them regularly. If you polish your nails, choose a color that isn't too bright or flashy, unless you're going out for the evening.

- ✔ Find a hairstyle that flatters your face and that you can maintain fairly easily. Make sure to keep your look up-to-date, too — try modifying your style every few years.

- ✔ If you color your hair, either to enhance your features or to cover gray, use a color that works with your skin tone, and don't do anything too drastic. The idea is to make yourself look better, not to make it obvious that you spend lots of money at your hair salon.

Grooming tips for men

Clothes may make the person, but personal hygiene may make or break a deal. Remember that being casual doesn't extend to poor grooming — always be clean and neat. Read on for a few important tips:

- ✔ You may think that skin care is just for women, but healthy-looking skin is an asset for anyone. Wash your face regularly, and use a moisturizer if your skin tends to be dry. If you have problems with acne or you have a wart or mole that you'd like to have removed, consult a dermatologist.

- ✔ Keep your hair well trimmed, clean, and neatly styled. That rule goes for facial hair, too! Make sure to shave any excess hair off the back of your neck between haircuts.

✔ Remove any hair that sticks out of your ears or nostrils.

✔ Keep your nails short, and file away any jagged edges. Check under your nails for dirt if you've been working in the yard or around the house, and promptly remove any dirt that you find.

Paying Attention to Your Body Language and Posture

Whole books have been written about body language. Psychology students can spend a semester learning how to read small gestures. Jury selection consultants think that they can separate the bleeding hearts from the executioners by watching how members of the jury pool stand, sit, and fidget. In the following tips, I skip the shrink-talk and go straight to the good advice on your body language:

✔ The person with whom you're speaking is the whole world. Don't let your eyes wander in search of someone else in the room. If you wish to disengage yourself, wait for a reasonable opening in the conversation and then be honest. Say that you have to greet an old friend or risk hurting his feelings. Promise to return (but don't say when).

✔ In groups, as in poker games, your facial expressions can betray your inner thoughts. Keep this in mind as you circulate at a party. When your supervisor hands out a new assignment, look enthusiastic. When you meet people at a social event, smile and look pleased to meet them.

✔ Folding your arms in front of your chest can be an innocent part of your normal fidgeting or a sign of rejection. The risk that people will assume the latter is high enough that you should avoid folding your arms.

✔ The signs of impatience — tapping your fingernails on a table or desk, tapping your toe on the floor, looking up at the ceiling, sighing repeatedly, looking at your watch every few seconds — are pretty easy to pick up. Teenagers are very skilled at indicating impatience, especially when an adult is trying to give them some good advice about good manners. It doesn't hurt to check yourself every few minutes to make sure that you aren't shouting something with your body that you wouldn't dare whisper with your voice.

Your body language communicates your feelings about others and about the social situation in which you're participating. Your posture communicates your feelings about yourself. When you stand with a slouch or sit with a slump, you're telling others that you don't feel confident and you'd like to be left alone. When your head is erect, your gaze is outward, and your backbone is as straight as Mother Nature made possible, you're inviting others to meet with you on equal terms. Mother was right; stand up straight!

Coping with Things That Sneak Up on You

The human body is full of surprises. No matter how much you try to control or suppress your body's natural functions, you may find yourself inadvertently forced to handle a bout of sneezing or a sudden wave of nausea. Your best bet is to know how to avoid or properly deal with the situation without additional embarrassment, which I help you do in the following sections.

Sneezes

Ah, the sneeze: anything from a gentle, ladylike puff of air to a moist explosion that could wake the dead. Here is a checklist of sneeze-coping strategies:

- Always carry a handkerchief or a small package of tissues. Reach for them at the first hint of a sneeze coming on.

- Forestall a sneeze at a critical moment (such as a priest's blessing over a newlywed couple) by pressing your extended index finger flat and firmly against your upper lip, just under your nostrils. This technique really works, but only temporarily.

- Sneeze gently. Practice sneezing without vocalizing.

- Turn away from people close at hand. When seated, try to bend toward the floor. You can also sneeze into the fold of your arm, which avoids those nasty germs from getting trapped on your hand or sprayed onto others.

- If a sneezing fit seizes you, excuse yourself from the room and return after your sneezing subsides (and you take a minute to compose yourself).

- If you have no other way to cope and absolutely have to use your table napkin to catch a sneeze, fold the napkin inward; wrap it in a second, unused napkin; and signal a waiter to request two replacement napkins. Say that you were forced to use the napkin for personal purposes so that it can be disposed of properly.

Indigestion

Indigestion has two meanings. Literally, the word refers to physical discomfort from something you've eaten. More commonly, in social situations, indigestion is just a polite synonym for belching. It happens to everyone occasionally, but belching can be embarrassing at a banquet, especially if you're seated at the head table near a microphone.

If you feel a belch coming on at a dinner or mealtime situation, use your napkin to cover your mouth, turn away from others, and forgo the pleasure of making a noise that would delight an 8-year-old. Loud belching is an acquired skill that can be unlearned in favor of quiet belching. If you're speaking to someone and an unexpected belch befalls you, say "Excuse me" and go right on with your conversation. Any statement you make in an attempt to mitigate the happenstance can only make it worse.

A human body that is determined to generate gas doesn't always limit itself to belching. If you're afflicted with any advanced manifestations, simply excuse yourself from the party until your system calms down. If you happen to pass gas without warning, don't pretend no one hears it. Quickly say "Excuse me," be discreet, and move on. Everyone is human and will occasionally have such moments.

Queasiness

The word *carsick* was invented for a reason, just as there's a reason for those little white bags in airliner seat pockets. People do get sick once in a while, and occasionally even the most well-mannered person in the world has to toss her cookies.

I recommend rapid movement toward the bathroom and the conclusion of your upset in total privacy. You have absolutely no reason to report on your adventures after you regain your composure and rejoin the group.

In an automobile, be extremely direct in addressing the driver. I recommend simply saying, "Pull over right now; I have to throw up." Any other message is likely to be misinterpreted.

As a last resort, when trapped by circumstance and absolutely doomed to the ravages of your upset, turn away from the group, grab a napkin or hand-kerchief, and trust in the sympathetic understanding of the others.

Part II
Fostering Well-Mannered Relationships

The 5th Wave   By Rich Tennant

"I always speak to the kids in a quiet and respectful way, but occasionally I wear this to add a little punctuation."

In this part . . .

One of the ultimate goals of proper etiquette is to make everyone around you feel at ease, so this part on building better relationships is an important section of this book. These chapters cover everything from your relationships with your children and other housemates to your relationships with your extended family, your friends, and your co-workers. Because the rules regarding behavior between men and women are ever changing, this part also includes guidelines on gender-specific etiquette issues. Finally, you can know whether to hold the door for her or him!

Chapter 4

Focusing on Courtesy with Your Family

*E*tiquette is often associated with experiences away from home. Before you prepare yourself for parties, dinners, and other social occasions, however, it's a good idea to put your own house in order. In this chapter, I offer a bare minimum of guidelines with the hope that you can be inspired to think about and practice good manners every waking hour. After you have doing the right thing at home down pat, you'll be fine out in the world. But an even better reason for etiquette at home is this: The whole family will get along better.

Somebody once said that you need love most when you're most unlovable. That same idea applies to courtesy. In a world where people are often hurried, stressed out, or aggravated by some prior experience, being courteous isn't always easy. But that's when extending courtesy is most important and most appreciated. Your considerate behavior can have a magical effect on those closest to you, and your determination to do the right thing enhances your own self-esteem. Best of all, if you succeed in surviving a "good manners challenge," your self-confidence will soar.

Being Considerate of Your Better Half

Adults who live together, whether in marriage or in some other agreement, begin the arrangement with an expectation of compatibility. Unfortunately, as time passes, familiarity often leads to shortcuts in communication. Here's some advice for communicating respectfully with your partner, no matter how long you've been together:

- ✔ Exercise expressive courtesy. Go ahead and say those nice things. Don't just enjoy a meal that your partner prepared; say that you enjoyed it. Don't just feel that your spouse or significant other is more pleasant than the unfeeling clods outside — say so.

- ✔ Always focus on the positive actions and characteristics of one another. If you must criticize, comment on the behavior and don't verbally attack the person.

- ✔ Choose to do what's right. Behaving like a polite adult all the time isn't easy. Taking the lead in exercising common courtesies when you feel rotten isn't easy, either, but that's part of the burden of adulthood. Accept the burden. Do what's right. Live up to the expectations of everyone in your household, especially your partner, and you can find yourself accomplishing things that you never thought possible.

- ✔ Always check with your spouse or significant other before you schedule an event or other appointment. Try to be respectful of each other's time. Don't keep each other waiting! And don't use manipulation to have your partner attend something you know he or she wouldn't enjoy. Compromise when there are disagreements.

- ✔ Don't snoop. Never rummage through personal things, read each other's mail, or eavesdrop on personal conversations, phone or otherwise.

- ✔ Promptly admit to mistakes and make appropriate amends, and always express gratitude, even for the smallest of deeds.

- ✔ Be alert to each other's emotional needs. Provide comfort when your partner is upset, distressed, or ill.

Setting a Positive Example for Children

There's no such thing as time off for bad behavior when you have children. Long before you think about teaching your kids some of the basics of good manners, they shape their own actions by watching and listening to you deal with telephone conversations, visitors, relatives, and so on. Parents are full-time role models for their children, and — without putting too much pressure on parents — the entire world depends on them to turn out civilized, polite members of the next generation.

In the following sections, I explain the basic rules of etiquette in a home and show you how to set expectations for proper behavior.

Laying down basic etiquette rules

When it came to etiquette, I tried to teach my children some basic rules. Here are some of the most important ones. I encourage you to copy this page and put it up on the refrigerator!

- ✔ Always say "Please" and "Thank you."
- ✔ Be responsible for your words and actions.
- ✔ Be polite when answering the phone (see Chapter 9 for more about telephone etiquette).
- ✔ Keep your room tidy.
- ✔ Pick up after yourself (no matter where you are).
- ✔ Don't leave your dirty dishes for others to clean up.
- ✔ Assist with family chores (I discuss chores later in this chapter).
- ✔ Learn proper table manners and use them (see Chapter 12 for details).
- ✔ Turn off the television at mealtime and when company is present.
- ✔ Agree to disagree courteously.
- ✔ Speak, but don't shout.
- ✔ Be willing to share.
- ✔ Be a good listener.
- ✔ Don't open a closed door without knocking.
- ✔ Respect others' privacy.
- ✔ Don't eavesdrop, snoop, or read others' mail.
- ✔ Treat others' property with respect.
- ✔ Don't take others' belongings without asking.
- ✔ Be kind to yourself and others.
- ✔ Practice patience.
- ✔ Leave things nicer than the way you found them.
- ✔ Think before you speak.
- ✔ Leave the toilet seat down.

Parents teach their children by setting a good example. If you're a parent or guardian, you *are* a full-time teacher. Children shape their own actions by watching and listening those around them. Being a good parent and helping your children practice good manners also consists of setting limits and rules, being consistent, and following through — don't just tell your kids what you don't want. Be positive and optimistic, and discuss the importance of treating each other respectfully. Remember to always maintain calm when disciplining your children. Aggressive discipline only results in aggressive behavior.

Establishing expectations for household harmony

The easiest way to maintain peace in your home is to make it clear to everyone what you expect from them in various situations. If you prepare children (and adults, too) for what they will encounter and explain to them what type of behavior is appropriate, you're bound to have fewer problems and squabbles. This section walks you through the various aspects of etiquette at home and helps you set the right expectations.

Don't expect perfection

When things don't go quite right at home or someone has lost his temper, discover how to forgive. Forgiveness is beneficial not only mentally but also physically. People who forgive tend to be less angry, depressed, stressed out, and anxious, and they also have lower blood pressure and heart rates than those who hold grudges.

Displaying acts of forgiveness can be a valuable lesson for children. Teaching the importance of simply saying "I'm sorry" and accepting another's apology graciously can be taught at a young age. If you conduct yourself by showing respect and consideration for others, your children will turn out civilized and polite members of the next generation.

When you want to forgive someone (and be a model for your children to do the same), you may find it helpful to look at the big picture. Is the situation and how you feel about it really having a negative impact on your life? If so, you may attempt to discuss the matter with the person that caused the hurt, or write him a letter. If the situation is having a major impact on your life, consider professional help or seeking spiritual counseling and guidance. Keep in mind that you benefit from the process and experience, as much as the person with whom you have the grudge.

However, if you have a hard time letting go of a grievance, you aren't alone. Don't feel pressured or be too hard on yourself if the feelings of forgiveness aren't there. Give yourself time. More importantly, consider that forgiveness doesn't mean you have to forget an incident, but rather that you can place a limit on how it affects you and your relationship with the other person. Remember that everyone is different, and some people may need more time.

Speak with civility

How you speak shows a lot about how much respect you have for yourself and others. In your family life, sticking to these principles helps maintain civility — and maybe your sanity, too:

✔ Teach your children to refer to other family members by name or title (and make sure you do it, too!). In other words, when speaking of a third party, say "Sally," "Jimmy," "Mom," or "Grandpa" — not "she" or "he."

✔ When correcting or scolding your children, speak with them out of earshot of others — your children will appreciate your courtesy. Similarly, they'll glow with pride when you make sure that others overhear your words of praise.

✔ Parents must speak respectfully at all times. Arguing, displaying rage or anger, raising voices, or using offensive language in front of children not only sets a bad example, but it also creates fear and confusion. Disagreements between parents should be settled in private.

✔ If you lose your temper in front of small children or teenagers, apologize immediately. If children are young, explain to them how you should have reacted and talk about feelings and emotions.

Some parents feel that there's something close and chummy about encouraging their children to address them by their given names. Instead of "Mom," I hear some kids say "Helen." In my opinion, though, this practice is unwise. As a parent, you need to be the authority figure, and having your child call you by your first name throws confusion into that relationship. Stick with "Mom" and "Dad" instead.

Create a routine

Children — and the rest of us, for that matter — thrive on routine. Knowing that certain events happen at certain times every day as well as what's expected of everyone is comforting and stabilizing.

Two of the most common complications to daily routine concern wake-up calls and lunch preparation during the school year. Kids often delay getting up, and countless parents mention the tedium of making sandwiches that won't get eaten at lunchtime.

To avoid problems in the morning, be prepared and follow these helpful tips in the evening:

✔ Have your children help you select their outfits for the next day.

✔ Make sure that your teenagers have their clothes ready before going to bed, even if it means that they need to wash and iron them.

✔ Have your kids put all their schoolwork and supplies in their backpacks before they go to bed.

✔ Prepare lunches or lay out money for buying lunch.

✔ Have your children bathe or shower at night rather than in the morning.

✔ Make your children aware of what time they need to be ready in the morning.

✔ Make sure that your children complete their homework before bedtime. Rushing to finish in the morning only creates anxiety!

Divvy up household chores

Sharing the household chores is important in learning responsibility and respect for others and for a household. Each week or month, trade specific duties so that one person isn't always responsible for the same chore. Doing so prevents boredom (for children and for adults) and teaches children the various jobs around the house.

The first rule of any well-mannered household should be to clean up after yourself. That goes for dishes, countertops, spills, toys, and dirty clothing. Children should also be taught to always leave things the way they were found. By teaching your children early that you expect this of them, you can have a happier life as a parent of teenagers.

A corollary to leaving things as you found them is that if it's empty, you throw it away or recycle it. Don't allow your children to put an empty milk carton back in the refrigerator with just a drop left, or a bag of chips back in the cupboard with just the crumbs! In the same vein, tell children that they're responsible for being good inventory clerks. If they eat or drink the last of something, they should tell the person who does the shopping. Parents can make this task easier by posting a shopping list for needed items.

Share fairly

For everyone in a household, the regular practice of doing your fair share, and not taking more than your fair share, is a large part of family etiquette. Sharing comes into play in many important ways, including the following situations:

✔ **Using the bathroom and the hot water:** When bathrooms serve more than one person, and when a number of family members need to make themselves presentable for the day ahead, the etiquette of sharing space requires that you use the bathroom for only your fair share of time. After one or two chilling experiences, everyone should have a pretty good idea of how long the hot water will hold out. Limit your time in the shower or bath to allow for others who also need hot water.

Time in the bathroom means more than just hot water. When others must also use the bathroom, get in and out in the minimum time you need for your routine. Consider moving parts of your morning routine, such as blow-drying your hair or applying makeup, to a bedroom or other place outside the bathroom.

The first person into the bathroom has the advantage of a dry floor, fog-free mirrors, and a clean tub. Before you exit the bathroom, take a minute to wipe down counter surfaces and the floor, straighten out the floor mat, towel off the mirror, and do whatever else is needed to give the next person a reasonably presentable bathroom. If you use up the last bit of shampoo, soap, and so on, you're responsible for replacing them.

- ✔ **Dividing food, drinks, and treats:** When four adults sit down to a pie sliced into four pieces, it's clear that everyone will get one piece. Put four children in front of four cupcakes, however, and the results aren't as obvious. Children need to be taught how to measure objects — particularly desirable objects such as cupcakes — and calculate fair share.

Adults can provide guidance for kids by thinking out loud. When three kids want fruit juice, place three clean glasses on the counter and make a show out of pouring equal portions. Your script can read, "Well, we didn't have enough for full glasses, but everyone got the same amount of juice."

- ✔ **Home entertainment:** Who controls the TV, how loud music may be played, what programs are suitable, and hours of use need to be determined. Set aside family time to make these decisions and set guidelines that give equal share.

- ✔ **Cost sharing:** You must decide who pays for what and any fair-share contributions your family should make for expenses. Create a family budget and make it clear who pays for what. If the family is planning a summer vacation, teach children to save or earn extra money and contribute to the expense.

- ✔ **Pet care:** Sharing the responsibility for providing food and water, brushing and combing, cleaning cages, and cleaning up your pet's accidents is fair. You can put up a weekly or monthly chore chart to assign children (and parents) to different days or weeks. Divide the list evenly and make notes when the chores aren't completed, and give your children praise when they are. You may also decide to set up a rewards and consequences system.

Warmly welcome all guests into your home

The adage "your guest is my guest" applies equally to children and their parents. Whenever any family member has a visitor, others must extend all ordinary courtesies. This means a friendly greeting, an offer of refreshments suitable to the hour, enough space so that the friends can enjoy each other's company without interference, and a proper farewell.

Teach your children to address and greet adults with a certain degree of formality. Explain that introductions require positive effort: You must speak. You can also guide your children to use other attributes, such as firm handshakes, a warm smile, good eye contact, and following the rules of introductions, that enhance a positive first impression. Help your children with conversation starters by asking the guest questions.

Just as younger people should address grownups by title, grownups should address young guests by name. If you don't know a younger guest's name, a self-introduction is in order, or your child can offer a voluntary introduction. See Chapter 7 for more tips on making introductions.

Acting Politely with Extended Family

Extended family relationships often turn on the very first words out of your mouth. The way you initially address various relatives, in-laws, and family friends can have a lasting effect on them and can shape the future of your relationships. Unfortunately for the rule makers, every family is unique. The following sections give you some guidelines to keep you in safe territory until you figure out what works best in your own extended family.

Respecting grandparents and other elders

Just as children have special needs and require special consideration, so do older people in your circle of relatives, friends, and co-workers. Nowadays, many more elderly people are in the United States, and the idea of designating a person as a senior citizen at age 55, 60, or 65 is rapidly falling by the wayside. Many folks in the workplace are beyond their 70th birthday, and knowing people who are in their 90s and beyond is becoming less unusual.

Senior citizens may have sharp minds and excellent professional skills, but as people age, they develop special needs. Consider those needs and accommodate older people, and you'll be rewarded with a much richer social life.

Many societies extend elaborate courtesies to parents and elders. In recent decades, American families have tended to be much less formal about such things. I think that there's a difference between informal and inconsiderate and that your treatment of elders falls under the umbrella of etiquette in several ways, as I explain in the following sections.

Addressing grandparents appropriately

New parents, as a courteous gesture, should ask their parents how they would like their grandchildren to address them. In many families, the decision of what to call the grandparents is based on tradition and culture. For example, Italian families may refer to grandma as "Noni" and great-grandma, "Super-Noni." Many times the title that sticks is simply because the children aren't able to pronounce the words. If this is the case, grandpa may become "Pa-pa" or grandma may be "Grana."

No matter what the family or children decide to call grandma and grandpa, as long as children are speaking respectfully and not calling their grandparents by their first names, forcing them to change isn't necessary.

Nowadays, it's not all that unusual for children to have four sets of grandparents. (This happens when grandparents on both sides divorce and then marry others.) Surprisingly, young children cope very well with this situation. Unless the various grandparents suggest names for themselves, have the children address them as "Grandpa Jones," "Grandma Murphy," "Grandpa Emerson," and so on. The formality of using the grandparent's last name eliminates confusion when referring to grandparents who may not be present and reinforces identities in the minds of the children even when the grandparents are on the scene.

You can usually address your spouse's grandparents with their last names appended, as in "Grandma and Grandpa Smith" (unless there is no ambiguity, in which case you can call them simply "Grandma and Grandpa"). Some grandparents don't wish to "sound so old" to their adult grandchildren, though. Ask directly what the grandparents prefer to be called. (I discuss what to call other in-laws later in this chapter.)

Living with mixed generations

Even though no official definition of "the family" exists, most discussions assume that a family consists of a mother, a father, and their children. But many households have one or two grandparents in residence, and perhaps even a grandchild or two. If your household has mixed generations, you already know that grandparents have special sensitivities, as do teenagers and the very young. This household must be governed by the best possible manners on the part of all members.

Common courtesies are an absolute necessity. When grandparents need help from the kids, saying "Please" and "Thank you" is a lot more effective than making brusque commands. The children must learn to give courteous greetings and farewells to the older folks: "See you later, Grandpa, I'm going to the library." "Hello, Grandma, I'm home from school." These simple messages help eliminate confusion as to who is present in the home.

All children need private space and possessions to call their own. This need becomes much more intense as kids become teenagers. Make sure that each family member has a room, or at least a piece of furniture, that is considered private. Many disputes arise when one person invades another's space, and figuring out how to respect another person's territory is an important part of good manners.

Assisting elders with limited mobility

A person in a wheelchair, walking with the assistance of a cane or walker, or affected by arthritis or other affliction of age always has the right-of-way. Your obligation as an able-bodied adult is to do what you can to help folks with limited mobility: Hold open the door, bring over the tray of hors d'oeuvres, volunteer to fetch a glass of water, do what you can to ease the way in and out of a car, carry packages or other burdens, and so on.

You owe this courtesy to every senior citizen, not just to your own relatives. Keep your eyes open for a chance to help while you're out shopping, moving in and out of a theater, and so on. At a restaurant, volunteer to go through the salad bar. Help with menu selections if the person has a visual disability. Pass things without being asked. When speaking to an elder who has a hearing impairment, face the person so that your body language and facial expression help her understand.

A loss of mobility doesn't equal a loss of interest in normal activities. Plan to include elders in family outings. Courtesy to elders implies an effort on your part to do whatever is necessary to help them remain connected with the world of activity around them.

Interacting with aunts, uncles, and cousins

The rule for addressing aunts, uncles, and cousins is "Titles up and given names down." Up and down refer to age. For example, you address an older aunt as Aunt Ida. A younger cousin is simply Henry. If somebody prefers a different form of direct address, respect that person's request. Children, however, should always include titles when addressing relatives who are older than themselves.

When dealing with your spouse's relatives, the general rule is to use the title that your spouse would use. In other words, your husband's Aunt Irene is also your Aunt Irene, at least for the purposes of informal gatherings. At a more formal affair, when you're making introductions, your script would be, "Roger, I'd like you to meet Alice's aunt, Irene Smith. Aunt Irene, this is Roger Black." Roger's response would be, "I'm pleased to meet you, Ms. Smith." (Note the use of the unspecific Ms. when the person's marital state is not mentioned.) I explain what to call other in-laws in the next section.

A time-honored way to show respect for elders

The Chinese have a custom regarding seating arrangements, especially in restaurants. The most senior person present is always afforded the seat that faces the main entrance. If the entrance isn't within sight, the honored position faces the main body of the restaurant. When you think about it, this arrangement makes sense, because it allows the honored elder to see what's going on without a lot of twisting and turning. I think that this is a charming way to show respect for elder people, and I recommend it for all family gatherings.

What about a relative your own age? The custom varies from region to region. In some parts of the country, certain titles, such as Cousin, are appended to the names: "Why, Cousin Nancy! What a delight to see you again!" Another regionalism that you may encounter is the use of Brother and Sister when addressing in-laws. "Sister Sally, would you like another slice of pecan pie?" Keep your ears open for these customs when you're away from home. In general, though, first names are appropriate when dealing with relatives nearly the same age as yourself.

When in doubt, you can confess your confusion by saying, "Honestly, I enjoy being with you, but I can't quite figure out what to call you. Please tell me what you prefer." This approach almost always works. If the answer happens to be, "You can call me whatever you wish, as long as you don't call me late to dinner," narrow the choices to either a more formal "Uncle Bob" or the person's first name.

Determining what to call your in-laws

You've probably heard the old story about the woman who called her mother-in-law "you" until her first child was born, after which she used the name Grandma. This little anecdote may seem harmless until you face the fact that names used in direct address are a very important consideration of courtesy.

If you can bring yourself to call your parents-in-law Mom and Dad, they'll probably be pleased. In many families, parents consider sons-in-law and daughters-in-law to be as close to them as their own children, and they appreciate that affectionate regard in return. But some people find this practice difficult, at least at first.

The safest tactic is to confess your uncertainty and ask your parents-in-law how they wish to be addressed. And be prepared to honor their response. If they ask you to use their first names, do so. If your mother-in-law asks to be called Mother Smith, so be it. If the answer is Mom, call her Mom. When everyone's parents are present, you may call your own parents Mom and Dad and your spouse's parents Mother Jones and Father Jones.

In all cases, using a pronoun instead of an actual name is an absolute no-no. When the person is within earshot, using words such as *she* and *her* is definitely not courteous, and the more you use them, the more rude they seem.

Sorting out a few other relationships

Re-blended families and former spouses fall into a gray area with no firm rules. Second (and successive) marriages often bring a confusing collection of relatives to family gatherings, and people have a lot of uncertainty as to how to address all these people. The following sections give you some guidance.

Ex-spouses

The ultimate test of your ability to maintain poise and good manners comes when an ex-spouse shows up for some plausible reason, perhaps to claim the kids for a visit. Even here, you should be on your best behavior. Address your spouse by first name. If an introduction is required, use this format: "This is my former husband, Jeffrey Allen. Jeffrey is Sam and Sylvia's father."

Stepchildren and other-custody offspring

If rules can be written for introducing and speaking about children from a previous marriage of your spouse, you can be sure that they won't work in your particular family situation. Children have very little control over the recoupling of their parents, and one of the ways they can assert themselves is to test your patience in this sensitive area. Begin with these conservative suggestions and see how things go.

Suppose your husband's ex-wife has custody of the children, and you get them every other weekend. How do you introduce the kids to your friends? Try, "I'd like you to meet Roger's son and daughter, Chad and Elizabeth." When you know for sure that things are okay between you and Chad and Elizabeth, you can experiment with, "And these are the children, Chad and Elizabeth." Talk it over with the kids before you refer to them as "our kids."

If the woman you married has a son from a prior relationship, I offer the same suggestion. Call him "Judy's son, Jeff" until you know for sure that you're on safe ground with the boy. Then you can go on to "This is our son, Jeff."

If you're a foster parent, introduce a foster child as "my foster daughter, Maria." The same goes for what your foster children call you. One of the goals of the foster-child program is the eventual reunification of natural parent and child, and foster children have a tough enough time without title confusion. You can let them address you as Daddy Sid or Momma Denise instead of expecting them to call you Mom or Dad. This rule is flexible, however; if a child seems to need to call you Mom or Dad, let it be.

Adopted children are exactly the same as those who are dropped into your lap by your own personal stork. Forget all about the legal details. These children are your real children, and you need make no reference to their adoption. If they want to talk about being adopted in later years, that's their business.

Half siblings and stepsiblings

Siblings who join the family from a stepparent's previous marriage are called stepbrothers and stepsisters, whereas siblings that result from a new marriage are half brothers and half sisters. Introduce your half siblings simply as "My brother Ralph" or "My sister Eloise" in general situations. As far as introducing stepsiblings, the family may decide to introduce them as stepbrother or step-sister, but it is perfectly fine not to mention "step."

Being a well-behaved blended family

When two people decide to remarry and bring children from previous marriages into the new marriage, several rules of conduct become crucial. Here are a few tips for newly blended families:

- ✔ **Sort out your discipline styles.** Issues to discuss include acceptable behavior and the consequences when children misbehave. Predictable rules make your children feel safe and secure.

- ✔ **Decide on each child's duties and responsibilities.** Together, work out jobs, expected behavior, and family etiquette. Assign chores so that children feel part of the household, not like guests in a stepparent's home. (See the earlier section "Establishing expectations for household harmony" for additional tips.)

- ✔ **Set precise and specific rules about visitation by ex-spouses.** Children need stability and predictability.

- ✔ **Make sure that grandparents and other extended family members, if involved before the divorce, remain just as involved in the newly blended family.** Grandparents and other extended family members may need to mourn the loss of the original nuclear family before they become part of the stepfamily.

- ✔ **Maintain family rituals in your home as you wish, and adapt to new traditions in the stepfamily as they develop.** Don't force new traditions, especially at first.

Keeping Faraway Relatives Close

There may have been a time when everyone in a family lived in the same city and had frequent in-person contact, but nowadays, it's much more common for relatives to be scattered all over the country. Some children go many years without ever seeing, or even meeting, all their aunts, uncles, cousins, and grandparents. Building and maintaining good relationships with your extended family (as I explain how to do in the following sections) is more than an exercise in good manners; families lend strength and support when it's most needed and appreciated.

Staying in touch is easier than ever, because most everyone has access to the Internet. This technology is a great way for children to communicate and keep in contact with relatives, especially faraway grandparents. You can send Grandpa in Poland e-mails daily or an instant message along with a live video.

Sharing big news and participating in life events

Tell everyone in the family about births, graduations, engagements, marriages, special honors, and, sadly, deaths. A personal note is best, but a formal announcement is better than nothing.

A formal invitation to a life event, even if you don't intend to be there in person, calls for a note of congratulation and a gift. If the relative is a distant one and you don't ordinarily exchange gifts with that branch of the family, your gift can be modest, but giving any kind of gift will surely help cement relations. See Chapter 16 for details on giving gifts and Chapter 17 for the scoop on celebrating major life events.

Your attendance at special occasions is another way to express your pleasure at being part of the family. Likewise, the presence, support, and expressions of love of far-flung relatives can greatly ease the terrible sadness of a funeral.

Visiting and vacationing

When you travel to a distant city to visit relatives, a little bit of consideration can save you a lot of uncertainty. Keep these suggestions in mind as you plan a trip to see relatives (for additional tips on being a good houseguest, see Chapter 15):

- ✔ Discuss the timing of your intended visit before you make definite plans. Be sure that the dates of your visit coincide with your relatives' agenda.

- ✔ Be definite and specific about arrival and departure dates. Don't stay longer than three days.

- ✔ Unless you know for sure that your relatives have adequate guest accommodations and expect that you will stay in their house, make reservations at a nearly hotel or motel. You can always cancel the reservations if Grandma insists that you stay with her.

- ✔ Don't expect to be waited on. Pick up after yourself, make your own bed, straighten up the bathroom, and so on.

- ✔ Pick up your fair share of the restaurant tabs, admission fees, and other entertainment costs.

- ✔ Graciously participate in any social activities that your hosts plan.

- ✔ Keep your eyes open to the general décor of the house. After you return home, send a little thank-you gift to your hosts or a gift card from their favorite store.

Making the holidays happy

Putting any extended family together in one place for the holidays is like turning on a pressure cooker. Those qualities that you consider endearing in your cousin who lives hundreds of miles away can suddenly become intensely annoying after three days in one small house. Etiquette during the holidays is all about taking the high road, avoiding unnecessary conflict, and sharing good times.

Generally, the eldest capable members of a large family have first choice of hosting the major family holiday gathering each year — Thanksgiving, Christmas, Hanukkah, Passover, or Easter. Make sure to take travel, small children, cost, and distance into account when deciding where to stage the events.

If some members of your family have a conflict with other members, the best way to deal with the situation is to tell everyone that the holiday will go on as planned, everyone will be invited, and if certain people choose not to attend, the rest of the family will miss them.

Keeping an even score

Within every extended family, you can probably find an elaborate system of keeping score. The details may not be written down anywhere, but you can bet that folks have a pretty good idea of where things stand regarding dinner invitations, birthday gifts, tradeoff baby-sitting, and other give-and-take situations. For the sake of peace in the family and for broader reasons of good manners, do your best to keep things on an even keel.

Invitations to meals, especially, should be equalized. They invite you, and then you invite them. It doesn't matter whether they invite you to a lunch and you invite them to a dinner, or you invite them to your home and they invite you to a restaurant — however you arrange it, meals must be reciprocated. Within your extended family, it isn't important to try to outdo your sisters-in-law when it comes to menu choices, but the effort of planning, preparing, and serving a meal and then cleaning up afterward should be distributed evenly over the course of a year.

Gifts, especially to children, should also be reciprocated. Although the value of the gift need not be the same, the thought that goes into the gift should be. If one of your daughter's cousins attends your child's birthday party and brings a gift that your child cherishes, try to send along something as thoughtful when the tables are turned.

Avoiding family gossip

You don't have to be a member of the British royal family to understand that every extended family experiences a steady stream of developments that challenge the patience and understanding of close relatives. Most families have ways of containing divisive issues and sticking together. If a relative who's in a difficult position brings up the subject and wishes to discuss it, by all means lend a sympathetic ear.

However, bite your lip and don't inquire about rumors. Gossiping isn't good etiquette. Although hearing negative things about another individual may be unavoidable, repeating that information isn't polite — and doing so can create particularly sticky situations within a family. Life is tough enough without some busybody forcing an unpleasant conversation!

Chapter 5

Appreciating the Art of Friendships and Relationships

*O*ne of the keys to happiness is having good relationships. After family ties, the closest bonds you form are with friends. And whatever kinds of friends you have throughout your life — best friends, fast friends, friends through thick or thin — having friends helps you through an awful lot on this planet.

Because no one is born with friends, you have to figure out how to make them. You have to put energy into friendships to keep them. Whether you consider yourself an introvert, an extrovert, or something in between, you can learn how to meet and keep friends.

Dating is just as important as forming and maintaining friendships, and etiquette plays an important role in the world of relationships. Enormous changes have swept through society in recent decades, and many "rules" regarding the behavior of men and women toward each other have evolved. What hasn't changed is the importance of putting others at ease, making them feel comfortable, and assuring that their needs are met. Etiquette between the sexes means give and take.

In this chapter, I let you in on the subtle etiquette to the process of forming and nurturing friendships and dating relationships.

Widening Your Circle of Friends

New friends don't magically appear. And as life changes, old friends may move away, get married or divorced, or develop new interests with new circles of friends. Never fear! The opportunities for new friendships are all around you. Just a little bit of effort on your part can yield a rich harvest of satisfying new relationships.

You meet new people when you get out of your house, break from your normal routine, and take part in activities that interest you. Once again, you need to push yourself slightly beyond your comfort zone. But I can practically guarantee that you'll be richly rewarded for taking this small risk.

The following are some great places to meet potential friends or new loves:

✔ **Sports clubs, such as running groups, volleyball and softball teams, and exercise classes:** These groups bring together people with at least one common goal: to be active and fit. Playing together on a team or encouraging each other to run farther or faster is a great way to form lasting friendships — and maybe to meet the person of your dreams!

I know a couple of 30-something runners who joined a marathon training group and found that they ran at the same pace. They wound up running together for a year, through rain and snow and sleet and heat. At the end of the training period, they realized that they were in step in both running and romance.

✔ **Committees and social groups organized by a church, temple, or other religious organization:** These groups can help you meet a wide variety of people, many of whom may live in your neighborhood.

✔ **Community service organizations:** These organizations enable you to give back to your community while widening your circle of acquaintances. Working together toward bettering your community may also make you feel more connected to your neighbors.

✔ **Continuing education classes:** If you take a class in a subject that really interests you — be it Italian cooking, a foreign language, flower arranging, architecture, or sailing — you can find yourself in the company of others who have similar interests.

✔ **Neighbors and neighborhood groups:** Make an effort to meet your neighbors, especially those who have recently moved in. Some of my best friends have ended up living next door to me. Take the incentive to meet your neighbors by offering to organize a block party to celebrate a holiday, hosting a back yard barbeque, or planning an event to raise money for a local charity. If you happen to have fruit trees or a vegetable garden, share your produce with neighbors. If you love to read, you can organize a neighbor book club and meet monthly.

Also, join neighborhood groups and organizations. Gail, a client of mine, told me that when she moved to a new city, she joined a dog-walking group to meet friends. Not only has the group been a huge success in producing great friendships and traveling companions, but her dog always has companions and a place to stay when she's out of town!

✔ **Online:** If you're single and like to meet someone or you simply want to find a community who shares similar interests, the Internet offers a variety of possibilities — from dating services to community message boards. (Check out the section "Internet dating" later in this chapter for more info on starting online relationships.)

Although the Internet is a valuable resource for meeting new people, don't give out your personal information to just anyone. Proceed in new friendships and relationships with caution. For more info on Internet safety and etiquette, check out Chapter 10.

After you meet new people, it's time to introduce yourself and make small talk; see Chapter 7 for the lowdown on these activities.

Maintaining Your Existing Friendships

Good friendships are the result of caring and hard work. Friendships are constantly changing and evolving, and good friends continually refine and renew the ties that connect them. I've learned that the three prongs to maintaining friendships are the following:

✔ When good fortune smiles on your friends, you help them celebrate.

✔ When bad news comes their way, you comfort them.

✔ When a special need arises, you do your best to help.

How do good manners affect your ability to keep friendships? A well-mannered person behaves nicely toward everyone, all the time, including the doorman, the mail carrier, the bus driver, the dry cleaner, domestic help, and even the dentist. People who are kind and who have a good word and a smile for everyone they meet are loved and popular and build and maintain long-lasting, loyal friendships. Keep reading this section for more friendship tips.

Sticking to a few do's and don'ts

You can't find a better gauge of your strength of character than your unfailing politeness. Good manners include an effort to keep friendships in balance. If you want a good friend, try to stick to the following tips:

- ✔ **DO respect your friends' and neighbors' private lives.** Don't show up on someone's doorstep without calling first (unless, of course, it's an emergency).

- ✔ **DO use tact, the quick awareness of others' feelings.** Be thoughtful about the remarks you make. An offhand remark such as "You look tired today" can cause hurt feelings.

- ✔ **DO be sincere.** You can be honest without being hurtful or telling people only what you think they want to hear.

- ✔ **DO be a loyal friend.** Loyalty is very important in good relationships.

- ✔ **DO keep track of birthdays and anniversaries and remember to send cards.** This gesture may seem small, but it can mean a lot to others. Who doesn't like to be remembered?

- ✔ **DO give as well as receive.** Be available and supportive in times of distress and trouble — and ask your friends for help when you're in need.

- ✔ **DO agree to disagree.** You don't need to agree with someone all the time. You can have separate opinions or beliefs without ruining your friendship.

- ✔ **DON'T make negative statements about a friend's spouse, children, relatives, pets, decorating, weight, or age.** You may remember the little mom-saying: "If you have nothing nice to say, don't say anything." Most people can complain and talk negatively about their own family, but when it comes to others saying negative comments about those they love or their taste in decorating, watch out! You don't want to step on any toes, so show kindness by speaking with respect and consideration.

- ✔ **DON'T overburden your friends with constant complaining about your problems.** Pay attention to signs that your complaints are dragging them down. If friends begin to avoid you, take it as a signal to lighten up.

- ✔ **DON'T take your friends for granted.** Having a casual, easygoing relationship doesn't mean taking advantage of someone's kindness or asking favors of her contacts or friends.

Keeping friendships in balance

Good manners include an effort to keep friendships balanced in terms of invitations extended, favors reciprocated, and kindnesses acknowledged. Friends don't keep written records, nor are friendships always exactly balanced, but most people have a general feel as to whether efforts to maintain friendships are being reciprocated.

Do your best to stay on an even keel in matters such as placing telephone calls, sending an e-mail, extending luncheon invitations, doing the driving, and suggesting activities to do together, such as an afternoon at a spa, a movie outing, or a fishing trip. A friendship can't thrive if one person alone takes all the initiative to keep the relationship going.

An invitation to your friend's house calls for a return invitation from you. When your friend grabs the check at lunch, remember the gesture and pick up the tab the next time you're out together. This general rule applies to most acts of friendship — a lift to the airport, a gift of homemade cookies, willingness to go along on a shopping trip, and so on. To be a good friend, be conscious of the kindnesses that your friends extend to you and reciprocate when you're able.

Nurturing friendships through entertaining

The ability to entertain well is one of the greatest assets you can have as you seek to maintain friendships — and bring new friends into your life. In fact, making and keeping friends is one of the main reasons that people entertain. Human beings are social animals and need to be with other people, and entertaining is one way to bring people together. By nurturing your friendships through entertaining, whether you host a grand feast or a casual dinner, the rewards are plenty — in the form of new friendships, closer friendships, or simply being invited to your friends' homes in return!

The success of a party depends not only on the host's organization and creativity, but also on the guest list. Making sure that everyone enjoys each other is essential. Remember that mixing your guests encourages conversation, so try to select an interesting and varied group. The goal is to make the event as enjoyable for you as it is for your guests. Here are some events that your friends may love to attend:

- A progressive dinner, in which the group has appetizers at the first house, the first course at the next home, an entree at the next, and so on, through dessert and coffee.

- A block party with your neighbors, which gives everyone an opportunity to meet new families or become reacquainted with old friends.

- Tea on a Saturday afternoon.

- A backyard potluck or picnic with badminton and croquet to celebrate the Fourth of July, Memorial Day, Labor Day, or the Summer Solstice. Don't forget to invite your neighbors!

- Hot food after a college football game on a crisp fall afternoon.

- When you're new to the neighborhood, an open house on a Saturday afternoon for the neighbors and their children.

- A barbecue and cold drinks after an afternoon at the ballpark watching the local baseball team.

See Chapter 14 for more information about hosting an event.

Handling financial differences delicately

Money matters aren't easy, especially when they come up between friends. However, a little dose of courtesy and poise can go a long way.

If you socialize with friends who have larger salaries than you and they invite you out to dinner or events that you can't afford, be honest about the situation, not pretending you can afford these things if you can't. You also shouldn't expect the friends with money to always cover your meals or tickets to concerts or other events. Instead, you can choose to make it clear beforehand that you will pay for yourself separately. That way, you can control the situation and what you will be expected to pay. Or, if you have the option of staying home or suggesting other restaurants and events that may cost less, do so!

Try your best to never borrow money from friends. They aren't your bankers. Many good friendships have been ruined by disputes about money. If you give money to a friend, it's best to think of it as a gift, not a loan. Don't expect to get it back.

Just as a good friend won't want to put you in debt, a good friend also enjoys picking up the tab occasionally. If you happen to make more money than some of your close friends, though, you shouldn't allow them to take advantage of your generosity, nor should you feel any obligation to always treat. Speak up, and learn to say no graciously.

Ending a friendship

Healthy relationships are mutual. The goal is for everyone to be a winner. However, if you're in a situation where a relationship turns negative and you're being hurt or taken advantage of by someone, your best option may be to end or change the relationship. Ending a toxic relationship isn't uncommon. For example, possibly you have a friend that is a constant complainer or always stuck in a drama, and you feel like avoiding them because the relationship is emotionally draining. In this situation, you may want to reassess the friendship.

If you feel that the friendship is worth maintaining, you have three options:

- ✔ Say nothing, stay for a while, and continue to be a supportive listener.

- ✔ Try being honest without being hurtful by writing a letter.

- ✔ Speak to your friend and let her know how you feel, but remember that you risk causing hurt feelings and damaging the friendship. Only you can make that decision.

If you decide to speak to your friend, write down your thoughts before talking, which can help you to be clear about what you want to say. And remember that it isn't always what you say, but how you say it. Be kind and sincere. You can say something like, "I feel terrible about all the things you've been going through; it seems like there is just no end in sight. I'm sorry, and I wish there was something more I could do to help you get through this. Possibly it is time you spoke to a professional." If you feel comfortable, you could even offer to go to with him when he goes to see a health care professional so he doesn't have to go alone.

If the reality is that your friend is self-absorbed and can't change, even after you write a letter or speak with him or her, maybe ending the friendship is the answer. In this case, face-to-face communication may be your best option. Speak with your friend and reiterate what you said in your letter or previous conversations. Be sensitive, sincere, and straightforward; don't make long excuses or apologies. Politely tell the person that you have less in common and ending the friendship may be the best thing for both of you. Having good manners doesn't mean concealing your true feelings, but learning to express them honestly and be true to yourself.

Be aware of what your needs are in a friendship. Also, try to understand what others may need. This way, your friendships can have the best chance of growing strong and healthy.

Showing Courtesy to Members of the Opposite Sex

Women fly fighter planes, serve as police officers, fight fires, repair heavy machinery, drive racecars, ride Harleys, and rule countries. In short, women can do every job that men do. Is there any reason for men to continue to open doors for them, offer them seats on subway trains, and offer to carry their heavy packages? In a word, *yes*. Common courtesy toward another human being shows a regard for the other person's comfort and safety. And no man should be surprised if a woman returns at least a few of those same courtesies when the situation calls for it. When you practice the "new rules" of courtesy, you're making a gesture of respect.

Equal rights didn't revoke the need for thoughtful conduct of ladies and gentlemen toward each other. If for no other reason, common courtesies help ease the strains of everyday life. When it's understood that a gentleman holds open a door and a lady goes first, women should accept graciously. And if a man spent just one day walking around in high heels, he certainly would appreciate a seat on a crowded bus.

If you're still a little fuzzy as to what is proper behavior around the opposite sex, the following sections are for you.

Tips for men

Just in case you aren't familiar with these demonstrations of gentlemanly courtesy, please make the following rules a part of your routine behavior:

- When walking along the city streets with a woman, walk to her left (closer to the street) to keep her from being splashed. If you're in a potentially unsafe neighborhood, walk on the building side to prevent her from being mugged.

- Take off your hat (even if it's a baseball cap) indoors, as the flag passes, and during the national anthem.

- In a restaurant, you lead the way if you're the host. If the woman is the host, she leads.

- After parking a car in unfamiliar territory, walk around and open the car door for your female companion. Look all around the car before opening the door.

- Rise when a woman enters or leaves a room or leaves or returns to the table. (The woman will usually exclaim, "Oh, don't get up" — but not until after you have already gotten up!)

- Hold a woman's chair and help to seat her. (In some restaurants, the maitre d' does the seating. In this case, stand until she's seated.)

- If you're telling a group of men a joke or story that you wouldn't be comfortable sharing with a woman, it's better not to tell it. Most people have experienced this scenario: A man is chatting with other men, perhaps telling an off-color joke, when a woman approaches the group. Suddenly, everyone stops talking, and the silence is deafening. Sudden silence in the presence of a woman is rudeness with a capital *R*. The lesson? Keep all public conversations suitable for a mixed audience.

Certain behavior that was once thought to be polite has faded into the mists of time. At a restaurant, for example, a woman is fully capable of declaring her wishes to the servers. She may also pick up the tab or order the wine, depending on which party issued the invitation or which one has the company expense account.

Tips for women

A woman of good manners knows how to carry herself gracefully. That includes knowing how to accept common courtesies extended by men. Allow a man to be a gentleman and accept his courtesies with a gracious "Thank you" — that includes courtesies that may seem a bit dated. You may accept the offer of a seat on the subway and allow a man to order for you in a restaurant, if that's what he does. If a man indicates that you, his female companion, should go first into an elevator, go ahead and go first. A man's attempt at gentlemanly behavior should be encouraged, even if he's a little behind the times.

Here are some other tips for women:

- ✔ Not only should you open your own doors, but you should also hold doors open for others, male or female.

- ✔ Regardless of the situational awkwardness, never give up your personal safety. Don't let yourself out of a man's car in a dimly lit parking garage, for example. If the man doesn't offer, tell him that you can wait for him to come around. Likewise, don't be a passenger in a car whose driver has had too much to drink, and feel free to insist that the man slow down if you think he's driving too fast (the same goes for men!).

- ✔ Women, like men, are expected to remove their hats when the flag passes by or when the national anthem is played.

- ✔ Never feel pressured to behave like ill-mannered men just to fit in. You don't have to pretend to be amused by foul language, off-color jokes, or X-rated films.

Surviving the Dating Scene

Dating among adults is a process of searching for a person you love and want to be with for a long, long time — perhaps forever! If you're a high school or college student, you probably know plenty about dating. You may have a bit of difficulty finding the "right" person for you, but at least you know how to behave. You have the advantage over older folks who, for one reason or another, are just getting back to the dating scene after being away for some time. Still, everyone needs to be reminded from time to time of the proper way to ask for a date, behave on the date, and follow up if you're interested in pursuing a relationship.

I cover just the basics of dating in the following sections. For more info, check out *Dating For Dummies,* 2nd Edition, by Dr. Joy Browne (Wiley).

Understanding what passes for a date today

A *date* is two people meeting at a certain time and place for the purpose of enjoying an activity together. Beyond that loose definition, anything goes. When a potential romantic partner asks you to meet for coffee for half an hour during the workday, consider it a date; when you're invited to accompany someone to a cocktail party, you're being asked on a date. A date may also be a jog in the park or opening night at the opera.

Going out on a date enables you to get to know a person one-on-one, and if you show yourself to your best advantage, that person can get to know you and to like you. An ideal date allows you to have some peace and quiet together — as well as some fun — so that you can focus on each other. Rather than being stressed out by the prospect of a date, view it as an opportunity to show off your best qualities — your intelligence, wit, kindheartedness, and creativity.

Meeting people to date

Women no longer need to sit home and wait for the phone to ring. One of the new rules of dating is that women can take the initiative as well as men. That said, finding and asking someone out on a date can be nerve-wracking for both men and women — but at least the pressure isn't always on the man these days. In the following sections, I explain how to meet potential dates.

Traditional ways of meeting people

In traditional dating, you normally meet and become acquainted with others from attending social and sporting events, the gym, parties, school, coffee shops, grocery stores, and work — the list is endless. And, of course, there's always the dreaded *blind date,* being fixed up by your friends.

Some of these traditional ways don't always give you an opportunity of knowing about the person beforehand, which can cause nervousness and anxiety. However, the experience doesn't have to be nerve racking if you follow specific guidelines of dating etiquette, which you can read about in the section "Behaving well on a date," later in this chapter.

Internet dating

If you're single and looking to meet someone, whether for a casual relationship or something more serious, meeting people online can be exciting and rewarding. While online dating sites offer you unique possibilities for finding a new love, you have to pay attention to a number of etiquette and safety tips when meeting new people on the Internet. You've probably heard about those people that have found true love and marriage — and you've also heard the horror stories from others who thought they had found the same, only to find heartbreak, cons, and scams.

Before you venture out into the virtual world of Internet dating, you need to remember that you can never really know whom you're talking to and what their real motives are. Most online dating sites have policies that you're required to follow, such as using a member ID or user name, so that your privacy is assured. Never sign up with an online site that doesn't provide or guarantee anonymous e-mail services.

Here's a short list of things you should and shouldn't do when meeting people online:

- ✔ Be open and honest about what you want: a fling, marriage, a long-term partner, friends, or just some fun?

- ✔ Be creative when describing what you enjoy, your unique personality, your background, and interests. Bragging about your accomplishments, places you've traveled, or people you know isn't necessary.

- ✔ Always be aware of the personal information you're revealing. Never give out personal details of where you live or work or your home phone number until you're certain of the person's identity.

- ✔ Use an e-mail address different than the one you normally use and keep this address as your main means of contact.

- ✔ Never feel pressured to meet face to face if you aren't ready. If you do decide to meet someone, make sure the meeting takes place in a public location and make someone you know aware of your plans. You should also set a time limit for your meeting a head of time. For example, if you say that you will have coffee for 30 minutes, you can have the option of leaving, or staying longer if you're enjoying the company.

- ✔ Always use common sense.

For more information, seek out Internet dating resources and books, such as *Online Dating For Dummies* by Judith Silverstein, MD, and Michael Lasky, JD (Wiley).

Asking for a date

Say you're at a cocktail party and an attractive person catches your eye. You introduce yourself, the two of you chat, and you find that you want to get to know the person better. Now what? Ask if you may call to schedule a get-together. A day or two later, summon up your courage and call to ask for a date.

When you're gearing up to ask for a date, expect the worst and hope for the best, as they say. The person you ask may well have another social engagement, have a heavy workload, or be involved with someone else. That person simply may not want to go out with you. Whatever happens, try to remember that getting turned down for a date isn't a major rejection, or even a judgment on you — it happens to everyone at one time or another. Keep your goal in sight: to find a person who wants to be with you. If you look long enough, you'll find that person. Lots of fish are in the sea!

When proposing a date, try to come up with an idea that's so creative, so fun, and so appealing that no person in his right mind would refuse. By making the date sound terrifically exciting, you can make the other person excited to accompany you. How do you come up with one of these fantastic ideas? Keep up with the latest happenings in your area. Think of creative themes. For example:

- You can get tickets to a baseball game and propose an afternoon at the ballpark with all the trimmings — hot dogs, peanuts, and Cracker Jacks, with a drink at your favorite ballpark-area bar afterward.

- You can go see an intriguing foreign film followed by dinner at your favorite corresponding Italian/French/Chinese restaurant.

- You can have dinner at your favorite French bistro followed by an evening of jazz.

Although most people simply call and ask for a date, a written invitation via e-mail may make your offer stand out. Writing enables you to set the right tone without running the risk of stuttering, sounding nervous, or tripping over words. Besides, turning you down immediately over the phone is easier than considering the invitation and calling you especially to decline. (You can specify in your invitation how you'd like the person to respond.) Make sure that your e-mail message is casual in tone and amusing in style and describes a wonderful event that you've planned.

Regardless of whether you call or e-mail, your invitation should be time specific, event specific, and sincere: "I have an invitation this Friday at 7:00 to attend an art gallery exhibit and Champagne party — I'd love for you to join me."

Accepting or declining a date

You should be considerate when accepting or declining a date; honesty is the best policy. The following are some guidelines you can use to either accept or reject a date invitation:

- To accept a date, be gracious and polite and respond in a timely manner, within a day or two.

- If you've already committed to another social engagement for that evening, simply say so with a simple "I'm sorry, but I already have other plans." Never try to cancel a previously scheduled engagement for a date. If you welcome the invitation but are simply busy, you can add, "I would love to see you some other time."

Last-minute dates are in bad taste, and you shouldn't feel bad about declining them.

✔ If you never, ever want to have a date with this person, say firmly but pleasantly, "No, thank you, I'm not available." Theoretically, you should only have to say this once, but sometimes you need to repeat the exercise once or twice to get the point across. Be kind to the other person — someday you may be in her shoes!

Knowing what to expect on a date

Whether the man or the woman does the asking, you can reasonably expect the following few things after you accept an invitation for a date:

✔ You should be given enough advance notice to get ready for the date. Three days beforehand is the minimum. So, to ask someone out for Saturday night, you should call by Wednesday at the latest.

✔ A date should be kept, even if a more enticing offer comes along.

✔ Both of you should dress appropriately and use good personal hygiene.

✔ Both people should make the best of a date if things don't go as planned, without complaining, yawning, or otherwise acting unhappy.

✔ Plans shouldn't change at the last minute.

✔ You can kiss on the first date only if both partners want to.

✔ Sexual favors shouldn't be expected from either person.

✔ The invitee should thank the other person at the end of the date, whether to compliment the planning of the date or to show that you enjoyed the person's company.

✔ The invitee should write or call to say "Thank you" the next day.

Behaving well on a date

These rules of conduct for going on a date would hold fast in almost any part of life, but they're particularly important when you're out with someone new and you're eager to make a good impression. Here's how to show yourself to your best advantage:

✔ Dress tastefully (for tips, see Chapter 3).

✔ Be thoughtful of the other person's feelings, space, and property. Go out of your way to put your date at ease.

✔ Ask open-ended questions about the other person's interests, hobbies, work, and travel.

✔ Avoid gossiping or using derogatory or off-color language, and don't make sarcastic comments that degrade anyone else.

- Don't boast or drop names.

- Don't reveal too much personal information or ask personal questions, such as discussing details of past relationships or break ups.

- Keep your promises.

- Don't talk about how much something costs.

- Always have cash or a credit card with you, even if you don't expect to pay.

- Say "Please," "Thank you," and "You're welcome."

- Use your table manners (see Chapter 12 for details), and don't overindulge in alcohol.

- Above all, be yourself.

Picking up the tab

The traditional rule that the man always pays has been replaced by greater equality. Every couple in an ongoing relationship works out their own financial arrangements. In general, however, when it comes to a first date, the person who issues the invitation picks up the tab. If one person says to the other, "Let's go out," that indicates that both will share the cost equally. If one of them asks, "May I take you out?" the partner who is asking intends to pay the full cost.

If you're a man and you're a woman's dinner guest, relax and be her guest. Her invitation implies that she'll pay the tab, and she should be allowed to do so. But even if you're the one that was invited (whether you're male or female), offering to pay your share when the bill arrives is polite. Your date will appreciate the gesture.

After the first date, the couple can split the cost of dining and entertainment. Nothing prevents a couple from agreeing beforehand to split expenses; this practice is common among plenty of people, from students to older folks on fixed incomes.

If you're on a limited budget, you have an answer to the dilemma of dating without spending lavish amounts of money: Substitute creativity for big spending. You can suggest a trip to see a new exhibit at the museum, followed by a picnic lunch, a lecture, or a recital at a local college. The right person will appreciate your creativity and thoughtfulness in arranging such a date, even if it doesn't involve roses, wine, and caviar.

Using proper phone etiquette after a date

The telephone can seem like tricky business when it comes to dating. And today, the phone itself isn't the only thing you have to deal with — you must cope with voice mail, text messaging, and other technological wonders.

Business phones are meant to serve the business, not your social life. If you phone a new love interest at her work location, make sure that you have a good reason for the daytime call and keep it short. Begin by asking whether the timing is convenient. Then say what you have to say, get the response you need, and promise to chat at length after working hours. The same etiquette rules apply when calling someone's cell phone, sending text messages, and writing e-mails.

Today's technology makes it easy to stay in constant contact, so don't overdo it, especially during work hours. See Chapter 9 for more on phone etiquette and Chapter 10 for tech etiquette.

Coming clean about vital facts

Nice people didn't discuss many subjects prior to the time when TV commercials dealt with every affliction known to humankind. Even now, you may have a number of little skeletons in your closet that you aren't ready to share with the latest light of your life. But you simply must declare the following few facts before your relationship moves from dinner to breakfast:

- ✔ If you harbor any sexually transmitted disease, you must say so. Even if your condition is held in check and is in remission by medication, you have to confess. Divulging this info is best done during a quiet moment together, with honesty and kindness — something along the lines of, "I'm very attracted to you, and before our relationship becomes more intimate, there's something we should discuss."

- ✔ If you're going to start a sexual relationship, discussing the risk of HIV as well as sexually transmitted diseases, and what you both are going to do about it, is important. That means raising the issue of taking an HIV test and using condoms. Having that discussion is only proper if you're intimate enough to be talking about having sex.

- ✔ If you're married, you have to 'fess up. You may be legally separated, you may be dreadfully unhappy, or your spouse may be on foreign assignment for the next two years, but your marital status is a matter of public record, and you must not keep it a secret.

As for the 100 other little details that may send a new lover running, you have to listen to your conscience. In general, you owe it to the other one to come clean about really important facts.

Knowing when to cease and desist

Liking someone romantically and finding out that your affection isn't returned is terribly difficult, but etiquette demands that you accede to those wishes by withdrawing in a dignified way. This means no late-night phone calls, no long letters, and no begging or pleading. On the other hand, the uninterested party should be firm but polite and unwavering when saying that he has no interest in a relationship.

If you call someone repeatedly and the person doesn't return your calls, your repeated failure to reach the object of your intentions is a good indication that your feelings aren't reciprocated. If the calling is all one-way on your part, stop calling — it wasn't meant to be.

Particularly for those people getting back into dating after an absence (because of divorce or the death of a spouse), dating is stressful. Many people give up after an initial rejection. Don't give up. If you run into a person who doesn't reciprocate your interest, don't take it personally. It happens to everyone at some point. Keep trying, and sooner or later you'll hit upon the right chemistry with a special someone.

Chapter 6

Showing Civility in the Working World

In This Chapter

▶ Enhancing your relationships at work

▶ Knowing how to behave in unusual workplace situations

*Y*our success in getting along with others in your workplace has a major influence on your career success. You can have excellent job skills and good productivity, but if you don't fit in with the others and your colleagues find you difficult to work with, you'll have a much tougher time winning promotions and advancing up the corporate ladder.

Another equally important reason to pay attention to the relationships that you form with others in the company is this: For better or for worse, what goes on at work comprises the most significant portion of your social life. You spend more time with your co-workers than you do with friends outside of work, and in many instances, you spend more time at your job than you do with your family.

Yes, you need to adhere to etiquette for conduct on the job. Men and women in military service are drilled in the details of military courtesy and appreciate the freedom from uncertainty that those guidelines provide. The rules of courtesy in civilian life aren't quite as rigid, but a code exists nevertheless. Incorporate the suggestions in this chapter, and you may find Monday mornings a lot less challenging. (For more details on behaving in the workplace, check out my book *Business Etiquette For Dummies* [Wiley]).

Building Positive Relationships at Work

Outside of your family, you live your most important social life at work. That's where you spend most of your time, where you interact with the largest number of people, and where good manners can lead directly to raises, promotions, and a pleasant work environment. Business school may teach you how to draw a graph of sales results, but it seldom shows you how to use good manners as a springboard to bigger and better responsibilities. Stay tuned. I tell you how to develop relationships at work in the following sections.

Through all the ups and downs of life on the job, let good manners be your trademark. Friendly greetings, cheerful participation in group activities, help for others when they need it, and a pleasant demeanor all contribute to your reputation as a whole person. When you practice good manners on the job, your co-workers will cheer whatever success you achieve and will be eager to put in a good word on your behalf if the need arises. And good manners are good business! They give one a competitive advantage and affect the bottom line. In a global market that is growing more competitive every day, you certainly want to have every advantage.

Relating to your boss

Is there still such a thing as a boss? In this era of team leaders and group-effort facilitators, identifying the boss isn't always easy. But you're on pretty safe ground if you consider the person who writes your performance reviews and gives you suggestions for improving your productivity to be your boss. Here are a few guidelines for relating to your boss:

- ✔ **Courtesy toward the boss begins with direct address.** Your supervisor is always Mr. Jones or Ms. Edwards until the moment that Mr. Jones asks to be called Ed or Ms. Edwards gives you permission to call her Josie. Nine times out of ten, you can get away with unbidden informality, but that tenth time can be a career killer. Stay with the formal title until you're told to use the first name. (See Chapter 11 for more details on how to address people at the office.)

- ✔ **The most important courtesy that you can extend to your boss is to give your undivided attention.** Take notes on her directions, ask intelligent questions, and be involved and responsive. All these things indicate respect.

- ✔ **Greet the boss as you would all fellow employees.** When passing in the corridor for the first time of the day, say "Good morning" or whatever is appropriate to the hour. When departing for the day, say "Goodbye" or

"Have a nice evening." If you and the boss are of the same sex and you happen to use the lavatory facilities at the same time, a simple nod is greeting enough.

✔ **Remember that bosses issue invitations and subordinates respond.** For example, your boss may invite you to take lunch with him, but you should be hesitant to initiate that same sort of suggestion. In the same vein, the boss should take the lead in the conversation. Subordinates should follow the tone and subject matter that the boss sets.

✔ **If you have any reason to complain about anything in the workplace, speak with your immediate supervisor.** Dealing with grievances is where etiquette meets company rules and regulations. Nothing upsets a supervisor more than learning that a subordinate has lodged a complaint with someone else. If, for some reason, the outcome of your discussion doesn't satisfy you, ask your supervisor to advise you of the next step in the process. Going over the boss's head is one of the worst offenses you can commit on the job.

Connecting with your co-workers

Every work situation has its own set of practices and procedures. Look around and you can see that folks in your department tend to dress alike, make similar arrangements for lunch, discuss certain topics at length and never mention other things, arrive and leave at certain times, and so on. In some countries, alikeness is part of the national character and is considered to be the very root of courtesy. That's not quite how things are in the United States, but even so, every workplace has established norms.

If you decide to make a personal statement by standing out (such as by always being on time for meetings, not calling in sick too often, or displaying a positive and upbeat attitude under all circumstances), be very sure that you know what you're doing and why you're doing it. Succeed in fitting in before you try to stand out.

Be alert to the special sensitivities and needs of your co-workers as well. As diversity in the workplace brings together people from different ethnic, cultural, religious, and national backgrounds, you need to have a much more tolerant and inclusive attitude than you do at home or within your private life. Keep the following suggestions in mind when relating to your co-workers:

✔ **Learn the accepted terms for the ethnic groups, religions, and nationalities of your co-workers.** Get rid of the slang and sometimes disparaging terms that you may have used in the past.

✔ **Don't identify or refer to others by race or ethnic identity.** People are people. Use names and titles and avoid other labels.

- ✔ **Companies select job titles with great care, so use those titles.** An administrative assistant isn't a secretary, and an information systems specialist isn't a computer jockey.

- ✔ **Older, more experienced co-workers are owed respect for their tenure and expertise.** In today's world, where very young people are often peers or even managers of older workers, you need to be watchful of your behavior in this area.

- ✔ **Be alert to people's special needs.** If one of your colleagues must be absent for a religious observance, for example, offer to cover his responsibilities for the day.

- ✔ **Pay attention to other's responses and personality types.** One of the keys to etiquette is to pay enough attention to others to be able to modify your behavior to accommodate each person. Appropriate responses to particular personality types are helpful for anyone wanting to be an effective colleague.

Always remember that your co-workers are a vital part of your social life and that good relationships on the job are paramount. However, be wary of that fine line that's easy to cross when co-workers become friends. Use moderation in your exchanges so you don't spend too much time socializing. If it's necessary to discuss personal issues or conduct urgent personal business in your workplace, be brief and discreet. The best rule is to discuss personal issues in private so you give your employer what he pays you for — your time, focus, and work done well.

One last guideline: Don't become known as a constant complainer or someone who brings a bad mood to your workplace. Bring a positive attitude to everything you do at work. You don't have to be rude or sarcastic to say no.

Working in a land of cubicles

Today's office environment is often described as open. Instead of floor-to-ceiling walls with latching doors, people have cubicles with half-high dividers. Such an environment offers precious little privacy for personal telephone conversations or confidential chats with co-workers. You can safely assume that your every utterance is overheard, so don't say anything that you wouldn't want published in the company newsletter. And try to practice selective deafness; don't listen in on the activities taking place in the cubicles adjoining your own.

Here are a few other guidelines for working in an open environment:

- ✔ If you have nervous habits, break them. Don't twitch, jiggle your leg, or tap pencils and other items on the table — that can be irritating to those around you.

- ✔ Never engage in personal grooming in your cubicle or in meetings. Do it all in the restroom or at home.

- ✔ If you need to eat anything in your cubicle, try to select foods that don't have strong or unpleasant aromas.

Extending courtesy to your subordinates

Libraries have shelves full of books offering management guidelines. The most important etiquette advice concerning your dealings with subordinates is this: Praise in public, and criticize in private. Never let others know that you find it necessary to chew out Richard for forgetting to lock the cash box, but if a customer sends a note of thanks for Richard's kind assistance, read the letter to the whole work group.

One of the most important courtesies that you can extend to those who report to you concerns awards, praise, and other honors that come to you in the course of your work. If you're honored for your performance, be sure to mention the contributions of others who made your achievement possible. If a ceremony of sorts is held, name those who helped. It's no accident that acceptance speeches at events such as the Academy Awards are the way they are. Share the glory of the moment with your whole team, and they'll be eager to help you be a winner in the future.

Showing respect to strangers and newcomers

A new face in the workplace calls for the courtesy of introductions and an expression of good wishes. If a third party hasn't taken care of introductions, take the initiative yourself. Here's a sample script:

> "Hello. My name is Jack Browne, and I'm responsible for computer maintenance. What would you like me to call you?"

Chapter 11 has the full scoop on business introductions.

In the event that a stranger appears in your workplace, approach the situation with both courteous behavior and a reasonable amount of caution. If your company gives identification badges to employees and visitors, look for a badge. Introduce yourself to the stranger and ask how you can help. Specific rules regarding security are usually outlined in a written document available to all employees; if your company provides such a document, follow company policy.

Handling Unfamiliar Situations

Countless unfamiliar situations arise in which you simply don't know how to behave: The boss asks you to escort an important shareholder through the facility. You're called to a high-level meeting involving managers several levels above you. A power failure knocks out the air conditioning in your office building and leaves everyone suffering from the heat and stale air. You get into a traffic accident while driving a customer to the airport.

Unfamiliar situations bring out the best in people who can behave as sensibly and gracefully as possible (as I explain in the following sections). Communication counts in these situations. Inform your supervisor at once. Inform the human resources office. Call plant security. Call the receptionist and ask for help. The people who have mastered the many details of etiquette seem to know everything, not because they actually do know everything but because they know what to do when they don't know what to do. In the business world, as in society at large, self-confidence and smoothness carry the day.

In every unfamiliar situation, consider the comfort of others. Ask questions and confess your uncertainty. In addition, phrases like "thank you," "please," and "excuse me" are how you can promote civility in your society, because they move people to feel more kindly, more forgiving, and more empathetic toward others. They're words that connect people — and they're free. So, don't be stingy when it comes to using them. People will appreciate your thoughtfulness.

Choosing to be assertive rather than rude

When a co-worker is rude or making disrespectful remarks, or arguments arise in meetings, exercising decorum no matter how challenging it becomes is always best. Sure, being gracious when everyone is getting along is easy. But it takes an extra dose of character to act like a civil adult when a situation becomes negative.

If you find you're on the verge of responding in a less-than-polite manner, take control, count to ten, and maintain your composure. You gain nothing by responding to rudeness with rudeness. People are more inclined to cooperate with those they see as considerate and courteous. They're also more likely to want to talk further and work with thoughtful people, because they see that type of person as someone more like themselves. Think thoughtfully and then speak. When you take the higher ground, you always come out feeling better about yourself and the situation. You don't want to gain a reputation as a hothead.

Keeping your cool doesn't mean you have to be a doormat, however. Try to keep your distance for a while. You can take actions later after everyone calms down. Depending on the seriousness of the situation, you may want to express your opinion in a formal letter or schedule time with your supervisor to discuss the event. Remember, problems that start off small can become big if you let them go on very long.

To be proactive, try using the following assertive skills to manage the political and power dynamics that run through most organizations:

- ✔ **Network.** Get people on your side (and you on theirs) with sincerity and mutual respect (not through bullying tactics or manipulation).

- ✔ **Manage intimidation.** Learn to speak up and get around the blocks that undermine your efforts.

- ✔ **Invite reactions.** Make it easy for your allies to respond to your requests or expectations. Be open to constructive criticism.

- ✔ **Be visible.** Get recognized and valued for your skills, special talents, interests, and past and current contributions.

- ✔ **Claim your right to ask for help, advice, information, assistance, and opinions.** Be specific, focus clearly on what it is you really want or need, and *ask* for it. If you don't grant yourself that right, no one else will respect it, or you.

Ducking the limelight

You may have found yourself in meetings where you feel that you're in unfamiliar territory. Survive by taking a seat away from the conference table or, if that's not possible, by sitting as far as you can from the head of the table. Remain silent unless called upon, and if you don't have a useful response, defer to another, more knowledgeable attendee.

In any situation in which you really feel out of place or out of your depth, paste a pleasant expression on your face and be quiet. Others are probably eager for the limelight and appreciate the absence of competition.

Asking for advice during meals

A business lunch or dinner gives you an opportunity to form stronger bonds with your colleagues, clients, and managers. If you're caught off guard, remember that you're only a human being, and asking for help is always appropriate. Your co-workers and even your manager may be just as perplexed as you are — or they may be flattered by being asked to display their expertise.

So if you're caught in a restaurant where the foods are strange, the wine list is incomprehensible, and the table manners are foreign, confess your need for advice. Ask your host for help. If necessary, ask your host to order for you. If you're the host, ask your server for advice. (You can also find more information about dining in Chapter 12 and wine in Chapter 13.)

Are you headed out to eat with a guest who has special needs? Ask about his preferences first. You don't want to take a vegetarian to a steakhouse, and a person who follows Jewish or Islamic dietary laws won't enjoy a barbecue place. Remember that you can always phone ahead and ask the restaurant about provisions for people with special dietary needs.

Bridging the language gap

It's a small world, and business brings people from all cultures together. You may find yourself in a meeting with a foreign visitor, or you may find yourself sent off to a country with a language you don't understand. A language gap is a great opportunity for good manners to shine.

The best course of action is a little preparation. With as little as a single day of warning, you can obtain a phrase book and learn a few words of common courtesy — "Good morning," "Please," "Thank you," "I'm pleased to meet you," "My name is Adam Smith," and "Goodbye." Making an effort to communicate in another person's language shows your respect for that person.

After you establish that you're friendly and interested in the needs of your foreign guests, things ease up considerably. Large companies almost always have at least one employee who can serve as an interpreter. Ask for assistance in locating someone who can help. (See Chapter 19 for more information about interacting with people from other cultures.)

Apologizing as your final fallback

You really did it. You spilled coffee on the carpet in your boss's office. You went through an entire meeting calling one of the participants by the wrong name. You broke the glass trophy that a co-worker won at last year's golf tournament. Don't try to make your official apology while other business is being conducted. Do your best to minimize the damage and, at the same time, continue with the business at hand. Wait for the meeting to end before you try to patch things up. Then express your apology in writing with a brief, sincere note. (Chapter 8 has general tips on writing a note of apology.)

Note that such a letter is most effective when submitted immediately after the incident. The longer you wait to express your regrets, the less effective your gesture is.

Part III
Converse with Care: Saying Everything Right

"The lost art of conversation isn't lost at all. It's been kidnapped and held hostage by your sister-in-law."

In this part . . .

You just can't avoid communicating with others. And whether you're small-talking with new acquaintances, writing notes to family and friends, composing business letters, or e-mailing strangers who live across the globe, each mode of communication has its own set of etiquette guidelines. The chapters in this part can help you navigate your way through any form of communication with your manners intact. I even include detailed information about some of the newer technologies (think of cell phones, Internet chat rooms, and the like) to help you mind your manners in these perhaps unfamiliar waters.

Chapter 7

Engaging in Polite Conversation

*P*eople seem to have lost the ability to converse with each other. If you need evidence, look around your culture. Popular after-work restaurants and cocktail lounges play loud music on the sound system. People flock to theater complexes showing 20 different movies. Cable TV systems offer 50 to 100 or more channels. Many people spend their days in front of computers and have lost at least some of their ability to use language to communicate with people.

 Although times change, the basic human need to interact with other humans doesn't. Those people who have been able to cultivate the skill of conversation have a leg up on others who are stuck behind a computer or buried beneath a stack of paper. To become an interesting conversationalist, first keep in mind these three principles:

  ✔ Put the other person at ease and avoid saying anything that may cause discomfort.

  ✔ Show that you really care about what's on the other person's mind.

  ✔ Engage in a genuine exchange of information and opinions.

If your personality is sparkling and outgoing and if you have a genuine fondness for face-to-face conversations, you may find the suggestions in this chapter easy to follow. On the other hand, if you're shy and you feel a bit uneasy about chatting with anyone outside your immediate family, you may need to work a little harder. The best way to do so is to force yourself to attend social functions more frequently and make an effort to circulate among acquaintances and new faces. In conversation, as with other skills, practice makes perfect.

You may find yourself in situations with conversational barriers, such as when you travel to foreign countries or converse with folks who are deaf or blind. For tips on communicating in a different country, head to Chapter 19. Chapter 20 has information on disabilities and etiquette.

Initiating a Conversation

Good conversation starters involve everyone in your group in a lively discussion. A talented conversationalist understands who is in the group and what's appropriate for the occasion. For example, introducing the topic of baseball and then going on and on about statistics with the one other person in the circle who is a fan of the sport isn't a good idea. The other people will feel distressed and left out. However, bringing up an interesting story that you heard earlier that day is a good way to involve the group in a lively conversation.

Some people are naturally at ease in social situations and never have trouble making conversation. Others are a little shy when it comes to small talk, especially with strangers. The following sections give you some suggestions for surefire ways to get a conversation started. You'll be chatting away in no time!

Being naturally shy is common for many people, but don't let that stop you from socializing. If you keep to yourself, you may come across snobbish or rude. You don't have to always carry a conversation (sometimes saying less is better than talking too much). If you aren't contributing to the conversation verbally, just remember to smile and nod when others are speaking.

The art of social introductions

Introducing people is one of the most important acts you do in your daily life, yet very few people know how to do it correctly. Introductions are important in creating enduring impressions. The goal for making introductions is to provide information about each other in order to give you a common ground to carry on a conversation. Use the following guidelines to make introductions smoothly:

✔ The secret to knowing the order of social introductions is to remember the rule "Identify the king (or the ruler) of the situation." Formal and informal social introductions are done by gender. The most important person (ruler) is the eldest woman in the group. When introducing her, you say her full name first. Always introduce men to women and younger people to their elders. In other words, boys, men, and younger people are the people being introduced and their names are stated second. For example: "Mrs. Miller, I would like to introduce my swim coach, Mr. Jacobs."

If no women are in the group, the first name spoken is that of the eldest man or most distinguished man. If you aren't sure of their ages, or if their ages are the same, introduce the man you don't know as well to the one you know better. Say the name of the person you know better first.

✔ If you're in a business situation, gender doesn't matter; determine who to introduce based on pecking order — the ruler is the highest-ranking person in the group. For example, when introducing your father to your college professor, the professor is the ruler, and you say his name first. (See Chapter 11 for full details on business introductions.)

✔ When introducing someone, provide some information that clarifies your relationship with the person you're introducing, such as "This is my father, Sam McKibbin."

✔ Generally, use full names when making introductions. Exceptions may occur when introducing less authoritative people to more authoritative people. For example, when introducing your college friends to your parents, you would use your friend's full names, but you probably wouldn't introduce your parents by theirs. You can simply say, "These are my parents." Or if they have a last name that differs from yours, you can say, "These are my parents, Mr. and Mrs. Swanson."

✔ If you've forgotten someone's name, asking the person to repeat it is fine. Your best option is to be honest, apologize for forgetting, and move on. No matter what happens when you're introducing someone, almost all things can be forgiven if you make a sincere attempt at courtesy and accompany it with a warm and engaging smile.

People like to hear their names, so when you say a person's name, what you're saying is that you have a genuine interest in that person. And that person is probably flattered that you remembered his name!

✔ When introducing yourself to others, always give your full name and tell them something (but not too much) about yourself. (Be sure to ask them questions, too; see the next section.)

Meeting and greeting obviously require positive effort: You must speak! But other attributes, such as firm handshakes and good eye contact, enhance the positive first impression you want to make. Try the following tips:

✔ Always introduce the people you're with to the new people you're meeting by physically looking at each person directly when stating their names.

✔ Extend your hand for a handshake when introducing yourself or being introduced.

> ✔ When shaking hands, remember to squeeze the other person's hand firmly, yet gently, and grasp the entire hand. The web of your thumb should meet the other person's thumb web.
>
> ✔ Always stand when you're introduced or are introducing other people to each other.

Depending on the formality of the situation, you shouldn't use a person's first name until some additional direction has been given to do so. If, however, you were introduced earlier in the evening and had some conversation, upon departure it is okay to say, "I'm glad to have met you, Tom." Or, if you're on the receiving end of the farewell, reply, "Thank you, Tom. Have a nice evening."

Asking questions

A good way to break the ice is to ask a question. It all begins with a resolution on your part to say something when you find yourself making eye contact with another person. Here are a few ideas:

> ✔ **At a wedding reception:** "Hello. Are you a friend of the bride?"
>
> ✔ **At a company party:** "My name is Howard. Do you work in the head-quarters building?"
>
> ✔ **At a dinner party:** "I heard our host introduce you as Captain Lawrence. My name is Judy Jones. Are you on active duty?"

As the other party, your duty is to respond with a reasonable answer. A simple yes or no turns off the whole conversation. Remember the power of question-and-answer and keep the ball rolling. Here are some sample responses:

> ✔ "Hi. I'm a fraternity brother of Jack's. We promised that we'd show up for each other's weddings. My name is Steve. What's yours?"
>
> ✔ "Yes, Howard, I work in the marketing department. You've probably seen my name on some memos — Betty Borden. Aren't you an accountant?"
>
> ✔ "I guess you could call it active duty. I'm with the police department. And if you call me Don, I'll call you Judy."

Some questions, however, are simply too corny to use as ice-breakers. No matter how strong the temptation, stay away from "What's your sign?"; "Do you come here often?"; or "What's a nice person like you doing in a place like this?" A little creativity goes a long way in the initial stage of a conversation. You're much more likely to get a good response if you take time to think of a good question to ask.

When you ask a question, be prepared to listen to the answer, try not to be thinking ahead about what you want to say next. For the details on effective listening, see the section "Listening: More Than Not Talking" later in this chapter.

Complimenting someone

You're always on safe ground when you start the ball rolling with a genuine compliment. To be successful, a compliment should be sincere, specific, and followed up with a question. For example, say you notice someone's accessory — earrings, eyeglasses, a button — and admire it. Here are examples of three approaches you could take:

✔ "Those are lovely earrings — and so unique! Do they have a story?"

✔ "I've never seen eyeglass frames like that. Where did you find them?"

✔ "That's an interesting button on your lapel. What does it mean?"

Here again, the power of a question starts a conversation or keeps it moving. If you're the recipient of the compliment, accept it graciously and help continue the conversation with a question of your own. For example:

✔ "Why, thank you! I picked up these earrings while I was on vacation in Thailand. Have you ever been to Thailand?"

✔ "It's so nice that you noticed. There's a new optical store at the mall. I thought the frames were great when I picked them out, but now I wonder if they're too big. What do you think?"

✔ "It's kind of you to ask. I got the button for 15 years of service with the county. Can you imagine working at the same job for 15 years?"

Finding Something to Talk About

After the initial greetings and pleasantries, what do you say next? The etiquette of conversation is governed by your sensitivity. Topics that seem perfectly reasonable at a backyard barbecue may be totally out of place at a bar mitzvah. If you're at a funeral, discussing the latest news about the breakup of your favorite star's marriage may be seen as frivolous and disrespectful to the occasion, whereas at lunch with a couple of close friends, celebrity news may be completely acceptable as a light topic of conversation. Make sure to give yourself a second or two of time to think about the situation before opening your mouth.

In addition to an appropriate subject, timing is also of the essence. At a cocktail party, a five- or ten-minute conversations may be the maximum in order to allow everyone to circulate. Pity the poor person who gets stuck in a corner, hemmed into a 30-minute conversation about bad news in the local economy! At a dinner party, however, you may be expected to keep up a conversation with the people to either side of you for the duration of the meal, which may last two hours or more.

The following sections give you more tips on appropriate — and inappropriate — subjects.

Surveying successful conversation topics

Successful conversationalists know how to introduce topics that interest just about everyone. If you need a few suggestions, here are some ideas for topics that usually spark a lively conversation:

- **Current events:** It's a good idea to scan a news magazine, a news-related Web site, or the daily newspaper before heading off to a social event to find upbeat, interesting, or unusual news.

- **Congratulations:** Offering congratulations to someone on an accomplishment, such as a graduation, promotion, or new baby, can get the conversation rolling on a pleasant note.

- **Good news:** Providing happy news about mutual friends is an upbeat topic that puts people in a good mood.

- **Cultural events:** Talking about the latest play, musical performance, or art show interests almost everyone.

- **Sports:** If a sporting event is of national interest, such as the Olympics or the Super Bowl, everyone should be able to participate.

If you notice you've hit an uncomfortable subject or a topic someone isn't interested in, as awkward as it may be, try to turn the conversation to another one of my small-talk topic suggestions.

Avoiding conversation killers and taboo topics

The most explosive conversational subjects are sex, politics, money, and religion. People tend to have strong emotions and can be highly opinionated about this group of troublesome topics. You can avoid a whole lot of trouble if you keep these simple cautions in mind:

✔ Any conversation about sex inherently can be morally, legally, and personally hazardous. Even in this supposedly enlightened era, many people consider sex to be a forbidden topic. They may take offense at sexual jokes or comments on the alleged sexual activities of others.

What's worse, if you bring up a sexual situation in your conversation, you may unwittingly implicate a third party known to your conversation partner. Or, in the worst-case scenario, you may wind up defending yourself if that person takes your sexual stories or comments as sexual harassment.

✔ The give-and-take of political conversations is a basic component of democracy, and you may feel perfectly justified in expressing a strong opinion. But the conversation can take an ugly turn when the parties are on opposite sides of an issue.

Stay alert for any sign that you're triggering an emotional reaction, and drop the subject with a comment such as, "I can see that we disagree. Let's talk about something a bit less divisive." Even if your mission is to win a convert to your point of view, you won't accomplish anything by making an enemy.

✔ In some ways, money is a greater taboo in American culture than sex. People become very uncomfortable when money is discussed in a group setting. You should never ask someone how much something costs or how much someone earns. Make any discussion about money in very general terms.

For example, an inappropriate comment is "I heard that Richard Jones bought a house on Columbus Drive for $150,000 — doesn't that seem like a lot for that area? But the only reason he could afford it was that his parents gave him $10,000 for a down payment."

A more appropriate comment is "Columbus Drive is getting to be a really nice neighborhood. I've heard that property values have appreciated considerably in the past year. In fact, Richard Jones just bought a house there."

✔ Religion means different things to different people. Some people quietly keep their religious beliefs to themselves. Other folks feel that they should be able to express their religious beliefs, and they may even make an attempt to convince others to join them.

If you have strong religious beliefs, bring them up only when you're asked about them and elaborate only upon further questioning. If somebody asks you to discuss some detail of your faith, by all means go ahead and explain. But be very careful about forcing religious beliefs on someone who may be unwilling to hear them.

If your conversation partner begins moving away from you for no apparent reason or looks disturbed, you know you've hit on an uncomfortable topic. The worst thing you can do if you've made a conversational faux pas is to slink off into a corner and hide or vow to move out of town and assume an alias. You're much better off taking responsibility for your blunder and face the consequences — with a little humor. Humor is the best way to diffuse a tense situation and change the subject to a more positive one.

When using humor to ease tension, make sure that you're relaxed, friendly and humble, not arrogant or cocky. Try to make others feel comfortable. For example, suppose you're having lunch with your boss and you're discussing home décor; you mention that you don't like French provincial furnishings, and then your boss tells you that her house is full of French provincial. Now you're in an awkward situation and need to do a little backpedaling. You may try saying something like this: "Though it's not my favorite, I appreciate the period and designs; all my close friends tell me I have no taste when it comes to decorating." Then make a solemn oath to yourself never to offer your opinion in such a harsh manner.

Keeping your personal life personal

Good friends can discuss almost anything, but people you meet at social gatherings aren't entitled to deeply personal details of your life. Moreover, something you think is interesting may bore another person. For example, if you just went through an illness and your friend asks you how you're feeling at a dinner party, give a simple answer. Something like "I've been back at work this week and really am on the mend, thank you" should suffice. A detailed explanation of the virus that struck you or the havoc that it wreaked on your digestive system isn't necessary.

Likewise, if you're at coffee hour after church on Sunday morning and an acquaintance asks about your children, briefly state the news: "Brad is in Phoenix working at a law firm, and Terry is starting a new job at a public relations firm in Boston after getting back from a tour of Europe. They're both doing well, thank you." Details about boyfriends or girlfriends who have come and gone or raises or grades that your children have received are more information than most pleasant conversations require.

The question "How are you?" is particularly tricky for some people. It's a formal artifact of our society and isn't meant to elicit a detailed response. Although you may be tempted to launch into an in-depth discussion of your failing health or your recent breakup, the only appropriate response to this question in a casual social meeting is "Just fine, thanks. How are you?"

Good manners start to overlap into self-defense when strangers start probing into your personal affairs. You certainly don't have to answer questions about your finances, your marital history, or anything else that you'd rather not discuss. Deal with a Nosy Nellie courteously but directly by looking her straight in the eye and asking, "Why do you ask?" or stating "I'd rather not talk about that." Doing so usually stops the current course of the conversation and allows you to introduce a new topic.

Listening: More Than Not Talking

George Bernard Shaw once said, "One way to be popular is to listen attentively to a lot of things you already know." Listening well is an act of generosity. To truly listen to someone is an unselfish act that you perform for the other person's benefit.

How do you learn to listen? Ask a question of someone, and then let that person answer. Really concentrate on what the person is saying. Don't interrupt or interject comments that shift the attention to you. Ask follow-up questions to what the person has told you. All these signals show the depth of your attention. Beyond that, I explain some special ways to be a good listener in the following sections.

You have two ears and one mouth. Use them in that proportion by listening more than you talk. Nothing is more flattering than someone who listens to you carefully and shows sincere interest in other people. Plus, the best way to learn is to listen — not to talk. If you maintain lively curiosity about life, people, why things happen the way they do, how things work, and what people do in their jobs, for example, you can always be at the center of good conversations.

Here's looking at you

Eye contact is the glue of a conversation. When you look directly at a person and pay attention to the conversation (rather than letting your eyes roam around the room in search of other social opportunities), you give a signal that, for the moment at least, the person you're talking to is the most interesting person imaginable. Looking away, especially at your shoes or the ceiling, indicates your wish to be far away.

In the United States and Europe, direct eye contact shows that you're an attentive listener. However, keep in mind that in most Asian countries direct eye contact is considered rude. See Chapter 19 for more information about behaving appropriately when you're abroad.

Just follow the prompts

Keep your conversation partner going with little prompts. A well-placed "hmmm" here and there indicates your understanding of whatever is being said and shows that you're following along. A gentle nod of your head now and then offers further encouragement. Failing to respond and keeping your face in neutral have the opposite effect — they may even bring the conversation to a dead halt.

A soft chorus of affirmations is another trick. Little phrases like "Of course" and "Well, I should say" and even "Oh, no!" act as prods to keep you in the game and show that you're listening closely. "Tell me more" often spurns additional embellishment on the subject at hand.

Winding Down a Conversation

All things (no matter how good or bad) must come to an end — and conversations are no exception. A good ending can go a long way, so take time to end the conversation on a positive note. People remember what they hear last the longest. The best way to leave a conversation is to smile and thank the other person for her time, but it isn't always that easy. For more detailed advice about how to gracefully leave a conversation, keep reading.

Reading the signs

Some people just love to talk more than others (it's okay to admit it). You may find yourself rattling on, especially when you're nervous or afraid of silence. If you're a talker, try to read the body language of people you're talking to and gauge when it may be time to politely end the conversation.

Watch for physical communication signals as well as verbal. A few clues that you may need to end the conversation include the following:

- The person you're talking to keeps looking at their watch or looking around.

- The other person becomes fidgety, shows facial tension, or acts bored; his eyes start to glaze over.

- The person you're speaking with doesn't add to the conversation.

- Your conversation partner's eyes are closed and a tiny trail of drool is making its way down her chin (an unlikely, but final clue that the discussion needs to come to an end).

If you find you've been monopolizing the conversation, simply apologize and throw the ball in the other person's court without drawing too much attention to your faux pas. You can do this by asking the other person questions about himself (nothing too personal) or his work — and then be a good listener. At this point, if he is ready, the other party will end the conversation.

Bowing out graciously

Say you've been conversing with a person at a cocktail party for 15 minutes. This person won't get off the subject of his job, his health, or his children — three of the topics that are most likely to bore other people. No rule says that you have to remain trapped in a conversation you'd rather end. How you extricate yourself is just one more measure of your mastery of good manners. Here are some examples of polite exit lines:

- "I didn't know that quantum electrodynamics was such a fascinating subject. Perhaps you can tell me more after I've finished saying hello to my cousin, who just arrived."

- "You know, that cat of yours sounds like a real character. I'll be thinking about her while I powder my nose."

- "Oh, for goodness sake! The time passed so quickly that I forgot to call my babysitter. Please excuse me."

You should never lie when trying to come up with an exit line. Make sure your reason for bowing out of the conversation is legitimate so you don't risk making the other person feel bad.

A polite person is never cruel to another — no matter how bored you are. Smile, shake hands, and part graciously. Close by saying "It was nice talking to you."

Chapter 8

Catching Up on Correspondence

In This Chapter

▶ Choosing the appropriate writing supplies

▶ Grasping the basics of form and function

▶ Surveying writing samples for common situations

▶ Finishing with an appropriately addressed envelope

*T*he telephone is close at hand. You can pick it up and dial the number of just about anyone in the world, and in a matter of seconds, you're in voice contact. You can send documents via fax. You can e-mail or text message anything from an informal note to a long text. You have so many communications options these days that the old-fashioned letter seems almost, well, obsolete! Call me old-fashioned, but I still believe that nothing is as thrilling as receiving a nice, long, handwritten letter full of news, intimacies, and real emotion — the kind of letter that you can read and reread.

A telephone call may be welcome, but it doesn't allow you to replay the conversation. You can't hold an e-mail in your hand, admiring the ink and penmanship. And a fax . . . well, it's nice for a cheery greeting, but when it appears on the machine, you can find nothing intimate about it.

This chapter gives you some helpful comments on the art of writing letters. (See Chapter 9 for information about telephone etiquette and Chapter 10 for information about e-mail etiquette.) The many details of letter writing communicate a whole lot more than just the words on the page. Follow along here, and you can pick up some insights that may have escaped you in the past. You can also gain a better feeling for what to write and what not to write.

I discuss only personal correspondence in this chapter. For the scoop on business correspondence, head to Chapter 11.

Stocking Up on the Hardware of Letter Writing: Paper, Pen, and Other Fun Stuff

To write a "real" letter (that is, one that doesn't involve a computer), you need paper, an envelope, a pen (and ink if you use a fountain pen), a postage stamp, a writing surface, and, probably, a wastebasket. Here are a few suggestions:

✔ Personal letters should be composed on something a bit more dressy than those dead-white 8½-x-11-inch sheets that you feed into your printer. Investing in a high-quality stationery is a good idea. I explain the types that you can choose from and their functions in the section, "Selecting the Right Stationery."

✔ Although most stationery comes with matching envelopes, you should consider suitability when selecting both your stationery and envelopes — much like matching your wardrobe. If the paper you're using happens to be thin, use an envelope with a color lining. These envelopes can add elegance and formality.

✔ Your personal stationery envelope should be the same dimension as the folded paper; only use those oblong envelopes for business communications. (See more on paper sizes in the section "Selecting the Right Stationery.")

✔ You can find many good quality and inexpensive pens on the market, such as ballpoint pens. Experiment until you find the pen that is comfortable for you, your writing style, and the paper you use. Most medium- to fine-point pens look good on various types of paper.

✔ Do you have a fountain pen? Real ink looks wonderful on high-quality paper. You can find disposable fountain pens preloaded with ink for just a few dollars. Those inexpensive pens work a lot better than you may think, and if you get to the point where you really like writing with pen and ink, you can spend anywhere from $30 to more than $1,000 for a fancy pen.

✔ Ink, too, says something about you. Writing ink comes in many colors. However, dark blue and black are the most formal and correct. The standard dark blue ink conveys a neutral message; your reader won't even notice the color. Black ink looks very assertive. Green, purple, and brown inks are unusual enough to identify the writer as a creative individual.

Red ink may appeal to you, but it is difficult to read under certain lighting conditions and on certain tinted paper stocks.

✔ While you're out shopping, stop at the post office and get some stamps that are more interesting than the "official" first-class stamps that they sell in rolls. Your stamp says something about you. You may wish to select a commemorative design that features a special interest or cause.

✔ Your desk is an important part of success in letter writing. You need a large enough surface to provide a resting place for your forearm and elbow. Otherwise, your writing may have a messy, wobbly look.

You can find an assortment of stationery, notepaper, note cards, and envelopes at most large office-supply stores. Yet, seeking out smaller boutiques or shopping online gives you additional options and a broad selection of interesting paper and supplies.

Selecting the Right Stationery

If you've decided that your days of scribbling on a legal pad and stuffing the sheet into the nearest envelope are over, congratulations! Now that you want to stock up on real, adult stationery, what on earth do you need? And what purpose does each type of stationery serve?

Using ruled, lined, or highly scented paper can be seen as poor taste. Instead, read the following section to get the details of what you *should* be writing on.

Half sheets

You should use this paper for most personal social correspondence. Half sheets are about 7¼-by-10½ inches in size, and sometimes paper for women is smaller (usually around 4-x-6 inches). The weight and texture of the paper can vary, but you may want to take these factors into consideration to choose the best stationery for you.

Consider the shape of the paper you buy based on your handwriting. For example, if your writing style is tall and narrow, it will look best on narrow paper, and smaller, wide handwriting is more appropriate on a square sheet of paper.

While women can use any color of their choice, from tan to cream to pastels, men traditionally have used only white, cream, or gray. Engraving is usually done in a darker complementary color — dark gray on gray or dark brown on tan, for example. If you want to be perfectly correct, your social stationery should have your name or your monogram at the top.

Because you shouldn't write on the back of the first sheet, make sure that you also purchase second-page sheets, which are plain, with no engraving.

Insert the paper into the envelope by folding it in half with the bottom edge brought up to the top edge and placing it in the envelope with the back flap facing you. After the paper is in the envelope, the fold of the paper should be on the bottom and the two edges held together at the top.

Foldover notes (informals)

Foldover notes are used for writing notes and informal invitations. They're usually white, cream, or gray and about 3¾-by-5¼ inches in size. You can have these notes engraved, embossed, or printed with your name or monogrammed in the center of the card's front. You may want to choose a colored border to match the letter and lined envelopes. Again, the weight and texture of the paper is a personal preference.

Any monogramming makes it impossible to write on the top inside part because of the indentation. You can write on the bottom half of the inside of the card and on the back side of the bottom half of the card. If the card is printed and not embossed or engraved, you can begin your note on the top side. Insert the card into its envelope right side up, with your monogram toward you as you insert it in the envelope. The card's fold should be at the top.

A woman may make her surname the middle initial (usually slightly oversized), flanked by the initials of her given and middle names — in other words, Lisa Beth Johnson would use the monogram LJB. If single, Brad Cameron Smith would use the monogram BSC. For a married couple such as Jill and Kevin Mathews, you would enter the monogram order as JMK. Married women would use the same order as a single person (first name initial, last name initial, middle name initial), and if they go by their husband's last name, they use that initial in the middle. Anne Marie Fox would be AFM. If a woman is married but uses her maiden name in business, she would use her maiden name initial in the monogram rather than her married name initial.

Letter paper for everyday use

Having some lesser-quality paper with your name and address printed on it to use for writing about personal business is nice to have around. For example, you may write to request information about the stock of a public company or to ask about the status of an order or a bill.

Even if you're using the paper for personal business, use white, cream, or gray for a professional look. Texture and weight isn't as important, but you may want to keep in mind that normally a heavier weight paper is more expensive.

Crafting a Well-Written Letter

Writing a letter is more than slapping some words on a page. Before you begin to write, you should take a moment to ask yourself why you're writing the letter and what you want your reader to know. A little bit of forethought can go a long way to writing a meaningful letter that communicates your intent. You should also take the time make sure your letter is well organized and easy to read.

In the following sections, I explain each element of a letter and how to format it. I also give you advice on choosing the most appropriate language.

Understanding the basics: Form and function

Informal and personal letters need not follow a rigid format, but you should follow the basics. I walk you through the nuts and bolts of formatting a letter in the following sections.

The address

If your address isn't printed at the top of the page, write it in the upper-right corner. If the recipient knows very well where you live, you can omit the address and simply use a dateline (see the next section).

The date or dateline

Indicate under the address the date and place you wrote the letter. The date-line can be as simple as "Chicago, May 20, 2007." Dating letters — and even postcards — helps the reader when he rediscovers the note a long time after you sent it.

The salutation

Depending on your relationship with the recipient, personal letters are appropriately led off with a simple "Dear Eloise," with a comma at the end — such as "Dear Dad," "Dear Cousin Marlene," "Dear Professor Rubin," "Dear

Dr. Jones," or "Dear Bobby and Nancy," "Dearest Carol," and so on. You can use either first or last names or what you would normally call them in person. A good rule to follow if you're uncertain is to err on the side of formality.

A salutation in a formal letter would include the use of titles. If you're writing a letter without knowing the name of the recipient, you can use the following salutations: "Dear Sir," "Dear Madam," "Dear Gentlemen," or "Dear Sirs."

In all letter styles, all text in the salutation is flush to the left, two spaces below the inside address.

The main body

The content of the body very much depends on your reason for writing, of course, but the main purpose of the letter is to convey some news with clarity while reflecting your personality and expressing your thoughts in a clear, simple, and touching manner. Your purpose for writing should be stated fairly early on in the body.

You may want to start your letter with something like "You will be glad to hear that. . ." or "What a wonderful surprise it was to see you on Thursday. . . ." A description of where you're writing and what you've been doing that day are also wonderful additions to the beginning of the letter. As you progress in the body of the letter, you want to convey news about what has been happening to you and to those you know. (I provide sample letters for specific situations later in this chapter.)

Leave a space between the salutation and the beginning of the body of your letter, and be sure to indent the first line. Leave good margins at both sides of the sheet, write as legibly as you can, and, when mentioning important details such as airline schedules or a vacation address, make sure that the item is easy to read. Print if your handwriting is a bit eccentric or is difficult to read.

Keep your paragraphs, sentences, and words short. Don't try to impress your reader by using unusual or long words — you want your letter to be as pleasant for the recipient to read as possible. Always double-check that the spelling, grammar, and punctuation is perfect.

News of good fortune is always welcome, but bragging isn't. By all means, tell your former neighbor that your little Jennifer is doing well at school, but leave it at that. You may be proud that Jenny's teacher said she is the brightest 9-year-old in history and is reading at the college level, but your former neighbor may resent it, particularly if her own child happens to be having a difficult time in reading class — and you don't know it. In a similar vein, your mother in Spokane will be interested to know that you attended to your dental needs, but she doesn't need to read about the agonies of a root canal job and your struggle to find the money to pay for the procedure.

Headings

If your letter is long and contains several unrelated subjects, you can help your reader by inserting headings where appropriate. You can't find any hard-and-fast rules for headings within a social letter, so you can invent your own. Two or three words, perhaps underlined, can separate unconnected reports and topics. Consider the following examples:

> ✔ <u>My job</u>
>
> The area manager tells me that I'm in line for a promotion before the year is out, and I'm looking forward to. . .
>
> ✔ <u>Leroy</u>
>
> We took him to the pediatrician a few days ago, and the doctor says that he is developing nicely. And he's talking like crazy! His vocabulary now includes. . .
>
> ✔ <u>The flower bed</u>
>
> Now that the weather is getting warmer, the tulips are in full bloom and the sunflowers are shooting up. We put some topsoil on. . .

The closing phrase

Ending a letter should be graceful, an expression of affection or friendliness. The single word "Love," "Fondly," or "Affectionately," or a phrase such as "Miss you," "Write soon," or "More later," works with family and close friends. Closing with "Warm regards," is fine when writing to someone you don't know very well. "With every good wish for a speedy recovery," or "All best wishes for happiness in your new home," may also suit the situation.

The closing goes to the right, after the last line of your text and before your signature. Capitalize the first word and keep the remainder of the phrase in lowercase.

Your signature

Sign the letter with your name — for example, Dad or Ronald. If you're less familiar with the recipient of your letter, or if you're unsure whether the person will immediately know you by your first name, sign your first and last name.

For example, in a note to your grade-school teacher who is retiring, sign your full name. The same goes for a thank-you note to someone you met recently who invited you to a large cocktail party (and may have included two other Daves in the group).

Using titles when signing personal letters isn't usually necessary. In other words, if you happen to be a physician, you can stay with Maxwell Farnsworth rather than Dr. Farnsworth, but the choice is yours to make.

Postscript

The *postscript* is a sentence or paragraph normally after the close of a letter (in other words, after the signature), usually denoted by the initials *P.S.* These initials are Latin for *post scriptus,* which means, "after having been written." Basically, the postscript translates to having an additional thought after the writer has completed the letter. The use of postscript is common in personal letters and not appropriate in business or formal correspondence.

Using the right words

A letter is a direct reflection of the person sending it, so you want to be careful to choose just the right words. Here are a few guidelines:

- ✔ Because purely social and informal letters are intended to maintain contact with family and friends, you can write whatever you would normally say in a face-to-face conversation, within reasonable limits.

- ✔ In a formal letter, you want to create a professional and positive impression that clearly expresses your thoughts. Be specific and be polite. All letters are a reflection of your taste, character, and even your appearance. Writing neatly and legibly with all words spelled correctly is of the utmost importance.

- ✔ To sound sincere and personalize the letter, use language and terminology familiar to the intended recipient.

- ✔ Visualize the intended recipient seated across from you while you're explaining the subject of your letter. Think about what you want to communicate to that person and the tone you want her to hear.

- ✔ Write a first draft of a letter on plain paper before you transfer the letter to your stationery. Doing so allows you to take a moment to contemplate what you're about to write (and also saves on good stationery by allowing you to make mistakes on scratch paper first!).

You also can try writing your letter on your computer first. This way, you can cut and paste words and sentences easily and also use the spellchecker and other features your word-processing program may have.

As in all communications, verbal or written, it's considered in bad taste to use any type of slang terms, name drop, or brag. Never start off a letter with "I know I shouldn't say this. . ." or "I shouldn't be writing this. . . ." This type of communication can reflect poorly on your self-confidence and self-esteem. And remember that letters can last forever, and your comments, relating of gossip, or scathing remarks about others may come back to haunt you, so choose your words carefully!

Writing Letters for Everyday Situations

So you may have that weekly letter to your Great Aunt Hilda down pat, but you may find yourself at a loss when faced with writing that thank-you note for the baby shower gift or that apology you need to write for a careless word that struck a nerve. But don't worry; in the following sections, I show you some samples of typical letters that you may have to write. And here's to hoping that you write some of them more than others.

Thank you

A thank-you note is a gracious way to repay kindness with kindness. A thank-you note — especially handwritten — expresses your gratitude and makes others feel appreciated. More importantly, it shows you're respectful (and who doesn't want to look good?). Yes, writing a thank-you note is necessary. Just saying "thank you" isn't enough.

Writing thank-you notes isn't terribly difficult or time consuming — it takes just a few minutes at the most! The excuse of having no time to write a thank-you note isn't acceptable. Think about all the time and effort, not to mention expense, that may have been involved in providing a favor, a gift, a dinner, lending a sympathetic ear, putting a party together, or other acts of generosity.

When you sit down to craft a thank-you note or letter, be yourself and write with sincerity. Your letters and notes should reflect your personality, as if you were talking with the recipient in person. Be sure to use the following basic elements in the structure of your note (see Figure 8-1 for an example):

- **Always use a salutation or greeting.** Depending on your relationship, you may use either a first or last name and appropriate title.

- **Keep in mind that three to five sentences are all that's necessary in the main body of your thank-you note.** Some additional tips about the body of your thank-you include the following:

    - Refer to the gift, deed, or act of kindness by name (not just "thank you for the present") or describe of the deed.

    - If you've been given a gift, say what you like about it and mention how you plan to use it.

    - If someone went out of the way to help you, mention the actual deed and how that person's support was beneficial.

    - A thank-you note isn't the time to talk about your vacation or other activities unrelated to the gift, good deed, or occasion.

✔ **Include a closing sentence.** You want your closing statement to flow with the letter or note. The closing sentence can be a final mention of your appreciation or something as simple as "I hope to see you soon." You never want a close that is too abrupt, long, flowery, or negative such as, "I am sure you are bored of reading this," or "you've probably heard enough."

✔ **Close your letter appropriately.** Depending on your relationship, a close can be personal ("Yours truly,") or formal ("Respectfully,").

Dear Patti,

I was so happy to receive the beautiful silk scarf you sent me for my birthday!

It is my favorite shade of blue and will go with so many of my outfits. I am planning on wearing it to the concert in Central Park next week. I wish you were coming with me!

Thank you for thinking of me and remembering my birthday. I hope we can get together soon.

Love,

Maggie

Figure 8-1:
A personal thank-you note should be short and sweet.

Here are a few additional tips on writing personal thank-you notes:

✔ Thank-you notes should be sent within 48 hours at best. If it happens to take a bit longer, don't apologize or make excuses why you're late.

✔ If you've been a houseguest and are continuing to travel, send a thank-you postcard from your next destination rather than waiting until you arrive home to send a thank-you note.

✔ If you find that you're still struggling with expressing your gratitude in writing, many how-to books are available and a number of Web sites provide examples and tips on writing a thank-you. Recommended books are *The Art of Thank You: Crafting Notes of Gratitude* by Connie Leas (Beyond Words Publishing) and *Writing Thank-You Notes: Finding the Perfect Words* by Gabrielle Goodwin and David MacFarlane (Sterling).

Congratulations

The goal of writing a letter or note of congratulations is to sincerely express your delight in hearing the good news. Although the length and wording of your letter depend on the occasion, be sure to acknowledge and pay tribute to the recipient without overdoing it with praise. Just keep the letter simple and on the subject at hand. If you're sending a note to a close friend or relative, you can use terms such as "Good job!" or "Way to go!" as an opener. Figure 8-2 shows a sample congratulatory letter.

Write as soon as possible after the special event or soon after you hear the exciting news. If you wait too long, you may forget or the excitement may have passed.

Figure 8-2: A congratulatory letter features a rich vocabulary.

Dear Jill,

On behalf of everyone in the Swanson family, I would like to congratulate you on your recent graduation from Stanford University.

We were not surprised to read about your impressive accomplishments written in the Saratoga newspaper. Over the years, watching you grow up, we have witnessed your hard work, dedication, and commitment to your education.

We wish you all the best in your future career and life endeavors, whatever they may be.

With love,

Betty Swanson & family

Apology

An apology can be a difficult letter to compose, because it usually means an admission of your guilt, a mistake you made, an inconvenience you've caused, or an unfortunate mishap such as forgetting an important event. Hopefully you won't have too many to write! But if you find yourself in a situation that needs an apology letter, this section is for you.

The letter needs to communicate your sincere regrets and, if necessary, a resolution to the problem it created. Just by writing an apology, you're showing the injured party that repairing the damage or relationship is important to you. Figure 8-3 is an example of a proper apology note.

Depending on the extent of the mistake, you may want to wait a while before you write the apology, giving the recipient time to calm down. However, write your letter of apology immediately if the offense wasn't too serious such as forgetting an appointment. Ultimately, you have to make the decision on the appropriate time to send the letter.

Sometimes doing a first draft and then carefully reviewing and revising it can be especially helpful when writing an apology letter. Read it out loud and put yourself in the place of the addressee and imagine yourself receiving the letter. Does it sound sincere? Does it address the issues?

Dear Karen,

Happy belated birthday!

I wanted to tell you how sorry I am for missing your big day. It was inconsiderate of me not to call. Work has been overwhelming — yet being busy is no excuse. I hope your celebration was fun.

Please accept my apology by letting me treat you to lunch this week. You pick the date and the place!

Warm regards,

Julie

Figure 8-3:
A letter of apology should be sincere.

Condolence

Writing intimately from the heart isn't an easy task, especially when expressing sorrow over a death. When writing a letter of condolence, follow these guidelines (see Figure 8-4 for a sample letter):

✔ Write as soon as possible.

✔ Be as sincere as you can, using simple, straightforward language and words of encouragement.

✔ Write short sentences and don't go into details of the death.

✔ Include something positive or a fond memory about the deceased person.

✔ Don't write quotes from famous poets or other writers.

✔ Try not to say that you know how the ones left behind feel.

Dear Carol,

I would like to express my sincere condolences on the recent passing of your dear mother. It's an especially difficult loss.

I'm glad your mother was able to come home for hospice care. I hope that not having to deal with the mechanics of a hospital in those final days provided some comfort.

Although I didn't know your mother that well, I did come to realize her great kindness and compassion towards those less fortunate. You were truly fortunate to have such a wonderful woman as a model in your life.

My thoughts and prayers are with you at this difficult time. Please pass my deepest sympathies on to your family.

Most sincerely,

Melissa

Figure 8-4:
A letter of condolence should be sincere and straight-forward.

Addressing Envelopes Appropriately

Whew! You've finished your letter, and now the time has come to send it on its merry way. Keep the points in the following sections in mind when addressing an envelope for a personal letter.

Including your complete return address

A complete return address comes in handy if your recipient wishes to post a reply or if by chance the letter can't make its way to the recipient. Print your name and return address legibly in the upper-left corner of the envelope. You can also write the return address on the envelope flap, although the United States Postal Service prefers to have it on the front.

Keep the lines of your return address aligned on the left. Write your street address and apartment number (if any) on one line. Start a new line for the city, state, and zip code. Use numerals instead of writing out numbers, and make sure that you use the postal code abbreviation for your state — for example, NY for New York, IL for Illinois, AZ for Arizona, and so on.

Listing the recipient's address and formal title

Your letter isn't going anywhere if you don't include the recipient's address on the envelope. The address should be written single-spaced with either a straight margin to the left or each line of the address indented a couple spaces. Either style, the address should be legible and in the center of the envelope.

The recipient's name and title should be on the first line. The second line includes the street address (or mailing address if the person you're sending the letter to uses a post office box). On the third line, be sure to include the city, state (in abbreviation form), and zip code.

Regardless of the informality of the letter itself, the address on the envelope should be complete, including the necessary honorific in the person's title. Even when writing to your sister, address the envelope to Dr. Denise Kaufmann.

Here are a few additional tips for how to handle titles in various situations (but mind you, not them all):

✔ **A couple is married.** Addressing a letter to a married couple may be harder than you think, so here are a few guidelines:

- When writing to a married couple, the man's name goes first. If the woman uses her maiden name only professionally or not at all, write the address as Mr. and Mrs. Charles Delavan.

- If a married woman has retained her maiden name (for whatever reason), an appropriate way to address the envelope is Mr. Charles Delavan and Ms. Susan Birkholtz (or if her last name is hyphenated, Ms. Susan Birkholtz-Delavan).

✔ **The spouse is deceased.** If the recipient's husband is deceased, don't address the widow by her maiden name, such as addressing Susan as Mrs. Susan Birkholtz, because that name indicates that she's divorced. Widows keep their husband's first and last names — Mrs. Charles Delavan. If the man is widowed, his name and title remains the same.

✔ **The recipient is divorced.** Address the letter to whatever name she is using. For example, if Susan and Charles got a divorce, address a letter to Susan as Mrs. Susan Delavan unless she has taken her maiden name again. In that case, you would write Ms. Susan Birkholtz.

✔ **A couple is living together but isn't married.** Place each name on a separate line, flush left, alphabetically. Don't link the names with "and."

✔ **The recipient is single.** Unmarried girls should be addressed as Miss until they are 21, when they can choose to be addressed as Ms. Officially, boys should be addressed as Master until age 8, when that title is dropped and the boy is simply called by his given name, such as David McDonald. At age 18, a boy becomes Mr.

✔ **A doctor is in the family.** If only the man is a doctor, use Dr. Bill Smith and Mrs. Elaine Smith. If only the wife is a doctor, you use Mr. Bill Smith and Dr. Elaine Smith. If Elaine goes by her maiden name, you use Mr. Bill Smith and Dr. Elaine Cox. If the man and his wife are both doctors, the envelope should be addressed to Dr. Bill Smith and Dr. Elaine Smith.

Staying neat

Handwritten letters are a mirror that reflects your character, taste, and mood. A messy envelope with misspelled words, scratch outs, and ink smears can reflect that same image of your appearance — an untidy and unorganized person.

If you mess up somewhere along the line, start over on a fresh envelope and do it right. Strikeovers, ink blots, messy erasures, and the like are signals that you don't really care, and of course you care!

Chapter 9

Today's Telephone Etiquette

*T*echnology is changing the rules of telephone etiquette so rapidly that many people don't know what's right or wrong anymore. In the not-too-distant past, telephone etiquette involved answering the phone and taking a written message. Today, technology not only has multiplied your communication options but also has made the number of opportunities for making an etiquette faux pas greater.

Before cell phones came into existence, for example, you had to use a pay phone or wait until you got home to make a call. Before voice mail and Caller ID were widely available, you had to answer your phone and talk to people you didn't necessarily want to talk to. But this isn't the case any longer. Today, you can make (or ignore) calls almost anywhere, anytime — and you may be unsure of what etiquette rules now apply.

This chapter explains not only how to answer the phone courteously, but also how to answer critical telephone etiquette questions you face in modern life, such as: Is it inconsiderate to screen calls, or should you answer no matter what? Where and when may you use your cell phone? Should you call a friend back if the person's number appears on your Caller ID box, but he didn't leave a message? To get some guidance, keep reading.

Making and Receiving Calls

The telephone seems to bring out either the best or the worst in people. If people are looking for an opportunity to be rude and unmannerly, the telephone lets them do just that. On the other hand, you can bring out the very best in the person on the other end of the line by going the extra mile in courtesy. You can reinforce your friendships and social contacts by exercising your very best manners, and you can do a world of good for your company by handling callers with sympathy, consideration, and a genuine determination to help. In the following sections, I explain how to place, answer, and end calls politely and how to handle several common situations during phone conversations.

Placing a call

Many people jump right into dialing a phone number without a lot of forethought about what's going to happen next. But to place a courteous and effective phone call, you need to follow these steps:

1. **Think ahead about what you want to achieve before you place the call.**

   Will you actually reserve a flight if the price is right and the schedule is convenient? Will you agree to make reservations if the other party approves of your restaurant recommendation? If you decide before calling what you want to settle upon or discuss, your phone conversations can be brief, effective, and satisfying to both parties.

2. **Adopt a pleasant tone with the person who answers the call.**

   When you make a call, your voice should sound warm, cheerful, and upbeat. Your pronunciation should be clear. Sound glad to speak with the person who answers your call. Even if the purpose of your call is unpleasant (such as to make a complaint to a store), sounding pleasant gets the conversation off on the right foot and makes the recipient of the call more inclined to help you in an equally pleasant manner.

3. **Establish the identity of the other party.**

   When you get another person on the line, establish the identity of the other party before moving to the business at hand: "Good morning. Is this Mr. O'Malley?" If the answer is a flat "No," you can say something like, "My name is Ed Anderson. To whom am I speaking?"

   Have a piece of paper handy and write down the person's name. That information may come in handy during the remainder of the conversation, or perhaps later, when you speak with someone else. Continue to address the person using the name he gives you.

4. **Identify yourself and your reason for calling.**

   Just as you want to know with whom you're speaking, the other party wants to know who you are and what you want. Settle this issue before you're asked. Say something such as, "This is Mike Morgan, and I need some help getting your brand of paint off my mother-in-law's curtains," or, "Hi. My name is Brenda Beeman, and I'd like to order a case of wine."

5. **Inquire considerately whether the timing of the call is convenient.**

   No matter whom you call or what time of day it is, begin your conversation by asking, "Is this a convenient time to talk?" If it isn't, volunteer to call back at a better time. Folks who have call waiting appreciate this little courtesy.

6. **Take notes during the conversation.**

   You can exchange a great deal of information in the course of a telephone conversation. Get in the habit of keeping a notepad near every telephone and making notes as you chat. Otherwise, names, dates, model numbers, phone numbers, addresses, and the like can get scrambled if you try to keep everything in your head. Don't trust your memory. Jot it down.

7. **Achieve closure.**

   When you've finished the business at hand and things have worked out well, say so: "Thanks for helping me. I really appreciate it" or "Thanks for changing my appointment. I'll see you next Tuesday at 11:00 a.m." Then end the conversation politely. Just say "Goodbye" and hang up.

What if the person you're trying to reach is unavailable, but someone else answers the phone? If it is a business call, you can ask to be transferred to the person's voice mail so you can leave a message (see the later section on voice mail) or you can leave your name, number, and your company's name with the person who answered the phone. If you're making a personal call and a friend or a family member answers the phone, politely ask when it would be a good time to call back, or you can leave your name and telephone number. Unless you have a very common surname, go ahead and spell your name for the person taking the message. And remember: It's never appropriate to ask where the person is!

If you've dialed a wrong number, tell the person on the line, "I'm sorry, I've dialed incorrectly" or "I'm sorry; I dialed the wrong number," and then hang up.

Don't just hang up when you reach a wrong number! This action is no different than just walking away from someone talking to you, and it leaves the person at the other end of the telephone line wondering who just called and whether the call was a prank or possibly someone casing their home to see whether the residents were away. Today, with Caller ID and other new phone features, you may find that you immediately receive a call back from the person you just hung up on! You can avoid that embarrassment by not hanging up.

Answering a call

If at all possible, you should answer your home telephone before it rings a fourth time. If you pick up the phone after four rings, the caller may expect to be transferred to an answering machine or voice-mail system or worry that you're in the middle of something and don't have time to talk. Portable phones that enable you to move around the house make it much easier to reach a phone quickly.

When you answer, identify yourself and your household: "Hello, Johnston residence, Joan speaking." If you live alone, a cheery "Hello" is appropriate. When you pick up the house phone and the call is for another person in the household, walk over to that person and give the message. Don't shout "Nathan! Phone!" at the top of your lungs.

If you get a call from an unknown voice and you hear, "Hello, who is this?" you can say, "This is Charlie. To whom would you like to speak?" Give enough information for a genuine friend to verify that he dialed the right number, but no more. For safety's sake, never give out your phone number if someone asks, "What number is this?" Instead, ask what number the person is trying to call.

Evaluating what's important when that phone rings

Your behavior when the telephone rings can amount to the world's fastest indication of how you feel about the importance of others. This immediate impression has become especially true with the enormous use of cell phones. Study the following list of scenarios and try to remember it, and you can avoid a lot of unintended hard feelings:

- ✔ **You're having a face-to-face conversation with another person — a family member, neighbor, or guest — about an important topic. The phone rings, and you say, "Excuse me," and pick it up.** You've just indicated that an unknown call from the outside may be more important than the face-to-face conversation. If you're expecting a truly important call, tell your companion ahead of time. Otherwise, let voice mail or your answering machine pick up the call.

- ✔ **You're on the phone with someone and the call-waiting tone chimes in your ear. You say, "Excuse me," and flash over to the other call.** You've just told the first party that whoever is calling on the other line may be more important.

> ✔ **In a call-waiting situation, you decide that the second call is more important than the first one, and you ring off the first call with a promise to "get right back."** The message? Call number two is more important than call number one.

Special circumstances may force you to engage in any of these rude behaviors from time to time. You may have to be slightly unmannerly to one person in order to avoid a worse offense to another, for example. Only you can judge the situation, but your choice to let a telephone call interrupt other business can inevitably cause hurt feelings. In almost every situation, good etiquette says to let your phone ring.

If you must pick up call waiting, be conscious of how long you leave the other person on hold. If you'll be any longer than a few seconds, offer to call the second caller back and resume your first conversation.

Ridding yourself of nuisances

Nuisances come in several guises: salespeople who call while you're trying to enjoy dinner with your family, heavy breathers who phone in the middle of the night, and kids who dial numbers at random and giggle. The following sections advise you on how to deal with these nuisances.

Dinnertime sales calls

You don't owe any consideration to sales solicitations made during the dinner hour or later in the evening. However, as a polite person, you can't bring yourself to be unmannerly no matter what the provocation. Just wait for the first opening and say, "Thanks, but I'm not interested. Goodbye." And with that, hang up the telephone.

Truly obnoxious sales callers don't require any conversation. If a caller is rude or harassing to you, you're within your rights to hang up the phone without a single word of explanation. However, you may want to ask to be removed from the calling list before you hang up so that you don't have to deal with callers from that organization again.

The United States National Do Not Call Registry, managed by the Federal Trade Commission, gives you a choice about whether to receive telemarketing calls at home or not. After you register your phone number, most sales call will stop after a month. If you continue to receive calls, you're allowed to file a complaint online with the National Registry. To register or for more information, you can head to its Web site: www.donotcall.gov.

Prank calls and other nuisances

The easiest way to deal with nuisance calls is to let your answering machine or voice-mail system do the work. Pesky callers are quickly discouraged when they can't reach an actual human being. If you happen to pick up a nuisance call, just hang up the phone without comment.

Every telephone company has a department that deals with nuisance calls and other telephone offenses. By all means, call the phone company, ask for the appropriate department, and describe your problem. The phone company has many resources to help you.

Handling a sudden disconnect

Suppose you're chatting with a friend, and suddenly the connection is broken. You wait five seconds and then dial the other party. You get a busy signal because the other party is also trying to dial you. This rigmarole goes on for what seems like a long time.

When a sudden disconnect happens to you, remember this rule: The original caller is the one who should attempt to re-establish a conversation, even if the cause was the called party's fault.

Ending a call that won't end

Ending a call can be a difficult task when speaking with some long-winded folks. You don't want to be rude, but you also need the conversation to come to a close. If you find yourself in this situation, consider the following advice:

- If you find yourself on the line with a Chatty Cathy you don't know, you can take the initiative to end the call. One way is to politely summarize the point of the call and thank the person for calling.

- If you know the talkative person you're speaking with, getting off the phone can be hard. Being truthful is always best, so don't make up an excuse just to get rid of him. Mention at the beginning of the conversation that you only have a few minutes to talk.

  At times, you may also have to be insistent. Being polite and firm at the same time really *is* possible. You can say something like, "I would love to chat longer, but I'm sorry. I really have to hang up now"; "Thank you for calling"; or "I'll call you back soon." (If you say you'll call back, make sure you do so.)

- If the person absolutely won't hang up, interrupt the best you can, continue to be firm, and say (perhaps repeating yourself), "I'm sorry, but I really must go."

A Wireless World: Minding Your Cell-Phone Manners

New technology has created a whole new set of etiquette conundrums. For better or worse, cell phones are a part of the modern world. In many cases, this modern innovation is definitely for the better. If you're in an emergency situation on the road, for example, a cell phone can be a lifesaver.

Countless articles have appeared in newspapers and magazines regarding the proper — and improper — use of cell phones. Today, cell phones are being used in many situations once reserved for conventional wired telephones. But nothing about a cell phone excuses the user from good telephone manners. Although most people don't mean to be rude, many get into a sort of bubble while talking on a cell phone; they're unconscious, unconcerned, and seem to forget the people around them.

For example, have you ever been stuck in line with someone who insists on talking nonstop on his cell phone (loudly enough for everyone in the place to hear the conversation)? Ever had the cell phone of someone two rows in front of you ring at the climax of a great movie you couldn't wait to see and then this person continues to carry on a conversation as if everyone in the theater paid to listen to her instead of the movie? Or perhaps you've tried to have lunch with a good friend, only to have him constantly take calls from other people during your meal? Are you ever guilty of these rude behaviors?

To know how to mind your cell-phone manners in today's world, keep reading the following sections.

The basics of cell-phone etiquette

A good general rule for knowing when talking on your cell phone is acceptable is this: Other people should have the option of not listening to your conversation; if they don't (unless it's an emergency), this isn't the time for your conversation. Either don't answer your phone or tell your caller you will talk later.

Here are some other tips for using a cell phone with the best of manners:

✔ Turn off the phone (or put it on vibrate) before entering a concert hall, theater, or any other place where people gather to listen to each other or to enjoy paid entertainment. Believe it or not, humanity survived back in the days when folks called their babysitters from pay phones during intermission or between courses.

Can it wait?

In a 2006 survey done by LetsTalk.com, an online wireless retailer, the majority of people surveyed agreed that most callers don't require immediate phone access. Yet most cell-phone users answer their phones in public places anyway, putting their personal wishes ahead of civility (which explains why so many of the cell-phone conversations you overhear are trivial). A large percent of survey respondents also agreed that in some situations sending a text message would be more courteous to those around them than making a voice call. (See Chapter 10 for details about text messaging.)

The same rule applies for places where people have a right to expect to be free from your private conversations — libraries, museums, stores, public transportation, waiting rooms, hotel lobbies, houses of worship, during class, and so on.

✔ Understand that walking down the street while engaged in a lively discussion — business or personal — looks ridiculous. If the communication is essential, duck into a nearby doorway or be as discreet as possible.

✔ Remember that a ringing cell phone followed by a muttered conversation in the middle of a meeting is plain bad manners. If you're expecting an important call, set the ring tone on vibrate and excuse yourself from the meeting if you must take a call. Otherwise, turn your phone on silent or turn it off entirely.

✔ Never initiate a cell-phone conversation while you're seated in a reasonably quiet restaurant. Do your communicating before cocktails or after coffee — and do it outside the restaurant. Many restaurants are taking a stand against patrons who insist on talking on cell phones at the table by having customers check their phones at the door.

✔ If a call is of utmost importance and you aren't in an ideal place to answer it, you can speak softly into your cell phone and say, "I'll call you right back" or "Hold, please," but nothing more; you can then excuse yourself appropriately and find a better place to take the call. Or, if your phone has text-messaging features, use it instead of calling the person back.

The dangers of driving while using a cell phone

You probably don't need one of the many recent surveys to tell you that driving while talking on your cell phone is distracting and dangerous. By talking on your cell phone while behind the wheel, you're putting not only yourself at risk, but also other people on the road. In fact, most states now have laws that require hands-free earphones while driving.

Law or no law, you should consider the benefits of using an earphone if you must talk on your cell phone while driving. Not only do you have both hands free to shift and steer, but the earphone also makes it much easier to focus on the road.

Using Voice Mail, Answering Machines, and Caller ID

The telephone comes with all sorts of gadgets that require proper etiquette. In the following sections, I explain how to use good manners with voice mail, answering machines, and Caller ID.

Voice mail and answering machines

Recording messages seems to be a time when we let our manners slide. In the following sections, I give advice on how to speak considerately and politely when leaving messages and recording greetings.

Leaving a message

If you're old enough, you may remember how almost everyone once considered answering machines to be insulting, including etiquette experts. But today, most homes in the United States have either answering machines or voice mail, and many people use them to screen calls.

Understanding why some people found answering machines and voice mail difficult to handle is easy. You've probably been in a situation in which you desperately wanted to speak with a human being, but instead you got a recorded greeting asking you to leave a message after the tone. Or, in the case of voice-mail systems, you get a mechanical voice saying, "Press 1 if you have red hair, and press 2 if you have fallen arches." Infuriating!

When confronted with these situations, especially in business, keep in mind that the person you called probably didn't have anything to do with creating the telephone system. It may have been designed and purchased by a cost-control expert who promised management that it would save money in the long run. So don't blame the manager of customer service. And don't take out your frustrations by leaving a nasty message. Just go with the flow — leave a pleasant message and wait for a callback.

When you get connected with voice mail or an answering machine, leave a simple message. Speak distinctly and clearly. Don't mumble or say "ummm" repeatedly. Identify yourself, slowly give a phone number where you can be reached, say why you're calling, wish the person well, and say goodbye.

If you dial an incorrect number and an answering device comes on, don't just hang up. The polite thing to do is to leave a message apologizing for the mistake. Doing so eliminates the possibility of a callback from someone who has Caller ID or some other callback feature.

Recording your greeting

If you own an answering machine or use a voice-mail system, make your greeting as brief as possible. A simple "You've reached the Jones residence. We can't come to the phone right now, but if you leave a message at the beep, we'll get back to you" will do. Make sure that your voice sounds pleasant and cheerful (try smiling as you're recording the message). Don't speak too loudly or use a shrill tone of voice.

A long speech, a recitation of a hysterical joke, or a taped musical interlude from your favorite rap artist isn't necessary. Your Aunt Selma who phones you from across the country doesn't want to pay long-distance fees while listening to an unnecessary speech. Get straight to the point.

Caller ID

The main purpose of Caller ID is to stop harassing or obscene callers, as well as unsolicited sales calls. What Caller ID and some of the new phone features have changed is the person who is in charge. Now the person being called has the control, instead of the other way around.

One of the main etiquette challenges that Caller ID presents is people who check their Caller ID and then track down the poor souls who may have called their number by mistake and demand to know who they are and why they called. It may be time for some rules of fair play, so the following list answers some commonly asked etiquette questions about Caller ID:

- ✔ **Should I tell people that I have Caller ID?** Yes, the polite thing to do is to notify close friends and relatives that you have Caller ID. Doing so can eliminate a lot of hurt feelings and embarrassment in the future.

- ✔ **If someone, even a friend, fails to leave a message, is it okay to call and see what she wants?** Yes, calling your friend back is fine. Just let your friend know that you saw from your Caller ID that she called.

  If you don't recognize the name or number, don't call the person back. The person may have dialed a wrong number and hung up upon hearing the voice-mail message.

- ✔ **If your Caller ID box tells you that someone you know (like a neighbor) is calling, is it okay to answer the phone "Hi, Scott" instead of the standard "Hello"?** Yes, that's fine. Again, announce to the caller that you have Caller ID, because people may be surprised that you know who's calling.

✔ **What's the polite response when someone tracks you down after you make an errant phone call or fail to leave a message?** Common sense and courtesy should prevail. If someone calls you to ask why you called, just tell the truth: that another call came in, or you simply decided to call back later. If the person is being polite with you, be equally polite with them.

Providing Telephone Guidelines for Children

You may have noticed a gray area between child psychology and etiquette for children. Telephone usage falls into this uncertain area. On the one hand, you want your children to learn how to communicate effectively, but on the other hand, you don't want them to take over the phone as their own personal property. Every toddler seems to have a time in his life when he falls in love with the telephone and looks forward to every opportunity to use it. A bit later on, when your child becomes a teenager, the love affair may become an obsession. And that can cause major headaches for you, the parent.

Safety is also something to consider. Every child who is old enough to manage a phone should know how to dial 9-1-1 and stay on the line. Don't overlook your responsibility to teach your children when and how to dial 9-1-1.

Here are some suggestions regarding children, phone etiquette, and phone safety:

✔ **Don't inflict toddlers on others via the phone.** When Grandma calls, don't put your 2-year-old on the line unless Grandma asks to speak to her grandchild. You may think that it's cute, but Granny may not be thrilled to get an earful of silence when checking in from London.

✔ **Discuss with other parents your desires regarding child-to-child calling times for preteens and teens.** Establish the best time of day and a maximum duration for calls between kids, and then enforce the rules. Even though most kids have their own cell phones these days, the parents are still usually the ones who pay the bills and should have the final word in regard to when and for how long talking on the phone is appropriate.

✔ **Teach children to answer the phone by saying, "Good afternoon, Miller residence."** (Have them substitute your last name and the appropriate greeting for that time of day, of course.) Also teach them not to get into conversations with strangers.

✔ **Teach children how to take a message.** If a child is old enough to answer the phone, the child is old enough to take a name and number and promise a callback.

- Make sure that teenagers participate in equal access to telephones in the same way that they participate in equal dessert at dinnertime. Establishing a time limit for each call and a between-call time interval is fair. Otherwise, you won't receive incoming calls for anyone else in the house.

- Don't worry if your Sally dials up her friend Roger to arrange a meeting at the mall. The old business about girls not calling boys has pretty much disappeared.

- Examine your monthly telephone bills carefully. You may discover that one of your children is using the phone in a way that displeases you. Kids tell each other about little scams and pranks that they can play with the phone. Discuss exceptional charges and notations with the child.

The telephone company has elaborate means by which it can detect these types of infractions, and it will contact the subscriber with full details. If you discover your child's telephone misconduct from the phone company, be prepared to take stern measures to prevent such behavior in the future.

- If your child has her own line or cell phone, consider placing limits on it. Your telephone or wireless phone company can provide useful limits on a telephone to keep your children — and your phone bills — safe. For example, you can arrange to block all outgoing 900-number calls and all long-distance calls. In other words, the youngster can use the home telephone only for local calls. Purchasing a calling card for cell-phone use can also limit large phone bills.

- Display positive cell-phone behavior with your children and teenagers. Remember, children learn by example; share the rules that I provide in the earlier section "A Wireless World: Minding Your Cell Phone Manners" and see that they're followed.

- Even if your children are old enough to stay home alone, it is still wise to ask them not answer the home phone when you're away. As an extra safety precaution, tell them to let the calls go to the answering machine or voice mail.

Chapter 10

Using New Rules for New Technology

● ●

In This Chapter

▶ Minding your cyberspace manners

▶ Acting appropriately with other high-tech gizmos

● ●

*T*he Internet has developed its own unique rules for how to behave properly. Although the Internet may seem to offer up a perplexing array of new etiquette situations, the old rules still apply — basic courtesy always means considering others' needs first. It requires you to make others feel comfortable, and that forms the basis of what's called *netiquette*.

Because the character of the Internet keeps changing and the lingo is awfully confusing, the rules of common courtesy may be hard to grasp initially. Add to this the fact that millions of people have access to the Internet, and that your etiquette faux pas has the potential to reach millions of people, and you may be a bit nervous about how to act on the Internet.

If you're just beginning to venture onto the Internet, pausing to familiarize yourself with its particular culture can make you feel immediately more comfortable. It's better to get a feel for the online culture now than to do it the hard way by having others correct you! On the other hand, if you've been plugged into cyberspace for a number of years, you may understand the rules of netiquette instinctively. Although the information in this chapter may not be totally new to you, knowing the rationale behind it is always helpful. Either way, being able to distinguish yourself as a considerate person to your friends on the Internet is important.

And because you can use many high-tech devices to access the Internet from almost anywhere (not to mention the many other features these gadgets offer), I include a section on appropriate usage of these contraptions.

Downloading Some Cyberspace Etiquette

Remember what it's like to experience a different culture for the first time? Whether that culture was a new school, a new town, or a foreign country, you may recall moments of being misunderstood by people in your new surroundings — perhaps because you said the wrong thing or dressed differently. Or you may remember taking offense at something that was said or done to you, only to realize later that the behavior was completely acceptable in that culture, and that no offense was intended.

You may have a similar experience when logging on to the Internet for the first time. People may offend you by what they write, and you may offend others without meaning to. Being a mannerly person, of course you would rather make friends than enemies. If you follow the basic principles in the following sections, you're less likely to make the kinds of mistakes that prevent you from making friends on the Internet.

The basic rule of etiquette in any circumstance is to have and to show consideration for the other party. If you just stop and think how the other person is likely to receive your Internet communication, you can go a long way towards preventing misunderstandings and not giving offense.

Know that behind every message is a human being

One of the main principles of Internet etiquette to remember is that you're interacting with real people in real time. Even though all you see are words on a screen, a flesh-and-blood person is behind them. This live human being deserves the same respect that you would offer him face-to-face.

Just because you may never meet your correspondent in person, and just because you're protected by the shield of your computer, doesn't mean that you can allow yourself to be a Dr. Jekyll in real life and a Mr. Hyde on the Internet. Rudeness isn't acceptable anywhere.

Don't assume that you can be anonymous on the Internet. You can use a nickname, attempt to hide your e-mail address, and adopt other tactics to hide your true identity and location, but somebody out there knows how to trace your message back to you. A law-abiding, courteous Internet user has little to fear from this fact of life, but you need to certainly think about it if you're tempted to misbehave.

Make yourself perfectly clear

The Internet is a unique medium of communication because you don't get any of the clues — facial expressions, hand gestures, and vocal intonations — that you get when you're speaking to someone in person or on the telephone. When all you have are words, you'd better be sure to use them carefully.

As a rule, Internet users don't appreciate subtlety. Your wisecrack or innocent comment may be intended as humorous, but words have a way of taking on innuendoes and double meanings when they travel across the Internet. Unless you're sure of your audience, think twice before you send or post anything that could be misinterpreted. If you're concerned that something you've written could possibly offend someone, you're probably right. Rephrase or delete it.

Before you hit that Send button or post a comment, proofread for typos and grammar. Also, use caution when using acronyms such as LOL that stands for "laugh out loud"; instead, spell out the acronym the first time you use it. These seemingly little errors can create unintended havoc for the reader who is trying to make sense out of what you've said.

Write only what you would say in person

As a mannerly person, you avoid hostile confrontations with people in public. The same should go for the Internet. Arguments on the Internet sometimes escalate into ugly exchanges. You should avoid direct confrontations unless you're prepared for an endless exchange of increasingly hostile messages.

Even in a friendly situation in which you routinely exchange messages with someone, beware of assuming a false sense of intimacy or immunity from the rules of etiquette when you're online. Before you post a message or send an e-mail, ask yourself if you would say the same thing to the person's face. If the answer is no, take a few steps back. Reread your message. Edit it so that you would feel just as comfortable saying it to the person.

Many a hot-and-heavy Internet romance has fizzled when the partners come face-to-face. Why? One reason is that the Internet can give you a false sense of intimacy, maybe well before you would feel that comfort level with someone in person. Use restraint in your Internet relationships. Take things easy, one step at a time — just as you would in the real world.

Stay true to yourself

The goal of participating in any form of social interaction — whether it is in a chat room, online message board, or blog — is to clearly express your opinions and insights from your point of view. Your comments are meant to enable readers to respond in a free exchange of their views or elaborate on the information posted. Here are some tips about the importance of speaking in your own voice and staying true to yourself while online:

- ✔ **Always be accurate and honest.** Exaggerating or telling lies will eventually be discovered and can affect one's reputation. Be prepared for the backlash or consequences.

- ✔ **Keep it real.** Write how you truly feel about the topic or issue. Don't just write to impress others.

- ✔ **Give credit where credit is due.** If you take material from another source, give reference to the book, article, or online resource and provide a link.

Remember that what you write may be stored forever

E-mail may be electronic, but it's still mail. Your written word may be saved for posterity. And yes, those words may be held against you — whether it's by your spouse, a friend, or a court of law. Of course, I'd like to assume that no reader of this book would be in that kind of legal trouble, but even law-abiding citizens need to keep the potential repercussions of e-mails in mind. Even if you diligently delete all incriminating notes from your inbox, they may still be preserved by someone backing up a mainframe computer in your office where all messages are stored.

Just because you aren't involved in criminal activity doesn't mean that you shouldn't be careful. Even if no one delves into your e-mail files, you aren't necessarily safe. Any message you send could be saved or forwarded by its recipient. You have no control over where it goes!

When it comes to posting messages on public boards or blogs, your words could be there for posterity. Let me mention one word: *archives.* These can be accessible to almost anyone at any time, so give careful thought to each thing you write or publish online.

Know some key vocabulary

Take the time to understand online lingo. Knowing some key vocabulary can not only help you communicate clearly, but it also shows that you're a savvy Internet user. Some common terms and acronyms include the following:

- **ASP (Application Service Provider):** An ASP hosts, manages, and deploys access to a packaged application to multiple parties from a centrally managed location. The applications are delivered over networks on a subscription basis.

- **Browser:** A shortened term for *Web browser,* a software application used to locate and display Web pages.

- **HTML (HyperText Markup Language):** The authoring language used to create documents on the Web.

- **HTTP (HyperText Transfer Protocol):** The basic protocol for the World Wide Web.

- **ISP (Internet Service Provider):** ISPs provide services that sell Internet access to individuals.

- **Network:** A group of two or more computers set up to communicate and share resources with one another.

- **Search engine:** A program (usually on the Web) that searches documents for specific keywords and provides a list of the documents and URLs where the keywords were found.

- **URL (Uniform Resource Locator):** Global address of documents and other resources on the World Wide Web. A URL uniquely identifies a Web page.

- **WWW (World Wide Web):** A term used usually in reference to the Internet; also called the *Web* for short.

For the lowdown on Internet vocabulary, check out *The Internet For Dummies,* 10th Edition, by John R. Levine, Margaret Levine Young, and Carol Baroudi (Wiley). You can also find a variety of Web sites such as www.netlingo.com and www.matisse.net/files/glossary.html that have a glossary of Internet terms and acronyms.

Find out how to flame appropriately

Flaming is what people do when they express a strongly held opinion without holding back any emotion. Flaming isn't just an insult — it's an in-your-face statement. Although I'm usually against such display of aggressiveness in dealing with others, I understand that it is common among some electronic bulletin board groups and more recently in blogs.

Netiquette allows flaming, which is a long-standing Internet tradition. When made and taken in the right spirit (which is to say, not mean-hearted), flames can be lots of fun, both to write and to read. Sometimes, I hasten to add, the recipients even deserve the flack they get. Here's an example of both inappropriate and appropriate flaming:

> **Inappropriate:** "That meeting was a BIG FAT waste of time!! I am really FED UP with going to these stupid meetings where we have to sit there and hear the same junk again and again from the idiots running this company!"

> **Appropriate:** "I don't understand the reason for the meeting today. We have covered that topic just recently and it isn't a good use of our time, especially when we have to keep recreating the wheel. Don't the execs know this is a loss in productivity?"

The first flame clearly shows the person is hostile and rude, almost out of control. You can still make your point by fanning the flame just a little, like in the second example, which shows that the writer is expressing a strong opinion yet is still in control, professional, and not attacking the individual.

Flame wars, however, aren't accepted netiquette. A *flame war* is any type of derogatory comment or personal attack against another person, which often leads to heated exchanges that continue for a period of time. It may be amusing for everyone to read a brief exchange of flames, but sooner or later, they inevitably become mean-spirited and frankly, start to bore everyone else. Remember, you're in a group for the camaraderie. See to it that you don't spoil it by flaming. Plus, it could be risky for your career.

Stay on the subject

If you're on an electronic bulletin board or blog, stay close to the topic at hand. For example, if you're in a Cocker Spaniel grooming conference, don't post a question on German Shepherds and Great Danes. If you can't resist the urge to stray from the topic or to write a personal reply to someone's posting, label the message *Private* and send it only to that person. Even though you may be excluding others, you're being considerate of their time, which is much more important!

An important corollary to staying on the subject is to know what you're talking about and to make sense. This guideline may seem obvious, but you may be surprised at the amount of babble on the Internet. Please, pay attention to the content of your writing. Don't pass on speculation or hearsay; bad information propagates like wildfire. In addition, make sure that your messages are clear and logical. It's perfectly possible to write a paragraph that contains no errors in grammar or spelling but that still makes no sense whatsoever.

Share your knowledge

The Internet was founded and grew because scientists wanted to share information. So, sharing the results of your questions with others on an electronic bulletin board or blog is especially polite.

When you anticipate that you'll get a lot of answers to a question, or when you post a question to a discussion group that you don't visit often, it's customary to request replies to your personal e-mail address instead of to the group. After you get all those responses, write up a summary and post it to the discussion group. That way, everyone benefits from the experts who took the time to write to you. Sharing your knowledge is fun, and people will appreciate your thoughtfulness.

Respect other people's time

Although you may be intensely interested in the answers to a question you posted, or you may feel that the e-mail you just sent an editor about a book idea is incredibly important, you must remember that you aren't the center of cyberspace. Try not to expect instant answers to all your questions, even though the Internet is a nearly instantaneous communications medium. And don't expect all members of a discussion group to be riveted by your arguments.

You should also respect the time it takes for people to open and read your messages. Face it: Some Internet connections are faster than others. For some people, just opening a posted note or article can take a while. No one is happy to wait ages for a message to download and then find out that it's a silly joke, a photo, or anything else not worth the trouble.

Don't abuse the Cc: button

Copying practically everyone on your e-mail is far too easy, and as often as not, people do. Doing so is very poor manners. Why? It shows a lack of consideration for other people's time.

You may think it an overly repeated cliché that people have less time today. Well, it's true, and do you know why? People have less time than ever before because they have so much information to absorb. Before you copy people on your messages, ask yourself whether they really need to know the information. If the answer is no, don't waste their time. If the answer is maybe, think twice before you hit the Send button.

Refrain from junk mail and chain letters

Don't become part of the junk e-mail problem. The Internet wasn't created for exchanging silly jokes, chain letters, or messages attacking other people. If you receive any of these annoying pieces of e-mail, my best advice is to simply ignore them. Hit the Delete key and move on to your next, hopefully more meaningful, piece of e-mail.

If a friend constantly passes along the annoying jokes and messages, a brief e-mail stating that you love a good joke now and again — but told in person — should do the trick. If it's a more serious matter (such as a personal attack) on an electronic bulletin board or blog, use private e-mail to address the issue one-on-one with the author or the system administrator.

Take care to send messages properly

Write e-mails with care. Thanks to that little Forward command, your messages can travel far and wide. I have a friend who wrote a witty piece about why it's great to be a woman and shared it with other women in the small Midwestern advertising agency where she worked. A year and a half later, I received the same essay from a friend living in London. It had made its way around the world and back to its point of origin in 18 months! After you send a message, you can never be sure where it's going to end up.

Here are a few guidelines for appropriately sending a message:

- ✔ **Always include a subject, even if a preceding e-mail had none, and identify yourself.** Doing this can help the recipient recognize not only who the e-mail is from, but also the importance of the subject matter.

- ✔ **Use a greeting and a salutation.** Jumping right in with a message is like calling someone and starting to state your business without saying hello first.

- ✔ **Answer all questions in a previous message.** If you don't have time to answer all the questions requested, tell the recipient that you will get back to her with the additional information.

- ✔ **Avoid using the words *urgent* and *important* in the subject line.** Nothing is more frustrating than to stop what you're doing to see what the urgent message is just to find out that Susie from Accounting bought a luxury vehicle over the weekend. Be absolutely certain your message is urgent before you choose to say so.

- ✔ **Don't request delivery and read receipts.** Some people consider this action a sign of distrust. However, if you're sending an important e-mail to someone who doesn't often check his mail, you may want to use this feature, or you could place a phone call the next day to follow up.

✔ **Try to respond to an e-mail within a day.** Even if you respond just to acknowledge receipt of the message and to let the sender know that you'll be responding soon, replying is the right thing to do.

✔ **Double-check the recipient's e-mail address.** Hitting that Reply All button by mistake when you meant to hit Reply to a single person is an easy mistake to make. Try to slow down and double-check because being in a rush or just careless can cause embarrassment and hurt.

Avoid sending large e-mail attachments

Sending large attachments can be annoying to recipients. Not all receivers may have the latest high-speed service and receiving a large document can take a long while to download. On occasion, some attachments even cause technical problems for particular computer systems. If it is absolutely necessary to send a large file, notify the recipient ahead of time and try to compress the attachment.

Document attachments are usually the cause of spreading viruses. Installing protective antivirus software or having a virus scanner in place on your computer is a good idea.

Watch your grammar and language

On the Internet, the only measure that people have to gauge who you are is how you represent yourself. So don't use offensive language, and double-check your grammar and punctuation. Complete sentences are appreciated in business and personal communications, so try not to ruin the English language completely by the overuse of Internet lingo and acronyms! Yes, e-mail is casual, but if people have trouble deciphering your content, they won't be interested in responding.

Use your spell checker! Some people may become impatient with too many grammar and spelling errors. Laziness or sloppiness in writing doesn't make a good impression.

Use lowercase letters

Don't use all uppercase letters in a sentence unless you're genuinely angry and want the recipient to know it. THIS LOOKS AS IF YOU'RE SHOUTING to an otherwise calm Internet user. Avoid doing this especially in business messages. You wouldn't shout at a co-worker during a face-to-face conversation and e-mail is no different.

When you send an e-mail message or post a message to a newsgroup, use uppercase and lowercase letters, just as you would when you type a social letter. However, if you really need to emphasize a particular word, you can occasionally use all caps for no more than one word per sentence.

Correct mistakes, but don't be self-righteous

Everyone makes mistakes, and next time, it might be you. (Knowing how the world works, after you correct someone's error, you will be next to make one!) How often have you seen a message from someone correcting another's spelling mistake — and that message itself contains a spelling error? Believe me, the experience is humbling.

Just because you may know more than others in certain areas doesn't give you the right to gloat, taunt, or lord it over them. When someone makes a mistake — whether it's a spelling or grammar error, a stupid question, or an unnecessarily long answer — be kind about it. Think twice about correcting someone. If someone writes "compleat" instead of "complete," is it really necessary to say anything? Probably not. A well-mannered person realizes that having good manners (or knowledge of spelling or grammar) isn't a license to go around correcting everyone else. In fact, doing so can be downright annoying and rude in and of itself!

If you decide the error is grave enough that it must be corrected, be kind. If possible, inform the person of the error politely, preferably by private e-mail rather than on a public electronic bulletin board. Give people the benefit of the doubt; assume that they are intelligent but just don't know this subject quite as well as they could or perhaps were in too much of a hurry. And never be arrogant or self-righteous in your message.

Don't be too informal in work e-mail

Just because you're sending an e-mail instead of a memo or making a telephone call doesn't mean you should let your professional standards relax. Although a touch of humor in the tone of an e-mail can be fine, make sure to preserve your professionalism. Although smiley faces may be helpful in social e-mails, try to avoid them in business. See Chapter 11 for more about communicating in the business world.

Staying Safe on the Internet

Without question, technology has made communication practically effortless. Thanks to the Internet, access to information, entertainment, financial services, and an endless amount of products from around the world have made people's lives and daily tasks easier.

Although most people agree that the Internet helps make their lives simpler, they also agree that it creates potential danger that allows opportunities for the bad guys to have access to their personal information, homes, and children. Information security is part of netiquette. After all, what could be more impolite than stealing someone's identity, fraud, spreading viruses, or online sexual predators?

It's not all bad news! Here are ways to preserve your family's privacy:

✔ Secure your computer with the installation of firewalls, virus-protection software, and spam catchers.

✔ Know that people you're communicating with on the Internet may not be who they say they are. Never give out personal information to any individual on the Internet that isn't associated with a reputable business or company. Be positive you know the true identity of the person before you provide information about your finances, family situation, social-security number, home address, or your phone number.

✔ Check the Web sites your children visit and look into software or online services that filter out offensive material. Minimize possible risks by teaching children that talking to a stranger on the Internet is no different than talking to a stranger on the street — and that they shouldn't be doing it.

✔ Make certain that all family members understand potential online dangers such as giving out personal information to chat room acquaintances, sending a digital photo of themselves, or making arrangements to meet someone.

✔ Be aware that ISPs (Internet Service Providers) have policies and rules about online behavior. If someone does anything online that is inappropriate, makes you feel uncomfortable, or you believe is harassment, contact your ISP immediately.

✔ Take the time to subscribe to agencies that provide alerts, such as the National Cyber Alert System (www.us-cert.gov). Individuals, businesses, and governments around the world all have a role in the culture of Internet security.

Using Other High-Tech Gadgets Considerately

Technology has made communication easier, yet at the same time, people have created this need for instant gratification — and their manners associated with these new devises has taken a drastic turn for the worse. In this new environment of high-tech gadgets where everyone is trying to fit more activity into less time, misunderstandings about etiquette are bound to arise. Examples of these techie tools include digital MP3 players like the iPod and wireless e-mail tools such as a BlackBerry or PDA, as well as the many features you can find on your cell phone beyond the ability to make calls, such as a digital camera or text messaging.

No matter what the device, the rule for when they're appropriate to use is the same: If you're in the company of other people who you need to pay attention to — for example, at a meeting or over lunch — or if you could potentially bother someone near you by using the gadget, don't do it! Leave it in your purse, your backpack, or your briefcase; you don't want to come across rude or be a distraction to anyone around you.

The problem isn't the technologies, but the way they're being used and abused. People seem to be more focused on their fancy gadgets than on respecting others. If you don't want to be seen as rude, here are a few manners to consider when using these handheld tools:

- **Pay attention to your surroundings.** Before using any handheld device consider your location. Answering e-mails on a BlackBerry or sending text messages on a cell phone is acceptable in semiprivate situations, such as in the airport, in a cab, on a train, or while waiting in a line. Just don't hold up the line by asking the person at the counter to wait until you're finished sending or reading a message! I see this often, especially with cell-phone users.

- **Be with the one you're with.** Public or social situations are different. Constantly checking e-mails or sending text messages in the presence of others is not only rude, but also distracting. If you're talking with someone, don't continually look at your PDA while she's speaking. If you receive an urgent or important message, then excuse yourself and find a secluded corner to communicate.

The same etiquette rules that apply to cell-phone use apply to the use of handheld devices. See Chapter 9 for more on this topic.

Chapter 11

Communicating in the Business World

*N*ot only is clear communication one of the best ways to ensure that your career advances, but it also guarantees that your office is a pleasant place to work and that everyone functions efficiently. Pleasant, clear communication that takes the rules of etiquette into account helps to create a positive environment in which people can work to their full potential, without the confusion and unintentional errors that miscommunication engenders.

In this chapter, you can discover how to make your point in business clearly and concisely. You can find out how to communicate to a group while following the formal courtesies of meetings, conferences, and other events. I describe the latest etiquette do's and don'ts of electronic business communications, including the phone and e-mail. Finally, you can also see how the written word can still be the best way to accomplish many of your business goals. (For more on communicating in the business world, please refer to my book *Business Etiquette For Dummies* [Wiley].)

Meeting and Greeting

In the business world, you meet new people all the time and for many different reasons. Being able to introduce people makes everyone feel comfortable in a new situation and is one of the most useful skills you can acquire in the business world. The ability to remember names, shake hands properly, and graciously accept a business card demonstrates that you're at ease and in control — and sets others at ease too. In the following sections, you can discover these skills and how to use them properly.

Making introductions

Generally speaking, in formal business situations, your host meets, greets, and introduces you to other guests. In less formal situations, people frequently don the role of host for their immediate circle and facilitate introductions. If you enter into a circle where introductions have already been made, introducing yourself is always appropriate. I provide general guidelines on making business introductions in the following sections. (Head to Chapter 7 if you want information on social introductions.)

Introducing two or more people

In social situations, a man is traditionally introduced to a woman. Not so in the business world! In business, introductions are based on a person's rank and position in a company. Whether that person is a man or woman, young or old, makes no difference. Whoever is the highest-ranking person is introduced to everyone else in order of their positions. In other words, "Big, may I introduce Small." Many people say "I'd like you to meet. . . " which has a completely different meaning. Meeting is accidental — introducing is on purpose.

The only exception is when you're dealing with a client. In that situation, you always introduce the client first, even if the person from your company ranks higher than your client. For example, you would introduce a vice president of your client's company, Nina Duseja, to the president of your company, Chris Berenson, in this way: "Ms. Duseja, I'd like you to meet the president of Acme Graphics, Chris Berenson."

When you're introducing two people who are of equal rank in the corporate hierarchy, introduce the one you know less well to the one you know better.

If you're in a group and you're making many introductions, give people a little bit of information about each other to help them start a conversation. You don't want to introduce two people and then walk away, leaving them with no information about each other's position or how they can relate to each other.

For example, you might say, "Mr. Morel, I'd like to introduce Mr. Guy Shaffer, the president of our company. Mr. Morel is the president of XYZ Company, and he serves on the international shipping council." If you normally address your client by his first name, Bill, then the introduction should be "Bill Morel, I'd like to introduce the president of our company, Mr. Guy Shaffer."

In a large group, introduce one person to a few people at a time. This way, you won't overwhelm anyone with too many new names and faces.

When you're leading a meeting and efficiency is needed, introduce people around the table or allow each person to introduce himself or herself to the group (see the next section for more about introducing yourself). For example, say you're in charge of the first meeting of a planning committee for the Girl Scouts. You have a disparate group of people, all volunteers, coming from all sorts of backgrounds. In order for the committee to work efficiently, everyone needs to know one another, including each person's profession and how she will contribute to the committee. As leader of the meeting, your place is to begin with introductions, such as in the following example:

> "I'd like to welcome everyone to the first session of the Girl Scout Council's planning committee. We have an exciting task before us, which is to lay out the activities that our scout troops will be tackling this year. We're going to need each of your talents and energy to accomplish this task. On my left is Michelle Palko, who is a graphic designer and will be helping us put together our brochure when we have the year's activities laid out. Next to her is Stacey Jordan, who is a camping guide and knows a lot about outdoor activities in our area. . . ."

Introducing yourself

Situations always pop up in which you need to introduce yourself. When that happens, you don't want to leave people standing there guessing your name. It's polite to take the incentive, walk over, and introduce yourself. You also want to save someone the embarrassment of forgetting your name, so be sure to offer a handshake and give your name. (For more on handshakes, see the section "Handling handshakes" later in this chapter.)

For example, if you're passing through your company's lobby and you see a new member of your client's company, you should stop and introduce yourself and your role. You can extend your hand and say, "Hi, I'm Mike Samuels. I'm the account executive on the Stainless Steel Council business and wanted to stop to introduce myself." At that point, the new member of your client's company should introduce herself as well: "Hi, Mike. I'm Sandy Durkin, and I just started with the Council on Monday. How do you do?"

Remembering the right names

Many people dread introducing or being introduced to others, especially in business situations. In the following list, I point out the top three fears people have about making introductions and some simple solutions for overcoming them:

✔ **Forgetting a person's name — either when you're about to introduce that person or after you were introduced minutes before and you completely blank out when it's time to take leave of that person.** If — quelle horreur! — you forget someone's name when you're about to make an introduction, don't make a scene. Simply say, "I've momentarily forgotten your name." The person should jump in and say, "It's Bob Clinton." You can say, "Of course, Bob. I'd like to introduce Cheryl Damien. . . ." Forgetting a name is only a big deal if you make it a big deal. Most people would rather have you ask for their names than to stand in a group and not be introduced.

If you have a lot of trouble with names or are in a job that requires you to remember lots of names (a minister or rabbi, for example), you can try repeating the person's name a few times to yourself after you're introduced. Or you can use the person's name immediately in the conversation after an introduction. It also helps to turn around and introduce the new person to someone you know.

✔ **Mispronouncing a person's name.** Should you mispronounce someone's name, simply apologize, ask for the correct pronunciation, repeat the name, and continue with your introduction.

✔ **Hearing a name but not understanding it.** Simply ask the person to repeat the name and then repeat it back to the person so you know you're saying it correctly.

If *you* have a name that's easily mispronounced, you can jump in and help the person making the introduction. You may find it helpful to find something that your name rhymes with or something that people can visualize.

The basic rule for etiquette is to make others feel comfortable — and be sincere! If your introduction and greeting is warm and gracious, a little mistake won't make that much of a difference.

If you've been introduced to someone previously, allow yourself to be reintroduced if you aren't recognized. Don't make an issue out of it. Never walk up to someone and ask, "Remember me?" Always stop and reintroduce yourself.

Understanding the importance of titles

Titles are very important when you're making introductions in a business situation, because the title puts the person into context for others — is this a marketing person, a salesperson, an engineer, or an accountant? This information is critical to everyone's comfort with one another.

Never assume that you can call someone by his first name automatically. You should use a person's title until you're invited to use the first name; stick with Mr., Ms., Dr., and General. If you aren't sure which variation — Mrs., Miss, or Ms. — a woman prefers, just ask. However, if you know that the woman is a physician, a Ph.D., or a military officer, use the appropriate title.

Of course, people often begin using first names very quickly, especially in the United States. This practice is fine, but still, make sure that the person invites you to do so first. Let the host or your superior set the example and follow her lead. When in doubt, err on the side of formality.

Handling handshakes

When you're introduced to someone, you should always stand and shake hands. A handshake is the physical greeting that goes with the verbal introduction. Not shaking hands is a clear form of rejection and is very insulting to the other person. In America, you're expected to offer a firm (but not bone-crushing) handshake and to make eye contact. A firm handshake with good eye contact communicates self-confidence.

For an appropriate handshake in American etiquette — for men and women — you should grip the other person's right hand so that the webs of your thumbs meet. Shake firmly just a couple of times and end the handshake cleanly, before the introduction is over. You perform this motion from the elbow, not the shoulder. A good handshake is held for three or four seconds.

You're expected to shake hands in the following situations:

- When meeting someone and when saying goodbye
- When renewing an acquaintance
- When someone enters your home or office
- When greeting a host and being introduced to people
- When meeting someone you already know outside your work or home
- When ending a transaction or leaving a business or social event

In some situations, shaking hands can be awkward. How do you handle these circumstances gracefully? Check out the following scenarios:

- If you're introduced to someone when your hands are full or you're carrying files or other packages, don't try to rearrange everything. Simply nod your head as you respond to the introduction.

- ✔ If you're having cocktails, hold your drink in your left hand while introductions are going around. Later on, you can switch your drink to your right hand. Because you shake with your right hand, you don't want to fumble with your drink or offer someone a wet or cold hand to shake!

- ✔ If you're wearing gloves as part of formal attire, always remove them before shaking hands. The same goes for wearing gloves outdoors — you should take them off unless the weather is bitterly cold.

- ✔ If the person you meet has a mobility impairment, always shake the hand that is extended. If you're offered the person's prosthesis, shake that hand. If you're offered the left hand, you can shake it with either your right or left hand. If shaking hands isn't an option, touch the person on the shoulder or arm as a sign of greeting and acknowledgement.

- ✔ If you meet a person with a visual impairment, advise a blind or partially sighted person that you're about to shake their hand. (For more on interacting with people who have disabilities, see Chapter 20.)

Is there ever a time when you don't shake hands? Yes! When the other person has her hands full, and putting everything down to shake your hand would be an inconvenience.

If nametags are worn, you should place yours on the right shoulder, because that's where other's eyes tend to go when you shake hands.

Avoiding other body contact

In business situations in the United States, body contact beyond handshakes is inappropriate, regardless of the closeness of the relationship you have with an individual. You and your friend at work may feel comfortable hugging or exchanging a kiss, but this behavior may (and often does) make others uncomfortable. And physical contact with someone in the workplace who is not an intimate friend easily may be construed as harassment.

Excessive physical contact includes patting, hugging, putting an arm around the shoulder, kissing, holding hands, or touching any part of a person's body for emphasis. Don't do any of these in any business situation.

Exchanging business cards

Your business card and how you handle it is a very personal part of business communication. It's like a handshake. The essential part of business card protocol is not only presenting a well-designed card on high quality card stock, but also, more importantly, knowing when and how to present your card.

Americans can thank the Japanese for the lesson in business card etiquette. For decades, the custom was to accept a person's business card in the course of introductions, glance at it, and slide it into a shirt pocket. Then Japanese business people began to make frequent appearances in American circles, showing people in the U.S. how to make a great impression by establishing business card–reading protocol. In the United States, people aren't quite as formal as their Asian tutors, but exchanging business cards has become an intrinsic part of the business world.

Keep in mind that in Asian cultures, business cards are seen as a gift, so waiting until someone offers the card to you is best. When doing business with someone from any culture, try to accept the card with two hands (thumbs and forefingers), read the card, and thank the person.

When meeting someone, wait a couple minutes before offering your business card; otherwise you can look as though you're overeager, abrupt, or pushy. Never hand out any cards that are soiled, damaged, or out of date. Your business card projects an image of you and your company.

When someone gives you her business card, try to do the following:

1. **Read the card (to yourself) as if it were a best-selling novel.** Taking time to read the card shows you're interested in the person and also lets you know what the person's title is, so you have a reference to start a conversation.

2. **Say the person's name out loud and verify that you had the right pronunciation.** For example, you can say something like: "Alfred B. Marquez. Did I say it correctly?" If the person repeats it again and you obviously didn't get it right, try again. Doing this step shows you care about pronouncing the name correctly and can help you remember it.

3. **Acknowledge the company the person works for.** Say something positive about the person's company as a sign of respect. For example, "We're very pleased to have an opportunity to do business with a company as well-respected as Widgets International."

4. **Mention the person's job title.** For example, "You must have a great deal to do as the manager of engineering. I, too, am an engineer."

This process beats the daylights out of taking the other person's business card and slipping it into your pocket. You may not get around to all the details of this little ritual, but at the very least, take the time to read everything on the card and express your gratitude for the information. And remember to treat the card as a gift — don't deface it in front of the giver.

In addition to using your business card as a means of introduction, you can include it as part of your business correspondence. For example, if you're sending flowers or a gift in a business situation, you can attach your card. Or you can use your business card when forwarding material or a résumé (not your own) to someone. See the later section "Corresponding in Business Situations" for more details on writing business notes.

Don't write notes on the back of a business card, because it can be considered disrespectful in many cultures.

Addressing Your Staff, Your Colleagues, and Your Boss

If you have a staff, your job is to make clear how everyone should address each other. Whether you decide to use Mr. and Ms. or to operate on a first-name basis, setting ground rules helps to establish cordial and respectful relationships.

Formality can depend on the culture of the company. If the environment is more informal, such as a small start-up business, you can usually relax the use of titles. When I worked for Apple Computer in the early 1980s, all the employees addressed Founder and CEO, Steve Jobs, as "Steve." In a formal or conservative working environment, encourage your staff to always stick with the title until they're invited to use the first name. When in doubt, always err on the side of formality.

Regardless of what you call subordinates in private, always use titles (Mr., Mrs., Dr., Professor, and so on) whenever anyone else is within earshot.

In a group of outsiders, a boss should always acknowledge the presence of staff members and make sure that they're introduced to the group. If you're introducing a client to your administrative assistant, make sure to introduce the client in the same way that the client should be addressed. For example, if you expect your assistant to call your client "Mrs. Fox," you should introduce her as such. Use your assistant's last name as well, even if you normally use her first name.

If you're a junior person on staff and unsure about how to address your superiors, always choose the formal route until you're informed otherwise. Calling your boss "Mr. Jones" and sounding respectful is better than automatically assuming that you can call him "Doug" and risk looking presumptuous. Even if you've been invited to use a first name, don't assume too much coziness with your boss. In American business, relationships are based on rank, and rank should always be observed and acknowledged.

Yes, people like to be informal in the United States. Still, you should avoid using nicknames in business settings — or you may well make Sparky look unprofessional in front of a client or superior.

You're likely to spend more time chatting with colleagues and co-workers than your boss, so these relationships are normally on a more casual first-name basis. Even if you do address your co-workers and colleagues by a first name, always introduce them by using a title or a first and last name.

Surviving Meetings and Special Events in a Mannerly Way

Meetings, conferences, and other events may masquerade as a chance to update the status of a project or a chance to catch up on industry developments, but they're really used as a way to learn about and measure other people. That's why communicating by using all the right verbal and nonverbal signals is important. The following sections tell you what those signals are and how to use them.

Standing out at meetings

Meetings provide you with an opportunity to shine in front of your superiors and your peers. Here are some tips that can help you do so:

- **Always think before you speak, and weigh your words carefully.** Whether you're running a meeting or a participant, always stick to the agenda. Do your best not to repeat yourself, blather on for too long, or be offensive to anyone present.

- **Don't interrupt when someone else is speaking.** No matter how wrong you think that person may be or how important you consider your addition to the discussion, wait your turn.

- **Always smile at colleagues and be friendly and open.** Smiling and being friendly shows you're a supportive co-worker; it can also help others to be more relaxed and comfortable.

- **Avoid confrontations and harsh words.** Using positive language is always the best option. Instead of, "You're wrong. If you took time to read the report, you would know. . . ," say, "I disagree because it seems to me that. . . ."

✔ **Be gracious in acknowledging your co-workers' contributions by using the word *we* when referring to your department or company's work and position.** Remember that if you take credit for things when they're going well, you must take the blame if they take a downturn.

One of the big etiquette faux pas in business today is acting rushed, which is particularly evident while in a meeting. When people look at their watches, clearly distracted, you (and your boss) know they aren't listening. If you're that pressed for time, you should decline the meeting invitation. However, if the meeting is mandatory and you have a previous appointment or commitment, let the chair of meeting and your boss (if appropriate) know ahead of time that you have to leave early. When you leave, exit quickly and as discreetly as possible. Depending on the formality of the meeting, you sometimes would stand and excuse yourself.

Going beyond words at meetings

You can demonstrate your good manners in quite a few ways. When you go beyond the words you use and pay attention to the other details of meetings, you impress others with your sensitivity and consideration. If you haven't thought about the following details, try to imagine the effect that they have on you and others in a meeting setting:

✔ **Seating height:** Equal eyes mean equal people. That's just a cute way of saying that differences in seating height reinforce differences in authority. When the boss sits up on a platform and everyone else must look up, the meeting is definitely not a gathering of equals. Look around at "eye height" and make sure that no one has an odd chair that sits low.

✔ **Blinding light coming in through windows:** Being blinded by the light is especially problematic in one-on-one meetings. If one person has to deal with direct sunlight coming in through a window and the other has his back to the light, the squinter is at a disadvantage. Good manners call for you to pay attention to details of lighting.

✔ **A desk as a barrier:** Many executives have comfortable chairs in their offices and conduct conversations while all parties are seated informally. When you sit behind your desk and deal with others, you may be sending a signal that you wish to remain distanced from the other parties. Think about this when you hold a meeting in your office.

✔ **Refreshments:** Offer to provide coffee, water, or some other ordinary on-the-job refreshment for everyone at the meeting, or forgo a refreshment for yourself.

✔ **Interruptions:** Try not to take telephone calls during meetings. Wave off others coming toward you for your signature. You're much more effective when you can concentrate on the business at hand.

Mingling and networking at special events

Being social and making contacts at business events can be beneficial for your career and make a positive and lasting impression when done well. However, many people are scared to death of conversing with others, particularly large groups of people, mostly out of fear of making mistakes. Most people tend to gravitate to those persons they know because it's within their comfort level. Further, they fear rejection of how a stranger might react to them, which increases the uncertainty they feel when approaching new people.

Don't fear! With a bit of practice and planning before your next event (and with the help of the following sections), you can discover how to converse confidently. (Check out Chapter 7 for more information on engaging in polite conversation and the earlier section "Meeting and Greeting" for the scoop on business introductions.)

Getting ready for an event

Special work events can be great opportunities for you both socially and professionally, so don't just show up without a little forethought and preparation. The following tips show you how to make the most out of an event and be a good representative for your company:

- ✓ **Be prepared.** Carry business cards, a pen, and small notebook.

- ✓ **Know what you want to accomplish at the event.** For example, your purpose may be meeting a certain number of people, or finding a particular resource.

- ✓ **Be well-informed.** What are the current events for today? Do you have small talk options ready for an evening event if you needed them? Bring a local newspaper or news magazine or check the day's news online and briefly note some possible topics of conversation. (For more on conversing, see the section "Conversing confidently" in this chapter.)

- ✓ **Avoid making negative comments.** You don't have to lie, but never slander your employer or co-workers. Even if the company is mismanaged, keep that to yourself. Come up with a few stock comments and answers about your company — what the company does, positive comments on the CEO, or information about new products.

- ✓ **Practice various ways to start conversations.** Consider commenting on why you're attending the event, asking other people why they're attending, or asking others to tell you something about themselves.

Conversing confidently

In business, as in social situations, people appreciate someone who knows how to make the conversation flow pleasantly. How can you become one of them? Check out the following tips:

- ✔ **Be friendly, upbeat, and enthusiastic!** Take the initiative in starting conversations. Avoid making negative comments on the room, the food, the guests, the host, or your company.

- ✔ **Don't be afraid to approach people — and especially reach out to people standing by themselves (the white-knuckled drinkers) or those who look obviously uncomfortable.** When you focus on the other person's comfort, you will lose your own self-consciousness. And, introduce people to each other. Be helpful, kind, and genuine.

- ✔ **Don't succumb to conversation faux pas.** Don't brag about your dream three-month assignment in Hawaii or ask about another person's age, weight, or personal possessions, such as clothing or jewelry. And by all means, don't drop names or discuss who you saw in the boss's office.

- ✔ **Speak clearly and use proper grammar (but don't be a nuisance by correcting everyone else's mistakes).** Don't use clichés or slang.

- ✔ **No interrupting!** Studies have shown that interrupting is hands down, the most annoying thing that people do in a conversation.

- ✔ **Try to spend no more than ten minutes with each person you meet.** Remember that both of you are at the event to circulate and meet a variety of people, not to spend the entire evening involved in one conversation.

- ✔ **Don't drink or eat too much.** You can't easily shake hands and juggle a drink and an hors d'oeuvre plate all at the same time. And staying sober can keep you from doing things you will regret back at the office. Your behavior is a reflection of your company, so when dining with clients or colleagues, you should follow standard etiquette rules for dining as outlined in Chapter 12.

- ✔ **Exchange business cards when appropriate.** Ask for other people's cards if you sincerely want to keep in touch with them. (I discuss the exchange of business cards earlier in this chapter.)

Whatever you say, remember that a business conversation is never kept in confidence. If you don't want something to be passed along, don't say it — and if you do, don't be shocked if it comes back to haunt you.

Following up

Industry events are a great place to make contacts. Always follow up with the people you meet, and the leads they give you. You should send thank-you notes to the contacts who gave you leads soon after the event, within two weeks (I cover thank-you notes later in this chapter). If your follow-through is weak, people may feel you aren't good for your word.

Send a thank-you note, but remember to also keep your sources informed of your progress. They have a vested interest in your success and probably want to support you as much as they can.

Talking Business with the Help of Technology

So many people work in front of a computer screen all day that they tend to forget the usual social graces — which include things they learned as children, such as how to answer and make telephone calls politely.

Every time you make or receive a telephone call at work, you're representing your company. And many times, the first contact a person has with a company is over the telephone, so the impression you make on the phone may be a lasting one. Therefore, you want to sound professional. This section gives you some tips on answering and placing business calls. In addition, I discuss other important technological means of communication, such as faxes, voice mail, and e-mail. (See Chapter 9 for general tips on phone etiquette.)

Placing a call

When you make a call, identify yourself and your company affiliation immediately: "Hello, this is Samuel Dixon from Lion Management." Don't feel put out if you're asked to state your business. Just explain succinctly: "I'm calling Ms. Cartland regarding the photo shoot that we have scheduled for tomorrow."

If someone calls you while you're waiting for your first call to go through, the first call has priority. You can say to the second caller, "Hello, Bill, I'm on the other line. May I get back to you in just a few minutes?" This way, poor Bill isn't left listening to a dead receiver on the other line.

If the person you're calling is unavailable, leave your name, company name, and telephone number with the person who answered the phone. Unless you have a very common surname, spelling your name is considerate. If you've tried to reach this person previously, ask when would be a good time to call. However, asking where the person is isn't appropriate.

Make sure to end the call on a strong, positive note, because people remember longest what they hear last. For example, you can say something as simply as, "I am so glad we were able to discuss the merger, and I look forward to meeting you on the tenth of the month. Have a nice day."

If you get a person's voice mail, give the date, the time you called, your name, your phone number, and a short message. Here's a good example: "Hi, Jim, this is Shirley Jones at Xenex Company. It's Wednesday at noon and I'm calling to check on the status of our paper order. Please call me at 555-1212. Thanks!" (I discuss additional voice-mail etiquette tips later in this chapter.)

Even though good etiquette requires you to return all phone calls on the day they were received, don't call back on the same day if the person you're trying to reach doesn't return your call. The only exception to this rule is if the situation is an emergency.

Here are a few other general guidelines for business calls:

- ✔ Stop whatever else you're doing and make the call a priority.

- ✔ Focus on speaking directly into the mouthpiece, slowly and clearly.

- ✔ Don't eat, drink, chew gum, smoke, shuffle papers, or have music playing loudly in the background.

- ✔ If you dial a wrong number, apologize and hang up.

- ✔ When your administrative assistant makes a call for you and the person is in, be on the line when that person picks up the phone.

- ✔ Avoid making personal phone calls at work. If you absolutely must make a personal call, keep it short. When making a personal call to a friend who's at work, consider the time of day. When your friend answers the phone, ask if this is a convenient time to call, and offer to call back at a better time if it isn't. Also, be very polite to anyone who answers the phone when you call a friend's place of business. Remember, how you act reflects on your friend and can affect his business reputation.

Answering your own telephone

The phone rings so often these days that it's easy to slide into bad habits, such as picking up the phone and answering with a brusque "Yeah?" Even if the phone seems to ring every five minutes, you must be professional each time you pick it up.

Because the telephone limits you to sending only verbal communication signals, you need to make sure that those signals are loud and clear. You have to convey both your personality and your attitude to the listener through your voice alone. Speaking in a flat, monotone voice makes you sound bored or depressed. Speaking too loudly and trying to inject too many inflections, on the other hand, may make you seem anxious. The ideal telephone voice communicates self-confidence and assurance.

This may seem hard to believe, but how you look when you answer the phone strongly affects how you sound to the person on the other end of the line. For example:

✔ If you're slumped over paperwork at your desk, you sound closed-off and preoccupied.

✔ If you're leaning back in your chair with your feet up on your desk, you sound very relaxed (perhaps too relaxed).

✔ If you sit up straight in your chair with your feet squarely on the floor, you sound "together," and that energy comes across on the telephone.

When answering the phone, try to sound enthusiastic (or at least alert). Smiling as you answer the phone is reflected in your tone of voice. Try it and see how positively people react.

Try not to let your phone ring on and on — you should answer it after two rings at most. Doing so makes you appear efficient, and the caller will feel important if you answer immediately. Always identify yourself with your name and department, plus a warm greeting for your caller.

Never answer your phone abruptly by simply saying "Yes." Never use slang or words that are inappropriate for business, such as *honey, dear,* and *sweetheart.* Articulate properly (for example, say "yes" instead of "yeah"), and don't mumble into the phone.

If a caller has reached the wrong person, assist her in getting to the right party. Don't shout for the intended recipient of the call, and don't slam down the phone. If you can't find the person, don't leave the caller waiting; take and deliver a message.

Answering someone else's telephone

These days, most phones seem to be answered by voice mail. However, getting an actual voice on the other end of the line is wonderful! If you answer someone else's telephone, you should follow some special rules of etiquette:

✔ **Answer as promptly as possible.** Give the name of the person whose phone you're answering and then yours: "Ms. Kaufmann's office, Crystal White speaking."

✔ **If the person is unavailable, take down the caller's name, telephone number, and message.** Say something like this: "I'm sorry, Ms. Kaufmann is unavailable at the moment. May I take your name and number so that she can call you back?" When you take a message, check the spelling of the person's name and company to make sure that it's accurate. On the message, note the date as well.

✔ **Don't screen calls.** Screening calls for others is a delicate issue. Doing so is terribly rude, and I would discourage your boss from doing so. If your superior is unavailable (even if she's in the office), say so immediately. Nothing is worse than asking for a caller's name, putting the caller on hold, and then coming back on the line to say, "I'm sorry, Ms. Kaufmann is out of the office." The caller will know that you're screening calls.

However, if your boss wants you to screen calls, then you need to decide if you're comfortable with that and try your best to not offend the callers. Ask your boss for a list of people that he must speak with so you can ask who is calling and not have to put the person on hold to check with the boss.

✔ **If the person is in but is on another line, ask the caller if she would like to hold.** Make sure to check back with the caller every 20 seconds so that you don't leave her hanging on endlessly. If the wait is going to be longer than a minute, let the caller know and suggest that the person return the call at a later time.

✔ **Be courteous to rude or angry callers.** Unfortunately, you may have to handle a rude or angry caller from time to time. Do your best to defuse the situation by being courteous. Let an angry person calm down before trying to discuss the situation, and don't lose your own temper. Know, however, that you have every right to hang up on someone who uses profanity.

✔ **Tactfully end conversations with chatty callers.** If you find yourself on the line with a caller who talks on and on, you may take the initiative to end the call by summarizing the point of the call and thanking the person for calling. You can say, "I will make sure to have Ms. Kaufmann call you back when she returns from New York tomorrow, and I'll let her know that you'd like a copy of that video. It's been a pleasure speaking with you, Mr. Talbot."

Or simply say that you're busy — politely tell the person that you have a project deadline, for example. Remember, you're on business time, not social time, and you don't have to feel guilty about cutting social conversations short. (This rule goes for someone stopping by your office to chat, too.)

Dealing with faxes, voice mail, and e-mail

First faxes and then voice mail and e-mail radically changed how people do business. Along with the good things that these technologies brought came new etiquette pitfalls.

You need to remember one common warning about these means of communication: What you say or write can easily be accessed by someone else. Although it's uncommon that a business associate may listen in on your business call, accessing your voice mail may be easy. Someone else can easily pick up your fax messages or read a computer screen over someone else's shoulder. Although nothing is wrong with sending information back and forth as long as the information is work-related and wouldn't cause problems if other people read it, keep these points in mind:

✔ Write or voice whatever you put into an easily accessible message in business language and tone, keeping in mind that it could be read or heard by someone other than the person for whom it was intended.

✔ If you receive or intercept a message that is intended for someone else, ignore it. Let your good manners stop you from reading or listening any further. Don't repeat any of the information to anyone. If it happens again, notify the parties involved that their messages are being directed incorrectly.

✔ When you send a confidential fax, notify the receiver that the message is coming through so that he, or a designate, can be there to pick it up.

✔ Be very careful what you write in e-mail. E-mail messages are often misinterpreted because e-mail allows for no inflections, facial expressions, and so on, and also because people often write messages hastily and fail to phrase the information clearly. In addition, many companies today filter e-mails for content that could be seen as inappropriate. Make sure to word your e-mail messages very carefully to minimize these problems. (See Chapter 10 for more information about e-mail etiquette.)

Corresponding in Business Situations

Just like a solid handshake or good phone skills, business correspondence can tell people a lot about you. Anything that you mail out for business is a reflection on your company, so make sure that you do correspond professionally. The following sections give you some guidelines on business letters, from the stationery you write them on to the information you enclose with them. (See Chapter 8 for general information on written correspondence.)

Write a note in these business situations:

✔ To thank someone

✔ To acknowledge a gift

✔ To congratulate someone (on a promotion, on a marriage, or upon acquiring an advanced degree, for example)

   ✔ To convey condolences

   ✔ To thank someone for a luncheon or dinner invitation

In the following situations, a phone call is sufficient:

   ✔ To acknowledge an associate's birthday

   ✔ To schedule or change a meeting

Selecting stationery

Whatever their business purpose, write your notes on quality 5-x-7 notepaper printed with your company name and your name in small, embossed letters. You can use cream, taupe, or gray paper — nothing bright and flashy unless you're in the entertainment or fashion business. Don't write business letters or notes on hotel stationery. Take your own stationery with you or wait until you're back in the office.

Never use company stationery for your own personal business. Likewise, you should make no references to your company affiliation on your personal stationery, although you may use titles such as Attorney at Law or Ph.D.

Building a basic business letter

When crafting a business letter, follow these simple rules of correspondence:

   ✔ Type the letter. To be professional, business letters must be legible. Although the letter itself should be typed, you should sign it by hand, in blue or black ink.

   ✔ Place the date on the upper-right side, with your address either centered on the page or after a space and below the date. Place the recipient's name and address on the left side of the page.

   ✔ If you don't know the gender or name of the person to whom you're directing your letter, the appropriate salutation is "Ladies and Gentlemen" or "Dear Madam or Sir."

   ✔ When you know to whom you're writing, you can usually use just the first and last name with no title — for example, Joe Smith. When you're writing to more traditional companies, though, use the more formal form:

      • Unmarried women: Ms. used with first and last name

      • Married women: Mrs., used with the first name and last name ("Mrs. Jane Smith," not "Mrs. Jack Smith"), or Ms.

- Widows: Mrs., used with the first and last name
- Men: Mr. used with first and last name

When you use a professional title in business correspondence, place it after the surname ("Joe Smith, MD" or "Jill Black, Ph.D."), except in the salutation ("Dear Dr. Black,").

Because the way people prefer to be addressed is changing these days, phoning the office of the person you're writing to and asking how that person prefers to be addressed is wise. For example, some women may insist on Ms., while others may prefer Mrs.

✔ When addressing a known person in the salutation, use the word *Dear* before the name and end the salutation with a colon rather than a comma.

✔ The most widely appropriate closing line is "Yours truly." Traditionally, "Sincerely" is reserved for social letters.

✔ Get the spelling and grammar right. This part of sending written correspondence is perhaps the most important. Choose your words carefully, and be sure to double-check the spelling of the recipient's name, company name, and address, as well as the recipient's title. There's nothing worse than sending your biggest client a thank-you note only to realize after you send it that you spelled her name incorrectly!

✔ Whether you save your letter on your hard drive or in a filing cabinet, make sure to save a copy of it for yourself. Why? Letters get lost in the mail and computers crash. So saving a copy for your records provides you with a convenient back up.

Remembering the importance of thank-you notes

Sending thank-you notes is so important — in business as well as in your personal life. Sending a thank-you note not only makes you look good, but it also shows that you respect the person who did something kind for you. Simply saying "thank you" isn't enough! You must put your gratitude in writing.

Writing a thank-you note takes a few minutes at the most and should be done promptly — within 24 hours of receiving a gift or attending a business event. Sending a handwritten thank you for volunteer work, charitable contributions, job recommendations, sales leads, customer referrals, a job promotion, or host for a business dinner is acceptable. You also can send a thank-you note after a job interview; it lets you make points you may have forgotten to make and demonstrates your written communication skills.

The general rule is this: If someone goes the extra mile for you, then a thank-you note is appropriate; if it is just day-to-day business, a verbal thank you is good enough.

Two to three lines is a perfectly acceptable length — you don't need to write several paragraphs. The best thank-you note is short and sweet, but it may require a bit of formality, depending on the situation. An example of an appropriate business thank-you note is the following: "Thank you for taking so much of your time to talk with me during the trade show last week. Your knowledge of the industry and client referrals is much appreciated and extremely valuable for my company. I will be in Los Angeles next month and will contact your office to schedule time to meet with you."

Although it may seem like a chore at first, writing thank-you notes can become second nature to you after you get in the habit of doing so.

If you're feeling at a loss for words in starting a thank-you note, try writing the words "What a (wonderful luncheon, fantastic evening at the theater, thoughtful gift)." The rest of the words should flow from there. Try not to start off with "Thank you." Instead, mention the event or gift or make a general comment first.

See Chapter 8 for general information on writing thank-you notes.

Part IV
That's Entertainment! Meals, Parties, and Gifts

The 5th Wave   By Rich Tennant

"Oh, will you take that thing off before you embarrass someone!"

In this part . . .

Entertaining may seem like just the opposite if you spend the whole time worrying whether you're behaving appropriately — or if you find out later that you weren't. This part guides you through both sides of entertaining: being a host and being a guest. You can discover how to eat meals with elegance and all about wine etiquette. I also give you tips on the gift-giving that so often accompanies special events. And because being a guest or being the recipient of a gift requires you to express your thanks, this part also covers the proper ways to thank people.

Chapter 12

Eating Meals with Elegance

* *

In This Chapter

▶ Acting appropriately after seating

▶ Looking at basic and formal table settings

▶ Mastering the two styles of dining: American versus European

▶ Going through the courses of a meal and handling difficult foods

▶ Dining in restaurants for business

* *

*P*olite dining at the table, whether the meal is formal or informal, has developed as one of the behaviors that sets human beings apart from animals. Nowhere else is a person's difference from beasts more evident than in eating manners and social behavior.

Polite behavior at the table, whether informal or not, hasn't disappeared or gone out of style. Table manners and etiquette are just a means to an end. Dining etiquette is important because it enables you to enjoy the finer things in life — good company, good food, and good conversation. (If you aren't convinced, think about how many people fall in love over dinner!)

Knowing about these refinements not only makes dining more enjoyable but also can give you a competitive edge in business. When you're confident of your manners, you're a more relaxed, savvy, and polished representative of your company. Most of my clients are corporate executives who understand that it's very important for their employees to develop these skills. Business deals are made over breakfast, and prospective employees are scrutinized over lunch. Why put yourself in the position of being in an interview not knowing which fork to use? If you're confident in knowing the rules, you can focus on more important things, such as getting the job.

In this chapter, I explain the basics of table manners, including table settings, eating styles, meal courses, difficult foods, and more.

Meals are meant to be eaten mindfully, in an environment of calmness, harmony, and balance. I call it the Zen of dining. Remember that people make character judgments based on the way you handle yourself in dining and social situations.

Behaving Properly After Everyone Is Seated

Knowing proper dining etiquette simply gives you more confidence in embracing new dining experiences, whether it's dinner at the White House, job interviews over a meal, or dinner at a friend's home. Dining etiquette today is more important than ever, but being proper is more than knowing which fork to use. You need to keep your behavior in check, and the following sections can help you do just that.

Using your napkin

After you're seated, wait for your host or guest of honor to pick up the napkin and place it on his lap. Use this signal as an indicator for you, the guest, to do the same. You can find the napkin either to the left of the forks, beneath the forks, or on the main plate. In a restaurant, the napkin may be folded in a fancy way and placed on the plate or in a glass. (I discuss table settings in detail later in this chapter.)

It's not necessary to fully open a large napkin; just fold it in half. However, you can completely open a smaller luncheon napkin. The napkin remains on your lap throughout the entire meal and should be used to gently blot your mouth. If you need to leave the table during the meal, place your napkin on your chair (for more instructions, see the section "Excusing yourself" later in this chapter.).

No matter what the occasion, you shouldn't flap your napkin around like a flag before placing it in your lap, and men (and women) shouldn't tuck their napkins into their shirts like a bib. Never use a napkin to wipe off lipstick or to blow your nose!

Note: In more upscale restaurants, your server places your napkin on your lap for you, and when you leave the table temporarily, this member of the wait staff will bring you a fresh napkin and place it to the left of your plate.

After the meal is over, the host signals the end of the meal by placing his napkin on the table. You should follow suit by placing your napkin neatly on the table to the left of your dinner plate, with no soiled areas showing. Don't refold your napkin, wad it up, or place it on your plate.

Knowing when to start eating

When should you start to eat? When your host or guest of honor begins to eat. If the first course is brought to the table in twos or threes and not everyone has food yet, don't begin to eat. Wait until all the people around you have been served the first course, and then begin to eat together.

In this situation, the host may encourage you to go ahead and begin eating. If the host does so, it's perfectly fine to begin eating. If you wish, though, you may continue to wait until everyone has his meal before you begin, chatting with the other guests in the meantime.

Minding your posture

You need to pay attention to your posture and body language. Heed the following advice:

- Always sit up straight at the table. It makes a good impression.

- During the meal, keep both feet flat on the floor or cross your feet at the ankles. Don't cross your legs at the knees, and don't prop your feet on chair rungs or table legs or wrap them around anything handy under the table (sorry, lovebirds — that includes playing footsie).

- Keep your shoes on! I've heard numerous stories about people who removed their shoes while dining. Their shoes were kicked around under the table, and when they got up to go the restroom, they had to search for their shoes. One woman told me that she had to almost crawl under the table to reach one of her shoes.

- You can rest your hands up to your forearms on the table, but don't prop your elbows on the table. Keep your elbows close to your body so that you don't bump into others and so that you can generally control your arm movements better. Between courses, or anytime you want to rest, you can place both hands in your lap or place one hand in your lap and the other on the edge of the table at the wrist.

- As you eat, sit up straight on the front three-quarters of your chair. This way, you shouldn't have to bend over your food; you can simply bring your utensils to your mouth. Don't rush when you lift your food from the table to your mouth. Don't bend closely over your plate or try to meet your utensils halfway.

Excusing yourself

If you must leave the table during a meal for any reason, do so with as little interruption to others as possible. Politely and quietly excuse yourself, lay your napkin on your chair, and leave without fanfare.

If you have to cough or sneeze while dining, simply turn your head toward your shoulder and cover your mouth and nose with a tissue or your handkerchief (or in an emergency, your napkin). If you have a fit of sneezes or hiccups or you must blow your nose with force, excuse yourself, go to the restroom, and take care of your business. Medication should be taken in the restroom as well.

Looking at Table Settings

The first step to informed utensil use is to understand where the basic utensils and dishes go on a dining table and how to use them. That said, take a look at the basic tools of dining, shown in Figure 12-1.

Figure 12-1: A basic place setting is one that most people recognize.

As you can see in Figure 12-1, you have a plate, a bread-and-butter plate, a napkin, several utensils (usually consisting of a knife, a fork, and a soup spoon — commonly called *flatware* or *silverware,* even if they're not silver at all!), and at least one glass. Sometimes you have a coffee or tea cup and saucer and a tea spoon (or dinner spoon) as well.

When you add a salad fork and a dessert spoon or fork, you've filled out the simple place setting that most people have come to recognize. Sometimes a salad plate rests on the table instead of being delivered with the salad, and sometimes the dessert utensils and dessert plate and coffee or tea cups and saucers (along with spoons) appear after the meal. But in general, these plates and utensils are what you see on the table when you sit down at most meals.

This setting is, however, an abbreviated version of a full or formal place setting, which can have any number of other utensils, plates, and glasses. If you saw the movie *Titanic,* you may remember the scene in which Jack (played by Leonardo DiCaprio) asks, "Are all of these mine?" Molly Brown (played by

Kathy Bates) whispers quietly in response, "Yes, start from the outside and work in." Better dining advice was never given!

In fact, the two most important rules to bear in mind about dining, whether casual or formal, are the following:

> ✔ Liquids are to the right, and solids are to the left.
>
> ✔ You start from the outside utensils and work inward with each course.

By examining a formal place setting, as in Figure 12-2, you can get a good idea of what each course will be. The following sections provide some details about the various parts of a formal place setting and how to use them.

Plates and bowls

The place plate, or main dinner plate, is in the center in front of each chair setting. In formal dining, you usually have an underplate, also called a charger, as well that helps decorate and balance the table. The bread plate is always to the left, slightly above the forks.

Note: Sometimes a small bowl and a small plate with a doily, a small fork, and a small spoon rest above the dinner plate. These dishes are the finger bowl and the dessert plate, respectively; I cover them later in this chapter.

If soup and salad courses are served, the soup bowl and salad plate are brought to the table and later removed. The soup bowl is placed on a service plate, which sits on the dinner plate. The salad plate is also placed on top of the dinner plate.

Utensils

Forks are placed to the left of the plate, and knives and spoons to the right (with the exception of the cocktail fork, which is placed on the soup spoon, as shown in Figure 12-2, or to right of the soup spoon). The dessert fork and spoon are placed above the dinner plate.

Depending on the course, the salad fork, which is smaller than the dinner fork, is normally farthest to the left when the salad is served first. Salad is sometimes served as the third or fourth course, in which case the salad fork is closest to the plate. (If fish is being served as the first course, a fish fork rests to the left.) Next is the dinner fork, which you use for the entree. The butter spreader is placed on the bread plate, on the left above the forks. The butter knife is on the butter plate.

To the right of the plate, starting from the outermost utensil, you can see the cocktail fork, the soup spoon, the fish knife (if fish is being served), the dinner knife, and then the salad knife nearest the plate. The cutting edge of each knife is turned toward the plate.

Finally, the dessert fork or spoon is placed horizontally above the place plate, tines of the fork facing to the right or spoon bowl facing to the left.

Glassware

In a formal setting, you usually have five glasses at the table. They are always to the right above the knives, because the majority of people are right-handed. If the glasses were to the left, you'd have to reach across your food to get them, possibly soiling your sleeve.

To suit the beverage with which it is filled, each glass is slightly different in shape and size:

- ✔ The glass farthest to the right is a sherry or aperitif glass. You use this glass first, because sherry is poured during the soup course.

- ✔ The white wine glass is next, which you use during the fish course or appetizer.

Figure 12-2:
A formal place setting has a variety of plates, utensils, and glasses.

Using salt and pepper judiciously

Although you find salt and pepper on nearly every table, good manners call for you to thoughtfully taste your food before you add any seasoning. The chef (whether your host or the chef at a restaurant or banquet facility) tried to achieve perfect seasoning, and when you reach for the salt and pepper, you indicate that perfection wasn't quite achieved.

If you're asked to pass the salt or the pepper, always pass them together. They should stay together on the table throughout the meal — think of them as a couple.

✔ Behind the white wine glass is the red wine glass. This glass is larger, with a fuller bowl that allows the red wine to "breathe."

✔ The largest glass is the water goblet, which usually sits just above the dinner knife.

✔ Behind and to the right of the water goblet is the Champagne flute. You don't use this glass until dessert is served.

For details about how to hold wine glasses and about drinking wine in general, see Chapter 13.

Other items in a formal place setting

Most table settings include salt and pepper shakers or grinders. At formal meals, you see very small, individual salt dishes with tiny spoons. These very petite dishes are called *salt cellars*.

At a formal dinner, you also have a menu card, which lists each course to be served, with the exception of the sorbet or intermezzo (I describe these later in this chapter). Your host may also include the wines offered with each course. The date, location, and purpose of the dinner are on the card at the top — this is the only (or usually the main) keepsake for guests, so the information should be there to identify what, where, and why. You may have a place card as well, which helps you find your assigned seat.

Mastering American and European Eating Styles

You can find two basic methods of handling and using silverware at a meal: the American style and the European, or Continental, style. You can use either version, but stick to one or the other.

Some experts believe that when knives and forks first became popular in Europe in the early 17th century, most people used the utensils in much the same way that Americans do now. Later, in the 19th century, the upper classes in Europe began using what is now called the Continental style. The practice spread, but not to the United States.

Fortunately, though, one task is the same in both the European and the American style: You cut your food the same way, as shown in Figure 12-3. Here are the steps you need to properly cut your food:

1. **Make sure the food you're cutting is in front of you, not on the other side of the plate.**

2. **Hold the knife in your right hand and place your index finger on the handle and a little of the blade if necessary.**

3. **Hold the fork with your left hand, tines facing down (with the curve pushing up).**

4. **Cut your food with slow, small back-and-forth motions, one or (at most) two bites at a time.**

Figure 12-3:
Cutting your food properly with a knife and fork.

The knife is held in your RIGHT hand. Your index finger should be on the handle and should overlap the blade no more than 1 inch. Hold fork, tines DOWN &, in your LEFT hand. Cut 1 piece at a time!

The rest of the eating process differs from style to style. I show you exactly what to do in the following sections.

Whichever method you use, you want to avoid the following blunders:

- Don't wave your utensils around while you're talking. You aren't conducting an orchestra!

- At no time should you hold your utensils in any other fashion. It doesn't matter if you're left-handed. (And for all you people who talk with your hands, no pointing with your fork or knife!)

✔ Never saw at your food; simply request a steak or meat knife.

✔ Never cut your meat into bites all at once.

✔ Don't place your utensils by their tips on the edge of the plate, letting them hang onto the table. After you pick up your utensils, they should never touch the table again. The utensils should be placed either in the rest position or finished position (see more below).

American style (The zigzag)

People in the United States and Canada are the only people in the world who use this method of eating, which is also known as the *zigzag*. In the American style, after you cut your food, you lay the knife on the plate near the top, cutting edge facing in, and switch the fork to your right hand. Holding the fork with your thumb over the end, your index finger underneath, and the tines up, you then pick up the food, either with the tines or by slipping the food onto the tines, and eat. (See Figure 12-4.)

Figure 12-4:
American-style knife-and-fork work is known as the zigzag.

Hold your fork like a pencil. Steady it between your middle and index fingers. (Turn your thumb up, not down, like you would a pencil.)

After you cut the meat, lay your knife on your plate. The cutting edge should always face the center of the plate. Switch the fork to your RIGHT hand before you raise it to your mouth.

After you finish a course, you place your knife and fork side by side in the 4 o'clock (sometimes called the 10:20 o'clock) position on the plate, the blade of the knife facing in, as shown in Figure 12-5. By using this *finish position*, your server knows that you've finished this course and that he can remove those dishes and utensils and bring the next course.

If you wish to rest between courses, you use the same position but space the utensils farther apart and slightly higher on your plate, as shown in Figure 12-6. This placement is called the *rest position*.

Figure 12-5:
The finish position in American-style dining is at the 4 o'clock position.

When you are finished with a course, place your knife and fork on your plate at the angle shown. This position means you are finished.
On a clock, it would look like the 10:20 position. Tips of knife and fork at the 10, and ends of handles at the 4.

Figure 12-6:
The rest position in American-style dining is higher than the finish position.

The rest position. Use it if you are talking, drinking, using your napkin.

European (Continental) style

If you're traveling in Europe and don't want to stick out in a crowd (or call attention to yourself), you may want to consider using the Continental method of eating. In the Continental eating style, instead of switching the fork to your right hand and placing the knife on the plate to eat, you keep the fork in your left hand and use it to pierce the food and bring it to your mouth. Remember to raise the fork to your mouth with the tines down, but turning your forearm toward your mouth, as shown in Figure 12-7.

The knife stays in your right hand, ready for you to use it again. If you must maneuver something onto the tines of your fork, gently nudge it with your knife. You may rest your wrist on the edge of the table while you hold your cutlery.

Raise fork, tines down, to your mouth.
Twist the wrist and raise your forearm
slightly. Keep the knife in your RIGHT hand.
You may add a small amount of the other
food to your meat on the tines of the fork.

To rest your cutlery in the Continental style of eating, you cross the fork (tines down) across the knife, cutting edge in the 10 to 4 o'clock or the 2 to 8 o'clock positions, as shown in Figure 12-8. Place your utensils in this position if you must leave the table, take a drink, or use your napkin. The finished position is the same as in the American style (see Figure 12-5); however, you place the fork with the tines down.

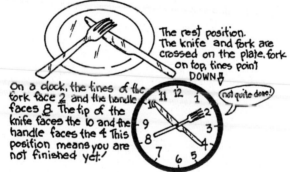

The rest position.
The knife and fork are
crossed on the plate. fork
on top, tines point
DOWN

On a clock, the tines of the
fork face 2 and the handle
faces 8. The tip of the
knife faces the 10 and the
handle faces the 4 This
position means you are
not finished yet!

(not quite done!)

Eating Each Course of a Meal

When you first sit down to dine in a formal situation, remember to touch nothing on the table until the host or guest of honor begins — not even a sip of water. The following sections walk you through a typical seven-course meal, giving you suggestions for what to do and not to do.

Bread

Bread is placed on the table or passed around the table. If a bread basket or bread plate is sitting in front of you, it's your responsibility to begin passing the bread. If the table is round, offer the bread to the person on your right, and don't help yourself until the bread comes back around to you. If the table is rectangular and you can see that the bread may not come back your way, help yourself and then pass to your right.

When bread is served half-sliced in a basket with a napkin, you take a portion of the napkin in your left hand and hold a section of the bread, without touching the bread, and you use your right hand to tear off one piece. The napkin is in the basket to cover and protect the remaining bread.

If you'd like some butter for your bread, take it from the serving dish and place it on your bread-and-butter plate, not directly on the bread. Never use the knife with the butter dish to butter your bread. If no knife rests on the butter dish, you may use your own butter spreader or dinner knife.

Don't butter an entire slice or roll at once. And don't butter your bread in the air above your plate! Break off one piece, butter it over the plate, and then eat it. If it's a crunchy hard roll, keep it as close to your bread plate as possible. And you can relax — it's not the end of the world if a few bread crumbs get on the table. The wait staff will sweep them away later in the meal.

Dipping, dunking, or wiping sauces with your bread isn't polite, except in the most informal gatherings or with certain dishes that are designed to do just that — such as fondues, certain au jus dishes, and olive oil. If you're dipping your bread into a communal sauce, never double-dip!

Soup

Soup can be served in a variety of bowls and cups, hot or cold. A clear soup is served with a large oval soup spoon (known as a *bouillon spoon*). A cream soup is served with a small, round soup spoon. At a formal meal, a sherry or aperitif may also be served with the soup course.

You eat all soups the same way:

1. **Hold your soup spoon or bouillon spoon the way you would hold a pencil, between your index and middle fingers with your thumb up.**

2. **Spoon the soup away from you toward the center or top of the bowl, and then sip the soup from the side — not the point — of the spoon.**

3. **Rest the spoon in the soup bowl while you pause.**

4. **After you've finished, place the spoon on the saucer or plate beneath the cup or bowl; don't leave the spoon in the bowl or cup.**

Serving food, banquet style

At banquets or in banquet-style serving, platters of food are served to you on the left. A serving spoon and a serving fork are usually on the serving platter, spoon with bowl up and fork with tines down. Take the fork in your left hand, tines remaining down, and use it to steady the food. Using the spoon in your right hand, lift the food and steady it with the fork while bringing it to your plate.

Serve the food in individual portions, as it is presented on the platter. Don't take more than one portion. If the food is presented as a whole — mashed, grouped, or in gels — take an individual portion with the spoon, using the spoon sideways to cut, if necessary. Then remember to return the spoon and fork to the serving plate as they came to you: spoon bowl-up on the right, fork tines-down on the left.

Soup is meant to be eaten quietly. Slurping or sipping loudly is considered rude. Keep in mind that this rule applies to Western culture — in many other countries slurping and making noise while eating is perfectly acceptable. Also, blowing on your soup or adding ice to cool it down isn't polite. If you're worried that your soup is too hot, gently stir it, or spoon soup from the edge of the bowl first.

Salad

Salad may be served before or after the main course. The placement of the fork tips you off (see the section "Utensils" in this chapter). If a salad is served prior to or after the main course, use the smaller salad fork.

In a basic table setting, you usually have only one knife. For this reason, some Americans seem to think that this knife is for the main course and that they can't use it for the salad. Not true! A fine restaurant or a considerate host always serves salad with the lettuce in bite-sized pieces. However, if you're served large pieces, cut one bite at a time by using the knife provided. Using your knife to cut lettuce is perfectly fine — just request a clean knife when the main course arrives.

If a salad is the main course, such as at a luncheon, use the entree fork. When a salad is served during a formal meal, you always have a salad knife. It is usually smaller than the dinner knife. (Refer to Figure 12-2.)

After you finish your salad (or any course, for that matter), never push your plate or bowl away from you. The placement of your cutlery informs the wait staff that you've finished.

Sorbet or intermezzo

A sorbet or intermezzo is normally served in a small glass similar to a sherry glass and sits on a plate and with a small spoon. A sorbet or intermezzo is usually served after the salad, though it may be served between the appetizer, soup, and entree to cleanse the palate. You need to have only a small taste; it's not necessary to finish the entire dish. When finished, place the spoon on the plate.

Entree

The main course is normally beef, chicken, duck, or lamb, and you eat these foods with a dinner knife and dinner fork. Finger foods, such as fried chicken, are usually served at informal occasions and not in formal dining situations.

If you're served a large steak, you may cut it into two or three sections, but not into many small pieces. (You may be given a special steak knife to help you cut the meat without sawing.) Otherwise, continue to cut one or at most two bites at a time.

Red wine is served with most entrees. These days, the rule of white wine with fish and chicken doesn't always apply — it depends on how the dish was prepared. For example, sea bass can be served with a rich veal reduction sauce, so either red or white would complement the meal. (See Chapter 13 for more on pairing wine with food.)

Finger bowl

A *finger bowl* is presented after the main course and before dessert arrives. Your server places it in front of you on a plate, usually with a doily under the bowl. The bowl contains warm water with a slice of lemon and occasionally a small flower. A small dessert fork and spoon are also on the plate (if they're not already above your place plate); you bring these utensils down and place them to the left and right, respectively, of where the dessert plate will go.

Dip just your fingertips in the water and dry them discreetly on your napkin. Remove the doily and bowl and place them to the left. A server then removes them.

Dessert

Dessert is normally served to you, along with a dessert wine or Champagne. If you're served ice cream, use your dessert spoon; if you're served cake with a sauce and are eating in the American style, you use either the dessert spoon or the dessert fork. (See the section "Utensils" for info on the placement of these utensils.) In a Continental-style setting, you use both your spoon and fork; hold your spoon in your right hand and your fork in your left, tines down. (I describe Continental-style dining earlier in this chapter.)

Fresh fruit and cheese are sometimes served as dessert. You eat these foods with a dessert knife and fork.

Dealing with Difficult Foods

Most etiquette guides assume that you eat from civilized menus that offer foods such as pot roast, mashed potatoes, broccoli, and blueberry pie. The standard etiquette rules work well with these types of foods. But real life is full of surprises, and today's multiethnic society encourages the serving of foods that fall far outside the conventional grasp of good manners. The following sections offer a few words of advice on various dining challenges.

You may find it helpful to practice these skills in privacy first. Then, the next time you're at a restaurant, try ordering some of the foods you feel comfortable with and try out the following techniques.

You may be served foods that are unfamiliar or difficult to eat. When you're unsure as to how to eat a certain food, the general rule is to wait and see how your host eats it.

Artichokes

Artichokes are delicious vegetables, but they represent the ultimate challenge to dinner guests. Regardless of your mastery of etiquette, artichokes are sure to test your table manners.

The fanciest way to serve artichokes requires the server to place a whole, steamed artichoke on a special dish that includes a small well to hold the vegetable upright. This special dish is accompanied by a separate, small dish of warm hollandaise sauce, mayonnaise with lemon, or melted butter.

To eat an artichoke served in this fashion, follow these steps:

1. **Use your fingers to break off an outer leaf (which practically falls away from a well-cooked artichoke).**

2. **Dip the thick base of the leaf in the butter or sauce, put the leaf — meaty side down — about halfway into your mouth, and then withdraw it through almost-closed front lower teeth, scraping the tender flesh away from the long strings of the leaf.**

The end result is a very small taste of artichoke.

3. **Repeat this ritual with the other leaves until you come to the center of the vegetable.**

4. **Use your knife and fork to excavate the tender and delicious bottom portion of the artichoke (called the *heart*); cut the heart into sections and dip with the fork into the sauce to eat.**

   While the prickly spines on an artichoke should be trimmed before cooking and serving, you may need to do this yourself before eating the artichoke heart. Remove the inedible hair-like thistles and lift them up and out of the bottom. Then, you can proceed with Step 5.

5. **Cut the heart into sections by using a fork and knife, pierce a section with your fork, and dip it into the sauce to eat.**

Bacon

When bacon is cooked crisp, you can consider it a finger food. When it's soft, however, use your fork and knife to cut one bite of bacon at a time.

Fish with bones

You can remove small fish bones with your fork or your forefinger and thumb and place them on the plate — as always, try to be discreet. The food goes out of your mouth the way it went in. In other words, if the food went in on a fork, use your fork to remove it. Always place discarded foods discretely on the plate to the side.

Foods that you eat with chopsticks

Westerners use various utensils to raise food to their mouths, chew, and swallow. But in many Asian countries, such as Japan, chopsticks are used at every meal as spoon, fork, and knife, making eating simple and practical. Using chopsticks takes a certain technique; however, it's easy to master with just a little practice.

To eat with chopsticks, remember the following tips (pictured in Figure 12-9):

1. **Hold your first chopstick in the web of your hand, between the bottom of the thumb and the index finger, resting on the tip of the ring finger; the bottom chopstick remains still.**

2. **Grasp the remaining chopstick as you would hold a pencil, between your index finger and middle finger with your thumb holding it in place.**

   This chopstick does the moving.

3. **Using your index finger and your middle finger, move the upper chopstick to pick up food (then and only then).**

Here are a few additional pointers for eating with chopsticks (see Figure 12-9):

- Don't hold chopsticks too tightly; mobility is easier if you hold them loosely.
- Don't hold chopsticks too close to the tip, because doing so makes you lose leverage, which makes it difficult to pick up food.
- Never suck on the chopsticks.
- If a piece of food is too big, you may cut it with your chopsticks or hold it with your chopsticks while you take a couple of bites.
- As with Western eating tools, never point, gesture, or talk with your chopsticks.
- Between bites, you place your chopsticks on the rest provided, or you may lay them across the lower dish or plate. Don't leave your chopsticks pointed upright in your rice or soup bowl.
- When finished with your meal, place the chopsticks diagonally across the top edge of the rice bowl or side plate.

   Never place chopsticks vertically over a rice bowl as in the position of 12:30, because this position is ceremonial, and don't place chopsticks on the table at any time — no different than your flatware.

- Never take or pass food from another person's chopsticks.

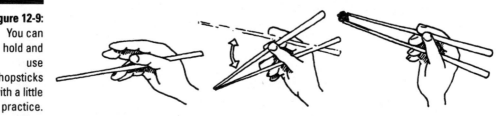

Figure 12-9: You can hold and use chopsticks with a little practice.

If you aren't ready to try using chopsticks, requesting a fork and knife is perfectly fine.

Olives and other pitted foods

Olives and other pitted foods are finger foods after they're on your plate, so you may pick them up with your fingers. Large stuffed olives are best eaten in two bites. Discreetly remove the pits with your forefinger and thumb.

If a salad contains olives with pits, eat them with a fork and take the pits out of your mouth with the fork. You *never* put your fingers in the salad. Set the pits on your plate.

Peas

Depending on which style of eating you're using — American or Continental (I cover both styles earlier in this chapter) — peas can present a challenge. But you have a number of ways to get peas onto your fork. If eating American style, either move them against the meat and scoop them onto your fork, or use a crust of bread to help push the peas onto the fork. If you're eating Continental style, you can use your knife or other food on your plate, such as mashed potatoes, and push or smash them onto the backs of the fork tines. You can also stab each pea (if you have the patience!).

Never use a spoon to eat peas, mostly because a spoon typically isn't on the table. Only children or possibly elderly people may be allowed to use a spoon if necessary.

Poultry

When you order turkey, it comes to you in nice, manageable slices. Chicken isn't too difficult, either, because you've probably eaten it from a young age. But what about game hen, duck, or quail? These foods show up on dinner plates every now and then. If you're lucky, the kitchen crew or the server will debone or cut the tasty fowl into manageable pieces that you can then handle with your knife and fork. Otherwise, try these approaches (listed in order of mannerly preference):

- ✔ Ask your waiter for help in disjointing the bird.
- ✔ Ask for a sharp knife if you don't have one.
- ✔ Do your best to separate the bird at its major joints.
- ✔ Pick up tiny legs and wings by a protruding bone and then eat the meat as finger food.

Place all bones to one side on your dinner plate.

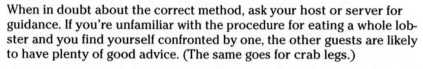

Shellfish and mollusks

Eating certain varieties of shellfish can be challenging, but with a little practice, even the most tantalizing and troublesome of mollusks can be mastered. Some of these foods are better left for nonbusiness affairs, but in case you have no choice, follow the guidelines below so you can tackle eating any type of shellfish or mollusk, no matter how awkward:

- **Lobster and crab:** Lobster and crab are almost always served in informal situations. The host provides bibs, and the host and guests generally accept that a lot of finger work is proper behavior.

   When in doubt about the correct method, ask your host or server for guidance. If you're unfamiliar with the procedure for eating a whole lobster and you find yourself confronted by one, the other guests are likely to have plenty of good advice. (The same goes for crab legs.)

- **Mussels:** Steamed mussels may be eaten with a fork and spoon or a cocktail fork. Spear the mussel, dip it into the sauce provided, and eat it whole.

- **Oysters:** Oysters on the half shell are usually served on ice or rock salt with a small dish of cocktail sauce or vinegar. They remain attached to the bottom shell by a slender little membrane. To free the meat from the shell, slip your oyster fork underneath the meat and wiggle it back and forth a time or two. Use your oyster fork to spear the oyster and dip it into the sauce. Eat the oyster in one bite. At an informal setting, it's acceptable to pick up the shell with your fingers and suck the oyster right off the shell.

- **Shrimp:** Shrimp can present special challenges. If it's served ready-to-eat in a cocktail appetizer, pierce the shrimp on a cocktail fork and bite off a succession of manageable pieces. If the shrimp are large, place them on your plate and cut them with the fork provided before dipping them into the sauce.

   Steamed shrimp served in their shells, however, is definitely a finger food. Before you tackle a serving of shrimp in their shells, make sure that you have a large fabric napkin on hand. Ask for a bib if you fear for the safety of your shirt or blouse. Usually, a large bowl is provided for the empty shells. If you don't receive a bowl, just accumulate the shells in a neat little heap on your plate.

- **Snails (escargot):** Pick up one escargot at a time, using the escargot tong that's provided (with the meal) to secure the snail. Remove it with a cocktail fork prior to dipping the meat into butter sauce. Many restaurants serve escargot already removed from the shell and placed in special dishes with sauce — a nice convenience.

Spaghetti

Eating spaghetti may look difficult, but really it's easy. You normally twirl spaghetti on the edge of your plate with your fork. However, you may use your fork and a place spoon if the table is set with one. The place spoon serves as a base of operation. Place a forkful of spaghetti strands (not too many!) into the bowl of the place spoon and then twirl it around until the strands are firmly wrapped around the fork in a bite-sized portion.

Cutting your noodles into bite-sized pieces is usually frowned upon, especially by the chef who takes pride in his noodles and their length. So when eating spaghetti, try to keep the knife at bay.

Sushi and sashimi

Japanese and Westerners alike love sushi! So — just what *is* sushi? Originally, sushi was created as a way of preserving fish — normally carp. From this practice evolved a large, varied assortment of sushi or *nigiri-zushi,* meaning "hand-shaped sushi."

Sushi, which is usually fresh, raw fish and vinegared rice, is served in hand-shaped, bite-sized pieces so that you can easily eat it with chopsticks (I explain how to use chopsticks earlier in this chapter). You can use chopsticks or a fork, but many aficionados prefer to use their fingers. No matter how you choose to eat sushi, you should eat it in one or two bites. Sushi is served with soy sauce and various condiments for dipping, with ginger provided as a refresher for the palate between courses.

Sashimi is the crowning glory of the formal Japanese meal. The raw fish is so important that the other dishes are merely garnishes. It's arranged artfully on beautiful plates with a variety of garnishes, which is a showpiece of the chef's skill — both his knife work and his mastery of the essence of Japanese cuisine.

Sashimi is usually eaten first, or early in the meal, before the palate is sated with cooked foods. Normally it's served in individual shallow plates, in small slices, or bite sized pieces to be eaten with chopsticks, never with your fingers. However, if you just can't master the chopsticks (and you aren't on a business trip in an Asian country), you can ask for a fork.

Making Deals While Breaking Bread

A lot goes into a meeting around a meal. From setting up the whole date to behaving properly, you must know what you're doing in order to set a favorable impression, so do your homework when setting up a business meal. Pay attention to the role of the guest as well because you may well be in that role someday too. For a thorough discussion of business meals, see my other book *Business Etiquette For Dummies* (Wiley).

Deciding when to meet

You must first figure out when you want to meet for your business meal — breakfast, lunch, dinner, or perhaps a simple cup of coffee. The different times of day have different implications about your meeting and its length, which I describe in the following:

- ✔ **Breakfast meetings** rarely last more than forty-five minutes or an hour. They imply a certain urgency and are often convenient when traveling.

- ✔ **Afternoon tea or coffee** is a relaxing, low-key way to spend forty-five minutes or an hour talking about business. Afternoon tea (originating in Great Britain) takes place between 4 and 5 o'clock and can include small sandwiches and pastries.

- ✔ **Lunch** is usually great for getting to know a guest a bit better and is the best time for discussing business. Lunch meetings can last one to two hours.

- ✔ **Dinner** is a more formal business invitation. Generally, dinner isn't a time to talk about business, but rather to get to know the other person, build a rapport, and enjoy each other's company. Dinner is rarely a first invitation; it usually follows a first meeting and can last two to three hours.

Working out all the details

After you've made a decision on the time, get to know a few good restaurants near your client or guest. Don't go to a restaurant new to you with a client. You want to be able to suggest menu items to your guest if she's never been there, which you obviously can't do if *you've* never been there.

Make two reservations (if necessary) at two different times on two different days. For example, reserve one table at noon and one at 1:00 p.m. for Tuesday and for Wednesday. Do this for at least two restaurants so you can give your guest the choice. You can say, "Taylor, I'd like you to be my guest for lunch next week. Would Tuesday or Wednesday work for you?" Then you can do the same for time preferences and location choices.

Immediately call to cancel reservations at the restaurant not chosen and confirm the time you choose at the other. Be sure to cancel the second reservation.

The day before, call your guest to confirm. Say something like, "Taylor, I'm looking forward to our lunch tomorrow at La Mere Michelle at 1:00 p.m. Is that still convenient for you?" Also, confirm the reservation with the restaurant. Ask for nonsmoking or a particular table, depending on what the client prefers.

If you're the guest, consult your schedule before accepting the invitation. You don't want to choose a date or time in which you will be rushed. Also, be decisive — you're trying to make a good impression, too, and you don't want to come across as wishy-washy.

Pulling it off

The day for your meeting has arrived, and now is the time to make a good impression. Arrive 10 to 15 minutes early, and be sure to have the maitre'd run your credit card with an 18 to 20 percent tip. (You may want to include a slightly larger gratuity for any special attention from the maitre'd or server.) Look at the table and decide where to seat your guest.

Wait for your guest in the lobby or near the front door. Don't have anything to eat or drink before your guest arrives, because you want to appear to your guest as if you've just arrived.

When your guest or client arrives, remember to shake hands, greet your guest by name, and present your business card properly (see a previous section on this topic). Allow your guest to follow the host to the table ahead of you and offer your guest the best seat.

After you're seated, make suggestions about the menu, but allow your guest to order first. Always match the number of courses you're having to your guest's order. For example, if your guest is only having a salad and a light pasta dish, you shouldn't go all out for the seven-course meal. And if she doesn't drink alcoholic beverages or order dessert, you do the same. Order foods that can help you keep your mind on business and that don't challenge your table manners or your wardrobe.

Never overindulge in alcohol at a business meeting, even if the restaurant does have the best martinis in town.

Don't talk about business until the client appears to be ready. Your agenda can wait until the end of the meal. Remember to mind your table manners and posture, keeping your feet flat on the floor. Your behavior at the table makes a huge impression on your guest.

Recovering from Distressing Mealtime Moments and Common Blunders

Sure, that whole Cornish game hen on your plate looks harmless, but you're faced with one delicate matter: How do you properly eat the thing without sending it into orbit?

Eating in any social setting may result in mishaps. Use the following tips to steer yourself out of common mishaps that can occur:

- ✔ **You drop a utensil onto the floor.** Never lean over and pick up the utensil (unless, of course, you're at your mother's dinner table and no servers or servants are present, in which case you may use your napkin to retrieve the wandering fork, walk it out to the kitchen, and get yourself both a clean napkin and a clean fork). In any situation where servers are present, beckon a server and explain what happened. The server will pick up the utensil and bring you a clean one.

- ✔ **You're served a piece of food that isn't cooked properly.** This situation can be especially dangerous with meat. If you encounter such a situation, call over a server and quietly explain the situation. Trust the wait staff to reappear with a different plate of food for you.

- ✔ **You find a foreign object in your food.** Again, find your server and tell him about the problem in a very discreet manner. Rest assured that your meal will be replaced quickly and may even be complimentary.

- ✔ **You dislike the food that is being served, or you're allergic to it.** The polite thing to do is try a little of everything; however, if you're allergic to a food, just smile and say "No, thank you." It's not necessary to say anything critical.

- ✔ **You have bone, gristle, or some other unwanted food item in your mouth.** Discreetly remove the food onto the tine of your fork and place it on your plate. If possible, hide it under a garnish or other food on your plate so that the people around you can't see it. Never spit anything into your napkin!

- ✔ **Food gets caught between your teeth.** If you can't remove it with your tongue, leave the table where you can remove the food from your teeth in private.

- ✔ **Food spills off your plate.** You may pick it up with a piece of your silverware and place it on the edge of your plate.

FAUX PAS

Beware! The most common dining mistakes

Knowing your way around a table is only the beginning. You must also know how to behave. When you're out to eat, try to avoid the following behaviors:

- Speaking too loudly
- Playing with your hair or earrings, or touching your face and head
- Pushing away the plate or bowl when finished
- Eating too fast or too slowly
- Using your cell phone while dining

- Poor posture
- Leaving your purse, keys, sunglasses, or eyeglasses on the table
- Elbows on the table
- Picking your teeth
- Talking with food in your mouth
- Chewing with your mouth open
- Using the napkin as a tissue
- Placing the napkin on your plate when finished

- **You can't eat all the food on your plate.** Asking for a doggy bag when you're a guest at a business meal or a formal meal is a no-no. Save the doggy bag for informal dining situations with friends and family.

- **The trick for the Cornish game hen weary?** Request that the server have it cut in half.

Chapter 13

Drinking In the Wonders of Wine

- -

In This Chapter

▶ Choosing an enjoyable wine

▶ Knowing what to do when your bottle of wine arrives to the table

▶ Figuring out how to hold all those glasses

▶ Opening (and enjoying) a bottle of Champagne

▶ Toasting the right way

▶ Drinking alcohol responsibly

- -

Americans have always had a complicated relationship with alcoholic beverages. In the 1920s and early 1930s, alcohol was prohibited completely. Traditionally, Americans drank mostly whiskey and other hard liquor, but today, wine and beer are much in fashion.

Wine in particular can pose etiquette challenges. A glass of wine is a pleasant accompaniment to a meal that adds a note of flavor and enhances the food that is served, but at the same time, the drinking of wine involves many rituals, including ordering, tasting, and enjoying. If you don't understand the rituals, you may find it somewhat stressful to select and order a wine.

If you're unfamiliar with the ins and outs of what makes a good wine and how it pairs with food, you may be tempted to avoid it altogether, especially in public. But a time may come when you have to deal with it, such as when you're the host of a business dinner at a restaurant. Relax: After you know a few guidelines, you can make your way through the process of selecting, ordering, and drinking wine. This chapter explains those guidelines.

This book can only touch on the complex topic of wine. You can find out much more about wine in Mary Ewing-Mulligan and Ed McCarthy's *Wine For Dummies,* 4th Edition (also published by Wiley).

Warming up to wine: The United States saga

Early historical writings, including the Bible, refer to wine making and the drinking of wine. Most cultures believed that wine was as significant as the meals they ate.

The popularity of wine in the United States is a relatively new phenomenon. Historically, wine was always very expensive, because most wine was imported and subject to tariff duties. Wine appeared regularly only on the tables of the wealthy.

Especially in the 1870s, when the temperance movement was in full swing, the drinking of wine was condemned, even though little was consumed. The efforts of these groups eventually led to national prohibition in 1919.

California had made wines before the Gold Rush, but when Prohibition took effect, manufacturing alcoholic beverages became illegal in the U.S. Thirteen years of Prohibition virtually ruined the wine industry, and only about 100 wineries survived in California, New York, New Jersey, Ohio, and Missouri by legally making sacramental and medicinal wines, salted cooking wines, and grape juice.

Today, American winemakers produce wonderful wines, and the popularity of wine is steadily increasing. According to the International Organization of Vine and Wine, the U.S. will most likely overtake Italy in total volume of wine consumed, ranking second behind France who's ranked first.

Selecting a Pleasing Wine

You and your guest have been seated, and you've been presented with a wine list. Now what? The following sections can help you choose a wine that both pleases your guests and complements your meal.

The purpose of wine is to enhance the meal and make your guest feel special. Select carefully, and you can make a good impression.

Who selects the wine?

Whether for business or for pleasure, navigating the wine list and ordering wine, as a rule, is done by the official host — the person paying the bill. As a host, you may pass the wine list around the table for others to inspect or offer to have one of the guests select.

If you regularly conduct business at a favorite restaurant, you may want to consider calling ahead and having them plan a menu and select a wine, or arrive early to discuss the menu, wine choices, and prices. (For more on eating out, check out Chapter 12.)

How much should you spend?

The first rule is to have a price range in mind before you order. A sensible guideline is to spend about as much on a bottle of wine as you spend on one complete dinner. Fine wines can vary in price from a few dollars to hundreds of dollars, so make sure that you know what you're doing if you select an expensive wine. (Because many wine drinkers have become more savvy about wine selection and prices, most restaurateurs now price their wines by doubling or tripling the price they paid and adding ten dollars.)

The most expensive wine on the wine list isn't always the most impressive. When you're looking for value, don't follow the trends; select lesser-known or local wines, which are normally priced lower because of lack of recognition.

If you're a beginning wine drinker or just not familiar with the wines on the wine list, ask for help from a knowledgeable wine specialist on staff. Better establishments have a wine steward, or *sommelier,* on hand to assist you. If you enlist this person's help, tip your wine steward 15 to 20 percent of the cost of the wine (in addition to the normal tip for the meal).

Be enthusiastic about your wine selection! Don't be afraid to ask your server or the wine steward for assistance, and mention how impressive the wine list is. Taste, learn, and drink what you enjoy. Personal preference should be the final deciding factor.

Which wine complements your meal?

Wine and food go together. The key to choosing a wine is to find one that won't overpower the food or be overpowered by it. The following are examples of wines that generally match certain foods:

- ✔ Light meat dishes (such as pork), poultry, or full-flavored fish (such as salmon) go well with a red wine such as Pinot Noir or French Burgundy.

- ✔ Lighter fish and shellfish dishes are fine with a light-bodied white wine, such as Chenin Blanc, Sancerre, Pinot Grigio, or German Riesling.

- ✔ Lobster or richer fish dishes are complemented by a full-bodied Chardonnay, Semillion, or Viognier.

- ✔ Chicken and pasta can go with either red or white wine, depending on the sauce. A heavy meat sauce is better complemented by a medium-bodied red wine, such as Merlot or Cabernet Franc, while a light vegetable or cream sauce goes well with a white or sparkling wine.

✔ Stews, roasts, game, duck, lamb, and other full-flavored dishes go best with full-bodied red wines, such as French Bordeaux, Cabernet Sauvignon, Petite Syrah, or Zinfandel.

If you're enjoying a spicier, ethnic meal, try these food-and-wine combinations:

✔ **Cajun:** Champagne

✔ **Chinese:** White Zinfandel

✔ **Indian:** Pinot Gris

✔ **Japanese:** Chenin Blanc

✔ **Mexican:** Chardonnay

✔ **Middle Eastern:** Syrah

✔ **Sushi or Sashimi:** Sauvignon Blanc

✔ **Thai:** German Riesling

Some international foods weren't designed to go with wine, so be creative and experiment with different varieties. Chefs across the country pour Champagne with everything from Asian-influenced main courses to Indian curries. The effervescence of Champagne can refresh the palate so that the spices don't overwhelm the wine. The right sparkling wine can make a meal memorable and create a festive mood. See the later section "Enjoying Champagne" for more information.

What do your guests prefer?

When selecting wine at a restaurant, also ask your guests whether they have any preferences. It's fine to offer or suggest an aperitif, Champagne, or white wine to be served with the first course.

Inquire as to what your guests' meal choices are. If everyone at the table decides to have a rich meat entree, then a red wine is appropriate. If guests are having lighter chicken or seafood dishes, suggest a lighter-bodied white wine. Occasionally, one guest doesn't drink red wine; if the majority of guests are having red wine, you may suggest that the guest order an individual glass of white wine.

One bottle of wine (750 ml) serves approximately four glasses. Make sure to request an adequate number of bottles for the number of guests; plan on your guests drinking two glasses of wine apiece. If more than four guests are present, choose a white wine and a red wine. In addition, if your guests order meals that are too different to pair with one wine, consider selecting a variety of half bottles (375 ml or 500 ml) or ordering by the glass.

If you're a guest, you have every right to avoid wine for whatever reason. Some people, for example, are allergic to sulfites, which are found in most wines. If you don't wish to partake of wine, just call over your server and say, "I will not be having any wine this evening." The server will remove your wine glass and then ask you for an alternate beverage order. Never turn your wine glass upside down!

Can you throw out those old rules?

Normally, you order red wines with red meats and other robust dishes and white wines with fish and other delicate entrees (see the earlier section "Which wine complements your meal?" for details). Yet some of these old rules are changing. Even wine experts don't always adhere to the basic guidelines — they drink what they like.

Oftentimes, you can find particular reasons to break the rules. And some dishes just don't fall neatly within the guidelines. Consider these situations, for example:

- ✔ What if you order oven-roasted sea bass served with a veal reduction sauce — do you order a white wine to complement the fish or a red wine to complement the rich veal sauce? If a dish has a wine base, say a Pinot Noir, a buttery Chardonnay is an excellent choice — or try to choose an appropriate Pinot Noir to match the sauce. You'll find it a sure hit. If you aren't certain, ask your server to make a suggestion.

- ✔ Suppose an unexpected guest drops by and stays for dinner. You're serving leg of lamb, and you have only white wine on hand. You don't need to omit wine just because you don't have the proper or recommended red wine. Just serve what you have and enjoy it.

The guidelines are there to allow you to get the most pleasure possible out of your wine and the food that you're having with it. Use these principles if you want to, but don't consider them to be ironclad rules that you can't break under any circumstances.

Savoring dessert wines

Dessert wines often go unnoticed or neglected. These sweet, rich-flavored wines go well with desserts of cheese, nuts, and fruit and are served best at room temperature (with the exception of a sweet Champagne). Particularly outstanding are sweet Marsala, Angelica, Tokay, Malaga, Cream Sherry, Port, Madeira, and Muscatel.

Examining the Wine

After you order a bottle of wine, your server brings it to the table and presents it to you. You can use this time to examine the label, making sure that you received the wine and vintage that you ordered. If you have the right wine, you then examine the cork and the temperature, as I explain in the following sections.

Checking the cork

If you do have the correct wine, the next step is for the server to remove the seal, take out the cork, and place the cork on the table next to you. Your job is to visually examine the cork. (It's not necessary to sniff the cork to see whether the cork is in good condition.) Unless the cork bears a different name than the label or the cork looks dry and crumbly (indicating wine not stored properly), you have nothing to worry about.

When opening the wine, the wine steward or sommelier should notice by the smell of the cork or visually by a dry cork if the cork is tainted. Occasionally, you may find a cork that is moldy, but it doesn't necessarily mean that the wine has been corked (spoiled).

Not all wine comes with natural corks. Now you can find wines in pretty much any price range with synthetic corks, or even screw tops, where corkscrews need not apply!

Determining the temperature

You may also want to feel the bottle with your hand to determine whether the wine seems to be at the correct temperature. Red wines are normally served at room temperature (not warm), and white wines are slightly (and I mean *slightly*) chilled so that the flavor and aroma are at their peak.

Serving precious red wine

Serving white wine is pretty simple: Just open the bottle and pour into the glasses. But serving red wine — especially an older, more precious red wine — is a bit more complicated.

In finer restaurants, the wine steward or sommelier usually serves a fine red wine. The bottle itself is placed in a cradle so that it tips at about a 45-degree angle, simulating its position in the wine cellar. This position moves the settled material, known as sediment, into a lower "corner" of the bottle. The wine steward then brings the wine from the cellar with great care so as not to disturb the sediment.

The steward also brings to the table a crystal decanter. After opening the bottle, he pours the wine into the decanter to aerate the wine, while taking care not to disturb the sediment. The steward then holds a candle beneath the neck of the bottle so that he can see the approach of sediment as the bottle empties into the decanter. A perfect performance results in a decanter that contains totally clear wine, with only a small amount of wine and sediment left in the original bottle. After 10 to 15 minutes of letting the wine breathe, the wine is now ready to drink.

Another way to aerate your wine is to ask your server to pour the wine immediately into wine glasses subsequent to opening the bottle. Leaving it in the bottle on the table will not adequately aerate the wine.

The server or wine steward may leave an ice bucket on or near your table to keep a white wine chilled. However, you may decide that the wine is cold enough — make the wine too cold, and it will not have any flavor. Politely let the server know that the wine is at a perfect temperature and that he may remove the ice bucket.

If the day is a very warm one, try a rosé style of wine that are served slightly colder than white wines. Rosé wines (many people used to call them *blush* wines) such as a White Zinfandel are pink in color and are wonderfully refreshing!

Tasting Wine: An Art and a Pleasure

The person who ordered the wine is normally the one who does the tasting, although the host may request that one of the guests do so. After you verify that you received the correct wine (see the section "Examining the Wine"), your server pours a small amount of wine into your glass. Properly taste the wine by following these steps:

1. **Look carefully before you taste because color can tell you much about the age of the wine.** Red wines lose their color when aged, and white wines can become deeper yellow or gold.

2. **Gently swirl the wine in the glass by holding the stem firmly while the glass remains on the table.** Swirling wine provides oxygen, which assists in releasing the aroma.

3. **Sniff the wine.** Many traits of the wine can be determined by the smell, because research states that the majority of taste is due to the sense of smell. The aroma of the wine can take on a variety of flavors, from herbs to a scent of smoke. A wine with a high alcohol scent is described as *heady,* and *perfumed* refers to a delicate bouquet.

Wearing heavy-scented perfume, cologne, or aftershave can ruin the wine-smelling experience for both you and others at the table. Keep the body fragrances to a bare minimum when you plan an evening that includes wine.

4. **Take a small sip, if you'd like.** It's not necessary to swish the wine through your mouth; however, if you want to taste the wine, you can hold the wine in your mouth for a moment before swallowing to get a first impression — was it rich, balanced, and pleasant?

Now is the time to determine your *overall* impression of the wine and to check that the wine hasn't spoiled. Wine is a foodstuff, and as such, it can spoil just like any other food. Even though it may be uncomfortable, if the wine tastes "off" to you, this is the time to say so. The usual remedy for spoiled wine is for the server to bring another bottle of the same wine. If that particular vintage isn't available, the wine steward will suggest or bring a similar wine.

Better restaurants will always offer to replace wine without hesitation. However, returning a bottle of wine if you only dislike the taste is impolite, especially if you ordered the bottle on your own.

If the wine hasn't spoiled, make a comment such as "Excellent. Please serve it." If you had assistance selecting from the server or sommelier, remember to compliment that person on his recommendation.

Don't make a huge production of the wine presentation ritual. The examining and tasting process should only take a minute or two without keeping your guests waiting for a glass of wine!

Getting a Grip on Wine Glasses

After you approve the wine, the server pours the wine clockwise to the right; women are first, and the host's glass is topped last. Wine is usually served in a clear glass, which shows off the vivid colors of the wine. The wine glass that is used has a particular shape for logical reasons as well.

Finer restaurants preset tables with at least two wine goblets: a long-stemmed glass for white wines and a conventional, tulip-shaped glass for ordinary red wines. (In some establishments, you also see a very wide-mouthed goblet with a deep bowl for older and more expensive red wines.) When you order wine, the server leaves the appropriate goblet on the table and removes the other(s).

Your red or white glassware should accommodate approximately 10 to 12 ounces of wine. You should never fill a wine glass higher than halfway in order to allow room for the wine to move when you swirl your glass. The wine will not breathe properly if the glass is filled too high.

The proper way to hold a wine glass is by the stem. That way, you don't get fingerprints on the bowl for the glass or alter the temperature of the wine. Here is some additional information about glassware:

✔ White wine glasses have long, slender stems so that you can hold the stem and thus keep the heat of your hand from warming the wine. The bowl of the glass is smaller than that of a red wine glass, with a more fragile look to complement the delicate flavor and clear color of the wine.

✔ A red wine glass has a shorter stem with a larger bowl to allow the robust wine to breathe. You hold the glass closer to the bowl because the heat from your hand releases the wine's flavor.

✔ Sherry and port glasses are small and open because these wines are more potent in aroma, flavor, and alcoholic content.

✔ Champagne glasses are tall and narrow and are designed to display the effervescence and flavor of sparkling wine.

Nowadays you can see stemless wine glasses at some of the trendiest restaurants. These wine glasses were introduced in efforts to demystify the wine drinking experience. Funny enough, a tumbler-like wine glass has been used by the Europeans for centuries. Many Italians drink wine out of glasses resembling small juice glasses. But if you're drinking a fine wine and you want to observe the color and not warm the wine, then use a glass with a stem.

During the meal, an attentive server watches your wine glass and refills it when it's close to empty. If you don't want a refill, leave a noticeable portion of wine in your glass.

An attentive host keeps an eye on the wine supply and orders an additional bottle if the situation warrants. As a gracious guest, make sure to compliment your host on her wine selection.

Savoring Champagne

Champagne is normally served before a meal or with dessert. This sparkling, bubbly beverage adds a festive air to any occasion, but you don't have to save the Champagne for a special day; it goes well with many casual foods — even Chinese!

Technically speaking, *Champagne* is the official name for sparkling wines made in the Champagne region of France. Sparkling wines made outside that region aren't officially allowed to use the name Champagne. Whatever you call them, Champagne and other sparkling wines come in a range of dryness: *brut* is dry, and *sec* is sweet. (You can find everything from extra brut, the driest, to demi-sec, the sweetest.) Generally speaking, you want to pair dry sparkling wines with savory foods and sweet sparkling wines with sweet foods.

Everyone loves hearing the "Pop!" upon opening a bottle of Champagne, but you need to open the bottle with a minimum of fanfare to protect your guests from a flying cork and to avoid losing any of its precious contents. Holding the bottle at a 45-degree angle from your body, making sure not to point it toward anyone, follow these steps:

1. **With your thumb over the cork, remove the foil and wire cage from around the cork.**

2. **With one hand about two-thirds of the way down the bottle and the other over the cork, twist the bottle while pushing down on the cork.**

3. **As the cork emerges, continue putting pressure on the cork so that it makes only a quiet hiss as it's released from the bottle.**

Giving a Proper Toast

The term *toast* comes from the old English custom of placing a piece of toasted bread in the bottom of the glass to enhance the flavor of beer or wine. After the toast was saturated with the liquor, the person would eat the toast. Who knows where that tradition has gone! Today, you can make a toast with Champagne, wine, or any other beverage (omitting the actual piece of toast, of course). Children, young adults, and those who don't drink can toast with water or whatever beverage they're drinking; doing so isn't bad taste or bad luck.

Who makes toasts and when? Toasting was once a man's job, and only men drank the toast, while women nodded and smiled. But now, it's perfectly appropriate for anyone to make or respond to a toast, regardless of gender. The host can and should propose the first toast to begin the meal — a welcome toast. If a guest of honor is present, the host also proposes a toast to that person over dessert.

Rising and sitting during a toast depend on the formality of the occasion. If the guest of honor is a dignitary, a very important person, or a distinguished elder, everyone should rise with the toast as a sign of respect. At large events where you want to command the attention of a room or more than one table, rising for the toast is traditional. Simply ask for everyone's attention, or rise and ask for everyone's attention in a larger gathering. After you have the floor, be respectful, take a minute or less to make the toast, and then be seated. At smaller occasions, if fewer than ten people are at the table, rising is unnecessary.

Don't use your silverware to clink your glass to gain everyone's attention. Also, clinking your glass to your guest's glass is actually seen as crude — and it can also break fine crystal! The custom of clinking glasses began in the Middle Ages for the purpose of spilling a little of the drink into the other person's glass to assure that they were not being poisoned — not a real danger today. Some believe that clinking also was thought to drive away evil spirits.

For a long time, the rule has been that you don't drink when you're the one being toasted, although some people feel that it's okay to raise your glass but not drink. Follow your preference in this matter, but to be perfectly correct, simply smile and nod to everyone if you're toasted to. The guest of honor responds to the toast by toasting and thanking the host. In fact, whether or not you're the guest of honor, you should always respond with a toast after you're toasted.

Drinking Alcoholic Beverages Sensibly

Whether you're the host or a guest, take care not to overindulge in wine or other alcoholic beverages. Nothing is less mannerly than losing control after drinking too much — and nothing can ruin an evening more quickly for everyone else. Make sure that you eat while drinking, and pace yourself by alternating alcoholic beverages with nonalcoholic ones.

Keep in mind that drinking any alcoholic beverages causes dehydration, so be sure to drink enough water!

Chapter 14

Hosting a Memorable Event

*Y*ou have no way of getting around it: If you want to be invited to social events, you must reciprocate by acting as host to your friends, family, and business associates. Excessive formality or a lavish party-to-end-all-parties isn't necessary, but as the host, you want to put your own personal touch on the event and make the experience as pleasant and memorable as possible.

Entertaining can run the gamut from something as simple as a midday luncheon to something as complicated as a formal dinner party for 50. In either case, just as a chef blends compatible ingredients to turn out a memorable meal, you blend the party's elements — guests, food, and entertainment — to create a memorable event.

You may be an experienced host who needs only a word or two of encouragement and perhaps a checklist to make sure that you haven't overlooked anything. Or you may be new to entertaining and require a step-by-step guide. Either way, you can use this chapter as your plan for hosting a perfect event. Along with practical and clever ways to stay organized and save time, I provide a few suggestions for unique ways to entertain without breaking the bank.

Don't get too caught up in making sure every person is entertained every minute of your party. Your guests will take the initiative. The success of your party depends on lots of laughter, good friends, delicious food, and everyone feeling welcomed and comfortable. If you're relaxed and make the comfort of your guests a top priority, most people will have a good time without ever knowing why.

Injecting Creativity and Organization into Your Party

The key to any successful event is planning. As a host, your motto should be "be prepared" (thank you, Boy Scouts!). Planning well in advance is the best way to ensure that you can handle the inevitable, unexpected glitches with grace. In the following sections, I discuss choosing the type of event to host, drawing up a guest list, and making a checklist of tasks to tackle.

If you think that organizing the event is more than you can handle, ask a friend to share the duties of hosting the party — doing so adds to the pleasure without adding additional stress. Just make sure your friend's duties don't keep him from enjoying the party. And, have a list of simple duties (open wine, pour water, light candles, and so on) ready in case other guests offer to help.

Determining the type of event to host

The first step in the planning process is to decide on the type of event you want to host. There are as many different kinds of parties as there are hosts. From an intimate formal dinner party for four to an outdoor barbecue and pool party for the neighborhood to hors d'oeuvres and Champagne before opening night at the opera, the opportunities for the creative host are unlimited.

For most people, the only limitations are time, energy, and budget. If your bank account won't support an elegant catered affair, don't fret! With some creativity, menu manipulation, and other tricks of the trade (all of which you can find in this chapter), you can replicate a catered affair for a fraction of the cost.

To decide which type of party you want to host, consider the reason for the party or event. Is it to celebrate a family member's birthday, a colleague's promotion, someone moving to another city, or a 30th wedding anniversary? Is your goal to raise funds for a good cause? After you take time to reflect on the purpose for the event, you can decide how best to celebrate it. For example, the visit of an out-of-town dignitary may be best marked by a dinner party with other luminaries in attendance. Your colleague's promotion may be best celebrated with cocktails at a restaurant near your office so that everyone can attend after work.

Be considerate of your guests' schedules and lifestyles when choosing a date for entertaining. For example, if you've chosen a weeknight, make sure that the party doesn't run late for those with early work schedules.

Mixing up a dynamic blend of invitees

The success of most events is measured by the mix of guests. (You thought the most important ingredient was the food? Well, that's a close second!) As you assemble your guest list, you want to consider inviting friends whose company you enjoy, guests whom you know mix well together, and those friends and family to whom you owe an invitation. All guests should feel special and know that they were invited because they have something special to contribute to the event.

Only you know for sure what will work and what won't regarding your guest list. For example, if Ken and Barbara had a perfectly amicable divorce and are now happily remarried to wonderful new mates, they may have no problem attending the same party. On the other hand, Ellen and Mike may be a different story. Ellen may have been left with no money, no car, three kids, and $10,000 in credit card debt, and she may have sworn to kill Mike if she ever sees him again. Take these essential pieces of information into account when you make up your guest list.

For some reason, people like to invite folks they know that don't get along with each other "just to see what happens." Please resist this temptation. If you have any doubt about certain guests getting along with one another, consult before you invite. Call your friend and ask her how she feels about attending a dinner that will include her ex-spouse. Make sure you extend that same courtesy to the other person as well.

The goal for the host or hostess is to try to select a dynamic blend of invitees. Have a good idea of who your guests are and what you can do to help them feel comfortable. As the host, you're bringing these people together, and your job is to help them interact. A good mix of people ensures a good party with polite conversation that is interesting, stimulating, and upbeat. Interesting people create interesting conversations and discussions, which will be the ultimate memory for your guests.

Checking tasks off your to-do list

After you determine the occasion and the number of guests for your party, make a party checklist. If you need a role model for planning a wonderful event, consider Santa Claus: Like Santa, you too need to make a list and check it twice — even if you're hosting a simple impromptu dinner for four. In planning any event, attention to detail makes the difference. If you start by making a list, you can remember all the details and stay organized. Things become hectic as party time approaches, and you don't want to forget anything at the last minute.

Need a reason to celebrate?

Each year a few annual holidays and events routinely call for a celebration (such as New Year's Eve, Fourth of July, and so on). But if you're in the brainstorming process, here are few extraordinary ideas that deserve some celebratory recognition:

✔ **Not-so-Common Holidays:** Election Day, Groundhog Day, Mardi Gras, April Fools Day, Summer or Winter Solstice

✔ **Worldly Holidays:** Bastille Day (France), Chinese New Year, Cinco De Mayo (Mexico), Oktoberfest (Germany)

✔ **Sporting Events:** Baseball season's opening day, Summer or Winter Olympics, Kentucky Derby, Indianapolis 500, March Madness

✔ **Hollywood:** Last or first episode of a favorite television show, Academy Awards, Grammy Awards

Following a party checklist also helps lessen the emotional stress and makes planning your event a much smoother process. When you bring together good food and good friends, you want to be able to enjoy yourself, too! The following sections provide checklists that you can use to keep your party on track.

If the guest list is large, consider hiring help. A hostess who spends the majority of an evening in the kitchen or running back and forth taking care of details can't give her guests the attention that they should have and in turn creates tension through out the event. If you can't afford a catering staff, consider hiring teenagers, whether they're neighbors or children of friends, to help you serve and clean up. If you have teenage children of your own, put them to work! They may enjoy helping and having a role in the event.

Three to four weeks before the event

Perform these tasks about one month before your party:

❏ Select a theme.

❏ Determine the guest list.

❏ Mail the invitations, including the location, attire, date, and time. (Phone invites if you're hosting a casual get-together.)

❏ Plan the menu. (Consider the season when planning your menu so that you can use the freshest foods available.)

❏ Prepare your grocery shopping list.

❏ Select a caterer (if hiring a caterer is within your budget).

❏ Book the entertainment (if hiring entertainers is within your budget).

❏ Purchase decorations and party supplies.

❏ Arrange to rent tables and chairs (if necessary).

❑ Check your supply of linens and tablecloths, and purchase or rent new ones if necessary.

❑ Make a bar shopping list if you're serving cocktails.

One week before the event

Tackle these tasks one week before your party:

❑ Call any guests who haven't responded to the invitation.

❑ Buy groceries and beverages.

❑ Check your dishes and glasses for chips and cracks; replace any damaged dishes or choose to use another set.

❑ Polish your silverware and silver serving pieces.

❑ Select trays and platters, noting which food you will serve on each.

❑ Plan your table décor, including the centerpiece, place cards, and candles or votives.

❑ Choose your favorite music to play at the party.

❑ Plan your outfit (take it to the cleaners if necessary).

One or two days before the event

The big event is nearly here! Be sure to check off the following tasks:

❑ Wash your dishes, glasses, and flatware.

❑ Clean your house and yard.

❑ Organize your serving dishes.

❑ Prepare food items that can be made in advance and refrigerate them.

❑ Decorate house and tables.

❑ Purchase fresh flowers and arrange them in vases.

❑ Coordinate last-minute arrangements with the caterer (if you've hired one).

❑ Have rental chairs and tables picked-up or delivered.

❑ Set up the bar, and have plenty of ice on hand.

❑ Make sure that your closet has extra hangers, or provide a coat rack if the season requires.

❑ Unplug, hide, or remove your television (unless you're hosting a party for a special televised sporting event).

❑ Put away valuable and breakable items that you cherish.

The day before the event

Take care of the following tasks the day before your party:

❑ Thaw frozen foods.

❑ Try on your outfit to make sure everything fits right.

❑ Mentally walk through your entire event.

The day of the event

It's show time! Attend to these final details on the day of your party:

❑ Prepare food that wasn't already made in advanced.

❑ Plate food on serving dishes.

❑ Tidy up the kitchen after food has been prepared and plated.

❑ Set up bar condiments and ice in ice bucket.

❑ Check your list twice, making sure that you've done everything you need to do.

❑ Allow yourself plenty of time to shower and dress for the party.

❑ Keep pets locked up (not everyone loves your dog or cat as much as you).

❑ Greet guests as they arrive.

Extending a Cordial Invitation

An invitation to a social event should be a well-thought-out process. Your invitation sets the tone and style for the affair, and your guests should feel welcomed and excited about attending! In the following sections, I explain the basics of creating invitations for your get-together.

Choosing the form of your invitation

Depending on the formality (or lack thereof) of your event, you can choose to invite your guests in one of three ways: in writing, orally, or via e-mail or the Internet. I cover all three options in the following sections.

In writing

Printed invitations range from the classic and formal (think of a traditional wedding invitation) to the creative and unusual (I once received an invitation to a Chinese-themed dinner in a Chinese food takeout container). If your party has a theme, use it in your invitation — for example, if you're hosting a wine-tasting event, you can design your invitation to look like a wine label. Whatever you do, don't forget to include the basics:

- ✔ When the party starts
- ✔ When the party will end
- ✔ What kind of attire is appropriate
- ✔ Where you're holding the party
- ✔ How to RSVP

Always let the guests know what the occasion is and, if you've designated a guest of honor, who she is. If you're hosting, say, a casual barbecue and you expect guests to contribute a dish or beverages, let them know in the invitation.

A mailed invitation for any formal event or dinner party is still the rule. However, sending a save-the-date e-mail beforehand is fine.

Orally

If you plan an informal gathering of friends or family, you can issue your invitations orally, either in person or by telephone. Make sure that you're clear about the time and date of the affair. Say something like this:

> "I'd love to have you join us for an informal brunch with a few other friends at my house a week from Sunday. We plan to get together at eleven, have a nice brunch, and play cards for a couple of hours."

Note that this invitation contains a lot of information. Your guests know how they need to dress and that others have been invited to the brunch. They know that the meal will consist of more than chips and dip, and they know that you expect them to leave after a couple of hours. Your guests will find all this information useful and will be grateful to you for providing it.

Via e-mail and the Internet

Another option for inviting guests to a casual social event is to send an e-mail invite or use an online invitation service, like www.evite.com or www.sendomatic.com. I describe how to go about these options in the following:

- ✔ **E-mail:** E-mail invites are quick and easy to get into all your guests' hands, that is, if they are online. Just as with the written invitation, the e-mail invite should contain all the pertinent information. You can add pictures or graphics to make it interesting, but not everyone may be able to download them due to their e-mail service.

Communication via e-mail is considered a more casual form of communicating, though you can send a nice invitation as an attachment. I usually suggest that if you're unsure, side on the conservative, more-formal side.

Be sure to suppress your guests' e-mail address so they will not have confidential e-mails for all your guests, unless you're inviting a close group of friends and relatives that know each other. Make sure you let the guests know that this information is only for them and their spouse or date! With e-mails, I have found my guest list has expanded because my guests decided to forward my invitation to others not on my list!

✔ **Online invitation service:** With online invitation services, your invitation is posted on a Web site so that the graphics and pictures are visible for all your guests. Many of these services often give you options to include maps, list of items needed for a potluck, weather updates, event reminders, and much more.

Your guests may be subject to the online provider's advertisements and or surveys. Please be considerate of your guests when using these services and make sure you know that they will not be bothered by Internet advertising.

Follow-up with a telephone call to those who have not RSVP'd via e-mail. In this era of Internet outages, spam filters and the like, they may not have received your electronic invitation.

Considering significant others and children

Always mention exactly whom you're inviting when you issue invitations. For a married couple, mention both names. For a single adult who you expect to bring a date, word the invitation as "you and your escort," "you and your date," or, if you know the name of the person's significant other, "you and Ian."

When you make up your guest list, be sure to include the people your guests won't leave home without. For example, you can't expect your friend Jason to show up for dinner unless you also invite the new love of his life, Cynthia.

Some people take their children everywhere, but unless you specifically mention them on the invitation, your guests should understand that children aren't invited. The only reasonable antidote is to be very specific in the way you address your invitation — make it read "Edward and Dorothy Smith" instead of "The Smith Family." If you want to include the little ones, state on the invitation, "You, Marvin, and the children," or write, "Children welcome."

If you have a feeling that one (or more) of your invited guests will want to bring along their children no matter how you word your invitation, telephone that person and say something along these lines: "We really hope you'll be able to attend our dinner. Did we pick a date when you can get a babysitter for the children?"

If perhaps your guests say that they thought they would bring the kids, be polite, apologize, and stick to your guns. Let them know you were really hoping to have an adult evening. You can be firm and gracious at the same time. Sometimes the way your request is received is just a matter of the tone of your voice. You can even mention that your next party will include children. Just keep your word.

Even after all your attempts, some people will still ignore the obvious and do what's convenient for them anyway. You can't do very much except take a deep breath and be as gracious as possible. Don't act too surprised when you answer the door, and remember to smile! Begin making introductions immediately — yes, even introducing the children. And be prepared with a few extra goodies, food, activities, games, and movies.

Designating guest attire

Your formal invitation should include a freestanding line that specifies how you expect your guests to dress. You can use the following guidelines:

- ✔ If you want to see the gentlemen in tuxedos and ladies in formal dresses, your safest line is *formal* or *black tie.*
- ✔ For suits and ties and cocktail dresses, use the phrase *semiformal.*
- ✔ For slacks, sport coats, and bright, coordinated outfits, use the term *business casual.*
- ✔ For events in which you'd wear shorts, jeans, or sportswear, mention *casual attire.*

Terms such as *semiformal* and *casual* mean many things to many people. If you're hosting a semiformal gathering, you may want to verbally explain what dress is recommended to guests when they call to RSVP. You don't have to be shy about calling the shots for your own party. But no matter what your guests show up wearing, always make them feel at ease. (See Chapter 3 for more details about clothing.)

Requesting RSVPs

If you're having an informal party, you can request telephoned responses to your invitations. Include on the invitations your phone number and a note to leave word on your answering machine or voice mail if you aren't home. With practically everyone having e-mail these days, you may also give your guests an option to RSVP via e-mail or a phone call.

If you're hosting a more formal party, you may want to include separate RSVP cards in your invitations. RSVP cards are note-sized cards that the invitees fill in and mail back to you indicating, whether or not they can attend the event. (Although the traditional rules of etiquette call for the invitee to respond to an invitation with a written letter accepting or declining the invitation, many people neglect this courtesy in today's busy world.) Always include with your RSVP cards an envelope addressed to your attention and affixed with the correct postage. Figure 14-1 shows a sample format for an RSVP card.

Figure 14-1:
An RSVP
card
includes a
deadline for
a response.

> *Please respond on or before May 20, 2007*
>
> *M*_____
>
> _____ *will attend*
>
> _____ *will not attend*

If you haven't received an RSVP from a guest, calling and asking whether that person plans to attend is perfectly acceptable. Just as a host has responsibilities, a guest also has responsibilities — and this is one of the most common mistakes that guests make. Guests are required to respond within a day or two of receiving an invitation.

Arranging a Tasteful Menu

Food is the showpiece of a social event. Your guests will have waited all day to taste your delectable dishes. A well-planned menu can have your guests "oohing" and "aahing," while a poor-planned menu can have your guests reaching for their coats.

Planning a menu should be fun. Your personal and familiar touches will make the menu and event special. Your menu can be as simple or as elaborate as you'd like it to be, whatever your budget and culinary talents allow. You may want to stick to simpler dishes for casual events and save the gourmet treats for more formal affairs. But remember that elegant and exotic don't always translate to difficult; these menus can be simple and easy to arrange. The following sections provide tips for menu planning from casual to more formal events.

You can never have too much food at a party. Have plenty of hot coffee, tea, and snacks on hand, too, for events that go late into the evening.

Planning a perfect menu for any type of event

Great cooks seem to have a knack for planning perfect menus, as artists create masterpieces. Considerations in menu planning are usually practical rather than artistic, but the secret lies with both. Not too often is a perfect menu an accident. Here are some guidelines that can help you create a menu that would please even the most discriminating guest:

- ✓ **Texture:** Include in your menu a variety of firm, chewy, smooth, crunchy, soft, and flaky foods.
- ✓ **Color:** Colors can stimulate the appetite as well as be pleasing to the eye. Use foods of bright, vivid colors for contrast and harmony.
- ✓ **Harmony:** Consider including a variety of compatible flavors and temperatures, using raw and cooked foods.
- ✓ **Seasonal:** Take cues from the season; pick fresh ingredients that are available during that time of year.
- ✓ **Safe dishes:** If you don't know your guests well or you're hosting a business meal, use simple ingredients for the main course. Appetizers provide you the opportunity to try something more adventuresome.
- ✓ **Time:** Estimate the time it will take to prepare each course, and select a menu with dishes that you can make ahead of time. Preparing the food while your guests are in attendance should be keep at a minimum. Guests expect to see you, not you slaving away in the kitchen. Keep your menu simple enough so that you can visit with your guests.

A considerate host makes sure that every guest can eat most of the food on the menu. So unless you know already, you may want to call ahead to see if any of guests have food allergies or diet restrictions.

Special occasions call for special meals. I hope that the two menus in Figures 14-2 and 14-3, which illustrate the previously listed tips, help to get your creative juices flowing.

The following sections feature additional hints and tips for both casual and sophisticated events.

Casual dining

If you're having a casual get-together, you want a menu that you can prepare and serve with minimum fuss. That way, if you must serve as host, cook, and server, you can handle the job with a little advance planning — and you'll have time to socialize with your guests.

Brunch on the Beach

Bucket of Crudités and Dip

Crispy French Bread

Assorted Shellfish on Ice

Grilled Herbed Salmon

Seafood Seviche

Mixed Greens with Avocado and Papaya

Sand Dollar Cookies

Blanc de Noir Sparkling Wine

Pinot Blanc

Figure 14-2:
The fun of a casual outing should be reflected in a menu.

Formal Dinner

Caviar Pouches

Roast Duckling with Orange Sauce and Wild Mushroom Rice

Sauté of Zucchini

Endive and Watercress Salad

Raspberry-Chocolate Torte

Champagne

Cabernet Sauvignon

Sparkling Muscat

Figure 14-3:
A formal event calls for extra-special food.

When deciding on a menu, don't bother looking for a dictionary definition of casual. Casual can mean whatever you want it to mean — just make sure that your prospective guests are in agreement with you. Among very close friends, casual may mean pizza ordered in and a couple of six-packs in a bucket of ice. Casual can also mean a three-course luncheon served at a nicely set table.

A buffet is an excellent way to serve a group of guests without having to traipse back and forth to the kitchen. Utilizing a buffet enables you to arrange everything on a side table, stack up the plates and silverware, and let your guests help themselves. The buffet concept can work beautifully if you keep a few rules in mind:

✓ **Make sure that you plan the timing.** After about one hour of cocktails and perhaps some hors d'oeuvres, it will take another 45 minutes for your guests to make their way through the buffet and consume a meal.

✓ **Unless you're planning a formal sit-down buffet with properly set tables, think of how your guests are going to manage to eat while holding plates on their laps.** Avoid pieces of meat that you have to cut, as well as long, unwieldy strands of pasta.

✓ **Food should be easy to handle because your guests will be serving themselves.** Think about individual portions that the guest can serve with a single serving spoon, fork, or tongs. Precarve meats such as roasts, ham, or turkey and cut small birds such as Rock Cornish Hens into halves.

✓ **If you're hosting a cocktail buffet at an open house, choose foods that taste good at room temperature (unless you have the use of chafing dishes or servers standing by to refill hot dishes).** A cocktail buffet should also include bite-sized foods, with small bowls of snacks and nuts placed around the room. The buffet may include the following foods: a cold pasta dish with chicken, a salad, a large basket of assorted breads and rolls, a platter of various cheeses, crudités with dip, fresh fruit salad, and a rich dessert (chocolate is always popular).

✓ **If you're intent on offering a more elaborate buffet menu for a large group, you must keep hot foods hot and cold foods cold.** To keep cold foods cold, arrange them in metal serving containers and then rest the containers on top of lots of ice in an even larger container. To keep hot foods hot, use electric warming platters or alcohol burners.

As foods approach room temperature — from either direction — the growth of bacteria is greatly accelerated. Instead of pleasing your guests, you may be at risk of poisoning them.

✓ **Arrange the food in the following order: entrees, side dishes, salads, bread, butter, and condiments.**

✓ **Prepare extra portions (make enough for 16 if you're expecting 12, for example).** Not only do you not want to run out of food, but some people may take larger portions than they can finish.

- ✔ **If children are invited, plan to have a few foods that they will enjoy — and a child's table can work out great!** The key is to make certain the children are all about the same age. Ask the older children or their parents ahead of time if possible. They may be at the age that they feel "older" than the other children. Normally children look forward to sitting at their own table because they aren't under the watchful eye of the adults.

- ✔ **Consider those guests who can't easily serve themselves in a buffet line.** Serve these guests first, or invite them to the buffet table just a moment before you issue a general invitation to dine.

Set the buffet up on a dining room table or sideboard. Also provide an open bar, plus sodas, bottled water, and fruit juice. Make sure to set the bar up a fair distance from the food to avoid traffic jams. At one end of the buffet, make a stack of large plates, utensils (a fork, a spoon perhaps, and, only if absolutely necessary, a knife). It's thoughtful to place utensils in large napkins to create neat, easy-to-grab packages. Be creative! You can tie these with a ribbon or cord, tuck in a flower, and place them in a basket for a decorative touch. You should also provide enough extra dishes and silverware so that people who go back for seconds can enjoy their new selections on clean dishes.

Make provisions for disposing of bones, fruit pits, peelings, and other inedible pieces of food, such as additional dishes set out for used food picks, shells, and shrimp peels, by placing a waste bin nearby. Otherwise, you may find unusual items in your potted plants!

If you'd like close friends or relatives to bring something to a casual event, or if they offer to, request specific items so that you don't have duplication. Never say no to a guest that offers to bring a dish.

Choosing a sophisticated menu

For a more formal event, your menu may vary, depending on the time of day and the degree of formality you want to achieve:

- ✔ A typical luncheon menu may begin with an appetizer or salad, followed by a main course (a cold dish such as cold poached salmon in summer, or a hot dish such as pasta in wintertime), and ending with dessert and coffee or tea. You can serve wine, but don't be surprised if your guests avoid alcohol during the day.

- ✔ For a small, casual, seated dinner, you can serve a substantial main course (including meat, vegetable, potato or rice, salad, and bread), plus dessert, with a choice of red or white wine.

- ✔ A more formal dinner would include a first course such as baked clams, oysters, or soup, followed by a main course and then dessert, with red or white wine at each course.

✔ If you want to pull out all the stops, a very formal dinner would include a light soup, a light fish course, a main course of meat or fowl, two accompanying vegetables (one vegetable and one potato), a salad and cheese course, a light dessert, a choice of red or white wine, and Champagne with dessert.

Deciding on a method of service

When it comes time to serving your food, planning the method of service beforehand is preferable. If you had decided on a buffet, well then the service is easily defined! Guests will serve themselves from a side table and they have the option of returning for seconds. All courses can be served buffet-style or you can choose to serve dessert at the dining room table after dishes have been cleared.

At a sit-down dinning, you can chose from a variety of service methods depending on the degree of formality, the number of guests to be served and the time needed to serve:

✔ **American or Plate Service:** Plates are prepared in the kitchen and delivered to the table one person at a time, similar to most restaurant service. This service allows you to be decorative with your plating. Ladies should be served first delivering the plate on the left. The advantage here is that you get faster and easier service and when the food reaches you it is hot — usually. This type of service is the least formal.

✔ **Family style:** Platters and bowls of food are put directly on the table and guests served themselves onto empty plates. Food is passed to the right (counter clockwise).

✔ **Service A La Russe:** In the Russian style, the server presents the decorated meats or other dishes in one whole piece on the platter then carves it in front of the guests. An arranged plate is then presented to each guest.

This type of service has been replaced by a form of service that uses a small serving table which is equipped with a portable stove where the foods were then carved and served. This service method is very common, and I'm sure you've experienced this type of showy service.

✔ **Butler Service:** Similar to a Russian service, the guest serves his own food while the server is holding the platter.

✔ **Service A La Francaise:** French food is served on platters. This type of service can be messy as food is moved from platter to plate. The server presents a pre-arranged platter and serves from the left. Each guest serves himself. This service is customary at formal dinners, especially in The White House, The State Department, and at Embassies.

> ✔ **Service A L'Anglaise:** In the English style, the server presents the arranged platter from the left and serves the guests. This service is more common and appropriate for banquets, because the portions can be limited and served to a predetermined number of guests. It offers a nice presentation, you can see the food, and it never runs out!

The type of service you choose is all a matter of preference, which is most comfortable for you and how it will fit within your style and budget.

Welcoming Your Guests and Making a Great First Impression

Etiquette means making others feel comfortable, and this statute is especially true when hosting an event. Welcoming your guest warmly, commenting sincerely how happy you are to see them, and making proper introductions make every guest feel special. More importantly, you give each guest an initial impression that greatly influences your guests' opinion of you, the evening, and even meal to come. This first impression sets the tone of the event.

In the following sections, I describe how to greet guests when they arrive, offer drinks, and make your way to the table.

Greeting at the door

As your guests arrive, do your best to greet them at the door. If you have someone else doing the greeting, make sure that you're close by and that the person welcoming your guests knows where you are at all times. If you're unable to greet every arrival, make certain to seek the guest out soon after she arrives and personally welcome her to your home.

I once attended a formal dinner in someone's home where a member of the catering staff greeted the guests. A few of the guests who hadn't met the host previously thought that the staff member greeting them was the host. Unfortunately, one guest after another shook the catering staff person's hand and said, "Thank you for inviting me to your home." Each time, the poor staff person had to explain who the host was — an awkward and embarrassing situation for everyone.

As host, you need to be prepared to receive hostess gifts. Accept all gifts graciously and have vases with water ready to go (out of sight) so you don't spend additional time locating vases and arranging cut flowers. If you receive wine or food items as a hostess gift, serving them isn't necessary. Thank the gift-giver and let him know you will enjoy his gift at another time. If the guest is overly persistent that you serve the wine or food, etiquette calls for you to do so. You can ask a close friend to assist with the hostess gifts so you're able to continue to greet guest.

If you're hosting a fairly large event, make certain you have arranged a safe and accessible area for coats, purses, hats, and other items. Consider providing a guest book and inviting your guests to sign in as they arrive. Not only is this a nice touch, but you'll also have a list of the guests who attended. If you need to send thank-you cards to the guests who brought gifts, you'll have their addresses handy, too. You can even make a notation later in the guest book of the gift that each guest brought.

If you're hosting an event in which most of the guests are meeting for the first time, consider using name cards. Doing so gives you the opportunity to have some fun and be creative.

Offering drinks

Normally, as your guests arrive, you should offer a drink or show them to the bar. In addition to a selection of alcoholic beverages, always have non-alcoholic beverages available during the cocktail hour. Keep cocktail napkins close at hand and offer them with the drinks.

If you plan to serve cocktails before a meal, anywhere from 30 minutes to an hour is acceptable. If the cocktail hour runs much longer than an hour, make sure to provide plenty of appetizers and snacks.

Serving a Champagne punch is a great alternative if you don't want to be busy opening bottles or pouring drinks during your party. Guests may help themselves! And mixing the sparkling wine with fruit juice or soda is easier on your budget.

Keeping an eye on the party for any sign of accidental overindulgence is a host's duty. Before-dinner cocktails, wine with dinner, and cordials afterward may sneak up on guests and impair their ability to make a safe trip home. Make sure to monitor your guests' conditions and, if you're serving mixed drinks, make adjustments to the strength of follow-up servings if necessary. Offer more nonalcoholic drinks as the evening progresses, too. If you have a guest who isn't fit to drive home, you can enlist the transportation assistance of another guest, call a taxi, or as a last resort, provide a guestroom for an overnight stay.

Be considerate of those guests who choose not to indulge in alcohol. Serve plenty of juices, soft drinks, and the like, and don't push anyone to have "just one drink." Think about the foods that you serve as well. If you plan to serve anything with an alcoholic content, such as the sauce on a dessert, make that fact known to your guests and have a nonalcoholic alternative available.

Mingling

As host, do your best not to spend all your time with just the people you know well. Mingle! Spend at least 15 minutes with each guest, and introduce people to others, remembering to say something about each person you introduce gives them a comfortable starting point for a conversation. (For more on social introductions, see Chapter 7.)

As you navigate around the party, always hold your drink glass in your left hand. This way when it comes time to greet someone or shake her hand, that person won't have a cold, wet greeting.

Coming to the table

If you're having a served, seated dinner (rather than a casual buffet, when people serve and seat themselves), at some point you must go to the table with your family or group. Be sure to follow these very specific ways to offer and take a seat:

- ✔ In formal situations, the men escort the women by the arm individually to their seats and assist them in being seated. (I discuss hosting formal events in more detail later in this chapter.)
- ✔ In informal situations, the men allow the women to approach the table in a group and then assist them in taking their seats.

Here's how it's done, step by step:

1. **The woman approaches her chair and waits to be seated.**

2. **The man stands behind the woman's chair and draws it back for her.**

3. **The woman enters from the right, and then begins to sit; when she is halfway down, the man pushes the chair gently beneath her.**

4. **After she's seated, she can move the chair closer or farther from the table as she wishes by holding the sides of the seat and scooting it forward or backward.**

5. **The man then seats himself to the left of the woman he just seated.**

If more women than men are being seated at the table, the men should seat the women on both sides of themselves and around the table before taking their own seats.

Women, be aware of where you place your handbag — never on the table or hanging on the back of your chair. If it can't sit in the back of your chair, set it on the floor slightly under you chair so that others won't trip over it.

Ending the Party

One of the toughest challenges for a gracious host is the delicate process of getting the guests to go home. Moving your guests homeward is really a two-sided issue, because guests are expected to exhibit their own good manners by knowing when it's time to leave.

The invitation is the first and best opportunity to let your guests know the proper time to leave. Say, or write, the times of the event on the invitation. Make it look (or sound) like this: "Jerry and I would love to have you join us between noon and 3:00 p.m. for a buffet luncheon at our home." (I discuss additional invitation etiquette earlier in this chapter.)

In the absence of a stated quitting time, don't rely on hints and subtleties. If circumstances dictate, make a matter-of-fact announcement that you need your guests to leave. Use subtle hints such as turning down the music and the lights. If you have some stubborn guests that refuse to get the hint, try asking a close friend to assist by having them leave, saying goodbye in a manner that other guests will notice.

Absolutely perfect manners require you to remain cheerfully hospitable until your guests leave without prompting. Absolutely perfect manners also require your guests to leave shortly after the final offer of after-dinner refreshments and a noticeable slowdown in conversation. Etiquette necessitates obligations on both sides.

As guests begin to leave, station yourself at the door, accept their compliments, and wish them a good evening. Don't apologize for the roast being overdone or the vodka running out — just say how pleased you were to have them at your party.

Something Special: Hosting a Semiformal or Formal Occasion

After you successfully host a few buffet luncheons on your patio and sit-down suppers for your close friends, you may feel ready to spread your wings and soar into the world of semiformal and formal entertaining. Say you have a 40th anniversary or a graduation coming up. These occasions are perfect opportunities to launch your entry into more formal entertaining. In the following sections, I provide you with some guidance that applies specifically to semiformal and formal occasions.

If you feel an obligation to host a fancy social affair and you can't imagine handling all the details yourself, you can always reserve a private room at a nice restaurant or hotel and let the staff handle everything. Or you can hire a caterer to come into your home and arrange everything from the seating to the flowers to a gourmet meal. However, there's no reason why you can't pull off a truly impressive affair on your own. So what if you overlook some small detail? What counts is your determination to be gracious and to provide others a good time.

Planning your event well in advance

The following steps can help you as you plan your semiformal or formal event:

1. **Set the date.**

   Plan your event far in advance to avoid conflicts with other popular events, and don't clash with religious or national holidays. Planning months in advance gives you ample time to coordinate the rest of your event.

2. **Rent the room, hire the caterer, and so on.**

   Popular places and service organizations schedule their work far into the future. If you have to change the date of your party to accommodate the help you need, do so.

3. **Write out an agenda for your event, setting the time and place for every activity.**

   You'll go over this exercise several times, making little changes. Nothing helps the planning process more than a minute-by-minute schedule — you may find yourself remembering to get help with parking, assigning a friend to assist with greeting guests, conferring with the caterer about hors d'oeuvres, arranging for music or other entertainment, and so on.

4. **Compose your invitation and obtain nice cards and envelopes, or confer with a printer about a more formal invitation.**

   See the section "Extending a Cordial Invitation" for more on invitations.

5. **Determine your guest list, make a sketch of the seating, and work out the seating placements.**

6. **Review your guest list and see whether anyone has special dietary needs.**

   If so, alert the caterer or arrangements manager, or make a note to yourself.

7. **If the party will be at your home, you may want to invite your neighbors. If that's not possible, inform your neighbors of what's on your calendar and ask them to tolerate a bit of temporary disruption.**

   Sending a small gift along wouldn't hurt, either!

8. **Address the invitations and the envelopes for the RSVP cards in longhand, and affix attractive postage stamps to both the inner and the outer envelopes.**

   Mail your invitations well in advance — five or six weeks isn't unreasonable for a semiformal or formal affair, especially around holidays such as Christmas and New Years.

9. **Find a place to store the RSVP cards as your guests return them, and keep a checklist of the cards that you receive.**

   You'll need to give the caterer the total number of guests. You may have to telephone a few invitees to determine their intentions as the date draws closer. If you haven't heard yet from a guest, you may want to call and say something like this:

   > "Hi, Bill, this is Joan calling. I'm in the process of confirming numbers with our caterer and am wondering whether you're planning on attending the costume party next Saturday night."

10. **Make a schedule for the big day and stick to it.**

    Remember to leave time to get yourself ready, as well as time to take care of quite a few last-minute distractions.

Choosing the right equipment for the menu

A semiformal dinner party is a splendid opportunity to use your wedding silver and your china and crystal. If you don't have enough matching dinnerware and silverware for the group, your caterer can provide whatever you need.

Different courses of a meal require different eating utensils — soup spoons for soup, salad forks for salad, dinner or entree knives and forks for the main course, dessert forks and/or spoons for dessert, and coffee spoons for coffee. (See Chapter 12 for the proper placement of tableware.)

You may also want place-card holders, napkin rings (unless you know how to do a nice folding job), water glasses, salt and pepper shakers at convenient intervals along the table, serving forks or spoons suitable for the relishes and other items, and, if you're employing a serving or catering staff, a little bell that you can ring to summon one of the servers.

Creating a formal seating arrangement

Certain rules govern where guests sit during a formal meal:

- ✔ The host sits at the end of the table. If a couple is hosting, the man sits at one end and the woman sits at the other.
- ✔ The male guest of honor sits on the hostess's right.
- ✔ The next most important man sits on the hostess's left.
- ✔ The female guest of honor sits to the host's right.
- ✔ The second most important woman sits to the host's left.

In many formal situations, you find yourselves at round tables, which facilitate group conversation and put everyone on an equal basis. Whatever the shape of the table, couples should be separated and men and women seated alternately.

When planning your seating arrangement you may want to start with the people whom you know. You're familiar with their personalities and their interests, and just maybe some of these people are natural talkers who you can sit anywhere. Ideally, you would prefer to have them near the difficult personalities and the quieter guest. You can even go as far as asking these friends (natural talkers) ahead of time that you would like them to sit next to the guest you know may be uncomfortable or difficult. This way, your chatty friend is prepared to diffuse the conversation if it goes off track. These people will know the polite thing to do is to be supportive and avoid negative comments and if necessary, be able to change the subject diplomatically and gracefully.

You can also ask your close friends ahead of time to bring up a particular topic of conversation that will encourage others to comment. This way the host doesn't have to be in charge of the conversation throughout the meal.

Many hosts use place cards to indicate where each guest should sit. Place cards don't have to be above the plate; they can be on the plate, on the napkin ring, or on the chair. And the meal doesn't have to be formal to use place cards.

If you're entertaining a group of close friends, you can make it fun by using place cards with various personality types, ask them to sit at the description they think best describes them. Use descriptions of personality types in good taste, positives such as "Romantic," "The Analyst," "Enthusiast," "Leader," "Flirt," "Comedian," and so on. This system will always get the conversation off to a good start!

Making your guests feel welcome

Before your guests begin arriving, make one last trip through the kitchen to verify that the cook or caterer is on track and to inspect the public rooms for stray newspapers, magazines, and personal items. Then position yourself near the front door and take a deep breath.

If you're brave and decide to be host *and* cook, the timing of the meal is critical. Be certain that the menu you plan allows you time to greet guests at the door — so out of the kitchen, please!

As your guests arrive, greet them, show them where to put their wraps, steer them to the living room or cocktail area, and invite them to request a refreshment. You're on safer ground if you avoid drinks and hors d'oeuvres yourself — shaking hands and hugging while holding a dish or glass is difficult. Likewise, leaving moisture or a few grease spots on other people's clothing is definitely bad form.

In the event of a spill or other minor accident, summon a server or other worker to handle the problem, move away, and then put it out of your mind. If you don't have help, take a few minutes to attend to the guest yourself. If all else fails, you may be able to offer a piece of your own clothing. It is gracious, also, to offer to send the stained garment for cleaning.

Introduce newcomers all around the room until the number of guests gets too large. When that time arrives, introduce newcomers only to the people who are closest at hand. Keep an eye out for shy guests who plaster themselves to the wall. Engage them in conversation and introduce them to someone you hope can draw them out.

Carrying cocktails to the dinner table is bad form, so as the host, you need to make it easy for your guests to leave their drinks behind before going to the table. You can have a tray near the cocktail area for used glasses, or if you've hired help, have them walk around the room to collect unfinished drinks and empty glasses.

Acting appropriately during the meal

In all that happens at this event, you're the leader. When the time comes, select an honored guest as your escort and move toward the dining room — other guests will follow. Take your seat right away and place your napkin in your lap as a sign that others should do the same. In a formal dining situation, no one sits down until the host(s) or guest of honor is seated.

As soon as the wine is poured, offer a short toast. For example, you can say something like, "Here's to the great pleasure of dining with friends." If a special occasion has prompted the dinner, suit your toast to the event: "To an absolutely wonderful fundraising season for the Society to Protect Cobblestone Streets." (Head to Chapter 13 for additional toasting tips.) Begin eating at once so that your guests may follow suit.

As the host, you have the responsibility to pace the meal. Don't eat too quickly or too slowly; watch the balance and harmony of the table. Don't rush through the courses or get up from the table too often, and don't continue to ask the guests if everything tastes okay.

As the host, it is important that you're comfortable. Your guests take subconscious clues from you. If you're laughing, talking to people, and having a good time, chances are greater they will too.

After dessert, when you rise from the table, everyone else will, too. Make sure that the slowest guest has finished eating before you stand. When you lead the way to the den, the patio, or some other room, others will follow. Try to engage every guest in at least a short period of personal conversation after the meal. Normally, guests should begin to leave an hour after the meal.

Chapter 15

Being a Gracious Guest

*I*n some ways, being a gracious guest is as challenging as being a good host. A good guest is a rare gem — a person who adds sparkle and zest to an event while helping the host in subtle ways that are undetectable to other guests. These people always seem to have a full social calendar and receive loads of fun invitations.

The rules of how to act with others and how to behave as guests in a polite and considerate manner are rules that have stood the test of time. Although some rules of etiquette have relaxed in this century, being rude or thoughtless will never be in style. When you're a guest, you should treat the host as you would want to be treated if you were the host.

In this chapter, you can discover everything you need to know about being one of those gracious guests who always get invited back.

Dressing appropriately is certainly a part of being a good guest, but because attire can get complicated, especially when you attend a formal or semi-formal event, I've devoted a separate chapter to it. For information about attire, see Chapter 3.

Responding to an Invitation

Unfortunately, people these days aren't taking RSVPs seriously! People have become extremely lax in this area, and consequently, the host is left with undue expense and hardships. Even those people who call and confirm can't be counted on to attend! (Almost as if they're awaiting a better offer, especially around the holidays.)

Every host or hostess has a horror story to share! Don't become part of someone's horror story. Always be considerate. The best way to show that you're socially gracious is "to do as requested." Following through with the host's request to communicate whether you plan to attend is a sure sign of your good manners and social skill. Follow these tips to respond properly to an invitation:

✔ The first step of being a gracious guest is responding to invitations promptly. A timely response to an RSVP is vital because the hostess plans the menu around the number of people to serve. I recommend responding within a day or two of receiving an invitation; however, a response within three to five days is acceptable. This reasonable amount of time allows you to check with your spouse or partner, coordinate calendars, or make arrangements for a babysitter. Any longer and you may leave the host wondering. Never assume that the host or hostess knows you're coming.

✔ If the invitation is telephoned and you aren't able to give the host an answer over the phone, say something like this: "What a lovely invitation! Thank you so much for thinking of us. I'll check with Tom and get back to you on Wednesday." Note that you should be specific about when you will be able to accept or decline, and be sure to follow through with your response.

✔ If the invitation is written, either RSVP to the telephone number (if one is provided), return the RSVP card, or write your own response. To accept the invitation, be sure to use the same wording. If the invitation invites "Mr. and Mrs. James Smith Jr." you don't respond with "Jim and Jane Smith." If you must decline, you don't need to give details. All you say is this: "We're sorry that we can't accept your kind invitation because of another engagement."

✔ For online or e-mailed invitations, your RSVP with an e-mail or using the electronic invitation response system is perfectly acceptable.

✔ If you see "Regrets Only" written on an invitation, you call only to say you can't come to the event — otherwise, you will be there.

✔ If you're unsure about going to an event, call and say you would like to attend; however, if you have a conflict, and if the conflict changes, you will immediately call to be sure the invitation is still open. This courtesy lets the host know that you did receive the invitation, and that you aren't simply ignoring it. If your plans change and you can now attend an event in which you had already declined, call at least three days prior to the event to be sure your attendance is still okay.

✔ If you've accepted an invitation and are unable to attend due to a valid reason (*never* a better offer), notify the host as soon as possible. In most cases all you need to do is make a phone call so you can offer an explanation and express your regrets. If you have enough time, you may send a short note, especially when the event is formal such as a wedding.

✔ If you previously declined an invitation for a legitimate reason, but you're now able to attend and want to go, you can call the hostess, explain the situation, and ask if you may change your regret. Only do this if the event is a large party, reception, open house, buffet, or any function that an extra guest wouldn't become a problem.

✔ If you're a guest and have forgotten to RSVP, you must rectify the situation ASAP. Call immediately and apologize. Be honest — no elaborate stories or excuses please! People know when you aren't telling the truth. Following up with a handwritten note is expected, thanking them for the invitation and also apologizing for forgetting. A gift or flowers is also a nice gesture.

Arriving at an Event

Being prompt is a guest's most important responsibility. The host carefully chose a time for the event to begin, and you must respect that choice by showing up at that time. Keep the following points in mind about timing:

✔ **Fashionably late is unfashionably rude.** When an invitation specifies a time, as most wedding and banquet invitations do, you're supposed to arrive at that time. If the affair is held in a hotel or other public place, getting out of the house a few minutes early won't hurt, just in case you get caught in traffic or have trouble finding a parking space.

✔ **You shouldn't arrive later than 15 or 20 minutes after the scheduled start of an event.** Arriving more than 20 minutes late to a dinner party is plain bad manners. Be on time! Period.

- ✔ **If the event is a dinner party and you're running late, phone ahead to request that the host start without you.** If you arrive late and the meal has already begun, don't disrupt the other guests or bother the host. Take your seat swiftly, and don't expect the other guests to stand and greet you.

- ✔ **Informal invitations that use words like *sevenish* imply a somewhat looser definition of arrival time.** At a private residence, when the host asks you to arrive around sevenish, plan to ring the bell between 7:15 and 7:30, and no later. Never, under any circumstances, arrive a minute before 7:00.

- ✔ **Arriving too early is as unacceptable as arriving too late.** Unless you're prepared to pitch in with the last-minute vacuuming or to open the Cabernet Sauvignon so that it can breathe, never ring a host's doorbell before the appointed hour. You're imposing another burden on a busy host who now has to entertain you as well as make the final preparations. If necessary, drive around the block a few times, stop at a local convenience store, or refuel your car to kill time.

As a guest, if you're met at the door by the host, thank them for the invitation. Engaging in a little small talk is okay; however, don't hold up the host if other guests are arriving. If necessary, offer introductions.

If no one happens to be greeting you and the door is left open (which is the case with some open houses or housewarming parties), don't be shy. Do your best to locate the host or a catering staff member. If necessary, ask where you can put your coat or hostess gift and begin to mingle.

Don't assume that additional company is welcome. The host carefully plans for the number of guests who returned an RSVP, basing the amount of help, food, and beverages on that figure. Don't bring an uninvited guest with you! If you happen to have an unexpected houseguest show up on the day of the scheduled event, you can call the host and ask if it's possible for you to bring a friend. Present the question respectfully, in a manner that doesn't put the host on the spot. You can say something along the lines of the following:

> "I'm really looking forward to attending your party tonight; however, I have a bit of a last-minute dilemma. My cousin, Jill, is in town unexpectedly and has asked if she can stay with me overnight. Would it be asking too much to bring her along? If this creates a problem with your dinner plans or menu, I do understand, and I'm sure Jill would be fine to be on her own tonight."

A gracious host would have extra food available and extend a *sincere* invitation.

Bringing a Gift

When you've been invited to someone's home, taking the host a small gift is always a nice gesture, even if the invitation instructs you not to. Bringing a bottle of wine, a flowering plant, or candy is a considerate way to show your appreciation.

Think about the host's hobbies when you select a gift. If you know that the host loves to garden or cook, for example, consider a gift or memento for that special interest.

Don't allow your gift to become a burden to the host in any way. For example, if you want to give cut flowers, try to bring them already in a vase so that the host doesn't have to take the time to arrange them. Gifts of food, wine, and special blends of coffee and tea are acceptable, as long as you let the host know that it's not necessary to open or serve them. The host most likely has already planned the menu so you should tell the host that you hope he or she will enjoy the gift of food or wine later.

Whatever you choose, the gift doesn't need to be wrapped or come with a card. And it's not necessary for the host to send a thank-you card. See Chapter 16 for full details on giving (and receiving) gifts. When presenting the host with the gift, the ideal way is to send it ahead of time or giving it to him it as soon as you arrive.

Mingling with Ease

Knowing how to mingle with other guests is part of the responsibility of being a guest who's always invited back. This isn't the time to be a wallflower. Try to mix with people other than your close friends. You already know what you like and what you think. Learning about other people — what they like and what they think — is just as important. Showing consideration should be the basis of communicating with other people. And one of the ways you do that is to have a conversation.

What is a conversation? It's what happens when two or more people exchange ideas. You give and take. You talk. The other person talks. The exchange moves back and forth. A conversation isn't one person doing all the talking while the other person does all the listening! And most of the time, conversations don't "just happen." You invite other people to talk with you.

As a gracious guest, you need to be able to start a conversation as well as participate in one. You need to know how to be patient and not interrupt; be a good listener. And you need to think about what someone is asking and respond appropriately, just as you need to think about what you want to say and say it clearly.

In the following sections, I cover the conversational skills you need and safe topics to bring up when you're mingling. For an extensive discussion of how to converse, see Chapter 7.

Handy conversational skills

Not everyone is a social butterfly by nature, but don't shy away from conversation just because this form of communication isn't innate. With the following tips and a dose of confidence, you can be mingling up a storm in no time:

- ✔ **Think about other people and care about them.** If you're shy or quiet, you need to learn how to open up to others and not always wait for them to draw you into a conversation. If you're an extrovert and extremely outgoing, you may need to learn how to rein in your enthusiasm and let other people have the floor.

- ✔ **Act as if you're a host, not a guest.** Reach out to people standing by themselves, the white-knuckle drinkers, or those that look obviously uncomfortable. Introduce people to each other. Be helpful, kind, and genuine. Don't be afraid to approach people. Strangers are merely friends you haven't met yet. If you focus on the other person's comfort, you can lose your own self-consciousness.

- ✔ **Be pleasant, cheerful, and upbeat when mingling, no matter what your mood.** If you've had a bad day, don't rain on anyone else's parade by talking about your negative experience — unless, of course, you want to be left standing alone. And when ending a conversation, say that you enjoyed talking with the person or that it was a pleasure meeting her.

- ✔ **Listen more than you talk.** You have two ears and one mouth. Use them in that proportion. Nothing is more flattering than someone who listens carefully and shows sincere interest in other people.

- ✔ **Know how to gracefully end conversations.** It is perfectly fine to simply say, "Excuse me, it has been nice meeting you" or "I've enjoyed our conversation." Then visibly move to some other part of the room.

- ✔ **Avoid making negative comments on the room, the food, the guests or your host.** In any social situation, making negative comments, especially when you're a guest in someone's home, is rude. You never know if another guest can overhear your comments. And, quite often, the person holding the party delegates the actual planning and details to someone else, and you could be speaking with someone that helped with the event.

Polite topics of conversation

When attending a social event, you stand a good chance of meeting people for the first time. To engage a stranger into a conversation, you should find some common topic of interest. Some common topics most people share include:

- ✔ Travel
- ✔ Children or pets (if you *both* have them)
- ✔ Hobbies
- ✔ Current news topics (preferably nothing controversial)
- ✔ Sports
- ✔ Careers
- ✔ Films
- ✔ Books

You should avoid any type of talk regarding physical injuries, sickness, accidents, or off-color language or jokes. Also, commenting on the host's home, décor, or food; spreading offensive gossip; or bringing up controversial subjects that could make others uncomfortable or angry is a bad idea. Keep your tongue in check!

Handling Any Situation Appropriately

Despite your best effort to be a great guest, you may find yourself in the middle of an embarrassing or uncomfortable situation. (Hopefully, you aren't the cause of it.) Or, you may simply not know how to properly deal with a situation, even a minor one. Instead of freaking out, try to appropriately and graciously handle such incidences, and try not to draw too much attention to yourself.

Here are a few situations you may encounter as a guest before and during an event and the right ways to handle them:

- ✔ **You aren't sure what to wear.** Dressing appropriately shows respect. A well-mannered host will let you know what the attire is for the event. However, if you aren't certain of the appropriate dress, call ahead and ask. One rule to keep in mind is that it's better to be overdressed than to be dressed too casually.

✔ **You inadvertently spill water or wine on the guest seated next to you.** Promptly blot the table. However, don't blot the other person's clothing. Make your apology, assist in pulling back the chair to let the person escape to the bathroom, and hope that your dinner partner comes back to the table in a reasonable state of repair.

✔ **You need to smoke.** Whether or not the event is a nonsmoking one, be considerate and go outside to smoke, away from the nonsmoking guests. Occasionally, accommodations for smokers are made, but always ask before lighting up. You shouldn't smoke cigars unless the host invites the guests to do so.

✔ **Alcohol is offered at the event.** Consume alcoholic beverages in moderation in all social and business situations. Nothing spoils a good party faster than forcing a host to cope with an inebriated guest who creates a scene that makes the other guests uncomfortable. A guest who overindulges rarely gets invited back.

If you've embarrassed yourself by drinking too much, call the host the next day to apologize. If you can't muster up the courage to call, send a note of apology. (I show you how to write apology notes in Chapter 8.)

✔ **You encounter another guest who is inebriated.** Don't antagonize the person or do or say anything to make matters worse. Although it's not a guest's responsibility, asking if you can assist the host in smoothing things over is a kind gesture. You can call a cab, offer to drive the guest home, or help take the guest to a separate room. Doing so affords the host the opportunity to continue entertaining the other guests.

✔ **You use a cloth towel to dry your hands after using the facilities, but you aren't sure whether to hang it back up.** If cloth guest towels are left out, leave the towel you used unfolded so that no one else mistakes it for a clean towel. A good host will supply paper hand towels; make sure to toss them into the wastepaper basket. Remember that behaving properly involves being courteous to the other people who use the same facilities.

✔ **While admiring the host's home, overwhelming curiosity strikes you.** It's never appropriate for a guest to pry or be overly nosey. No checking out the medicine cabinet in the bathroom or opening dresser drawers. If you're interested in looking at a book on a bookshelf or other item, ask for the host's permission beforehand.

Knowing When the Party's Over

Just as a good symphony ends on a beautiful chord, a party, too, should end on a nice note. You certainly don't want to catch your host yawning at three o'clock in the morning while you sip away at the Courvoisier.

Take the hint (and take a hike)

You know it's past time to go home when. . .

✔ The host is walking guests to the door saying goodnight.

✔ The host dims the lights and turns the music off.

✔ They close the bar.

✔ The orchestra plays "Goodnight, Ladies."

✔ The catering staff has packed up and left.

✔ The guests of honor have departed.

✔ The janitorial crew is waiting around with brooms in hand.

A well-mannered guest should stay at least an hour after dinner ends. If the majority of the guests stay and all are enjoying the evening, you certainly may stay longer. No matter when you leave, always thank the host for inviting you. Say something along the lines of, "Thank you for having us. We had a wonderful evening." Try not to engage the host in a long goodbye, which keeps the host from entertaining the other guests.

If you must leave an event early, try to be discreet and make your exit quietly. You don't want the other guests to think that the party's over.

Being a Well-Mannered Houseguest

When you're invited to someone's home for a weekend or longer, knowing what to do to maintain harmony is essential. Sharing living quarters can bring out tensions between guests and hosts like nothing else — and it's up to you, the guest, to do your best to avoid tense situations.

Here are some tips that are sure to please your host:

✔ When asked to spend the weekend with friends, never assume that bringing your pets, children, friend, or family member is acceptable if you aren't directly told or invited to do so.

✔ If you have special dietary requirements, please let your host know before you arrive. Offer to make a meal or take your host out for dinner. You may also want to bring some of your own food, but again, let your host know beforehand.

✔ As a gesture of appreciation, bring a small gift for the host. A picture frame, candles, a flowering plant, or a nice bottle of wine or liquor is appropriate. (For more on host gifts, see the earlier section in this chapter, "Bringing a Gift.")

✔ During your stay, you must adapt to the host's lifestyle. Don't try to run the show — be open to the host's suggestions for meals and recreation. If the host sleeps late, be considerate; don't expect him to get up earlier to entertain you. I always like to have a good book or magazine on hand for a little quiet time and give my host a break!

✔ Many homes now have a wireless home network allowing for access to the Internet. Asking your host whether logging on to his home network is acceptable. However, don't download large files that slow down the system or spend the entire day on the Internet. You are there to visit!

✔ Keep your voice down late in the evening or early morning, and if the guest room has a television, keep the volume low.

✔ Clean up after yourself, make sure not to leave your belongings strewn around the house, and make your bed. When your stay is over, empty any wastebaskets and ask your host where to put the used bed and bath linens.

✔ Be as clean and thoughtful in your host's bathroom as you would in your own bathroom. Pick up after yourself! Don't splash water everywhere, don't throw anything on the floor, and don't forget to flush! If you make a mess around the sink, use a paper towel to clean up your spatters. Men should keep the seat down.

✔ If your host takes you out on excursions to see the local sights or you go out to breakfast, lunch, or dinner, you should pay your own way or better yet, treat your host. A good guest would also offer to purchase the gasoline if they take you sightseeing.

✔ Know when it's time to go home; don't wear out your welcome. If you agreed to leave on Sunday afternoon, don't extend your stay until Monday morning. Remember the old saying, "Fish and houseguests begin to smell after three days."

Following Up with a Thank-You Note

Following up with a thank-you note, card, or letter of appreciation is a must whenever you're a guest. If you've attended a party or celebration, you're expected to send a thank-you note within a few days (the sooner, the better!). If you were a weekend guest in someone's home, send your thank-you note as soon as you return home. If you happen to be traveling, you can always drop a postcard in the mail when you arrive at your next destination.

Follow these guidelines for writing a thoughtful thank-you (see Chapter 8 for more on the ins and outs of correspondence):

✔ A thank-you note should be handwritten on good-quality stationery. A thank-you card is also acceptable, but make sure that you include a handwritten note inside.

✔ Don't send a note with smudges or words that are crossed out. Try writing your note on scratch paper and then rewriting it on the stationery.

✔ Be sincere, using warmth but not being overly expressive or sentimental.

✔ Always proofread your note for spelling and grammar mistakes before you seal it in the envelope.

Figure 15-1 is an example of a thank-you note for a party, and Figure 15-2 is a sample thank-you note if you're a houseguest.

Figure 15-1:
A thank-you note for a party compliments the hosts.

Dear Jean and Tom,

What a fantastic dinner party! Jim and I had a wonderful time. It was so nice to meet Dr. Bastian while he was in town. And your pork loin dish is always a hit. Thanks so much for including us.

Love,

Betty and Jim

Figure 15-2:
Include specifics from your visit when you write a note of thanks.

Dear Missy and Russ,

Alex and I had such a wonderful weekend, and all thanks to you. I can't believe how much fun your Jet Ski is! We so enjoyed the barbecue on Saturday night, too. Thanks for all you did to make for a very relaxing weekend.

Fondly,

Lisa and Alex

Chapter 16

Giving and Receiving Gifts with Class

In This Chapter

▶ Explaining the giving and receiving process

▶ Giving gifts thoughtfully

▶ Thanking people for the gifts they give you

▶ Declining, exchanging, or returning a gift

*O*ne of the great pleasures of life is giving to others. If you have a large family or a big circle of friends, it may seem that every month offers an occasion for giving. Between birthdays, weddings, graduations, anniversaries, holidays, moments of affection, and appeals from a good cause, a reason to give always seems to be there. The decisions you make regarding your selections of gifts and the way you present them are always a matter of personal choice, but you need to consider some important etiquette guidelines. I outline those guidelines in this chapter.

I believe that when you give, you receive even more. Sometimes, that comes true through reciprocated gifts! When it's your turn to get a gift, you also need to keep etiquette in mind. You have definite actions to take, and a few mistakes to avoid, as the recipient of a gift. You may even find yourself in certain circumstances in which you should politely turn down a gift. This chapter provides you with advice about receiving gifts in a way that not only delights the giver, but also displays your good manners!

Looking at the Basic Responsibilities of the Giver and the Recipient

No discussion of good manners can divide the action of giving a gift from the action of receiving a gift; the two halves of the process are inseparable. Each party has obligations that are easy to understand.

A giver must do the following:

- ✔ Choose an appropriate gift for the recipient.
- ✔ Present the gift in attractive wrapping.
- ✔ Ensure that the gift arrives on time.
- ✔ Give the gift freely, with no strings or conditions attached.

A recipient bears equally an important burden: You must acknowledge the gift promptly with a thank-you note.

If you're receiving several gifts at once (on the occasion of a significant wedding anniversary, for example), writing down a description of each gift and the name of the gift giver in a diary may come in handy at a later date. See the section "Expressing Your Thanks for a Gift" later in this chapter, for more information about receiving gifts.

Walking through the Gift-Giving Process

Giving a gift isn't a simple matter of spending as much as you can afford on an item and handing it over to the lucky recipient. (Well, it can be, but you risk creating an awkward situation if you do so.) You must decide whether to give a gift at all, select a gift that's appropriate for the occasion, wrap the gift attractively, and deliver the gift in the proper manner. The following sections demystify this process and guide you through each step.

Determining whether a gift is in order

How do you know when a gift is in order? Begin by keeping a good year-round calendar and clearly noting significant days for close family members and friends. Review your calendar frequently to remind yourself of upcoming birthdays, anniversaries, and holidays that require gift-giving, such as Christmas, Mother's Day, and Father's Day. Invitations to weddings, graduations, religious milestones, and the like also alert you to ceremonial gift-giving occasions. When you receive an invitation, make a note of the event in your calendar and mark a date a week or two before the event to shop for a gift.

Some occasions may throw you a curveball. Is a gift required at your nephew's birthday party? Should you give your son's girlfriend a high school graduation present? The answer depends very much on your personal situation, but if you're wondering whether to give a gift, you probably should. In the case of a party, you may want to ask the host whether other guests will be bringing gifts and then follow suit.

Here are some additional reasons and occasions that may require gifts:

- Meetings with business clients
- Baby showers and births (see Chapter 17)
- Thank-yous
- Illnesses
- Congratulations (such as for a job promotion)
- Housewarmings
- Retirements
- Moving away
- Welcoming of new neighbors
- Host gift (such as for a dinner party or overnight stay)
- New family pet
- Romance
- Back to school
- Sympathy (see Chapter 17)

Some of the most memorable gifts aren't for any special occasion at all. Surprising someone with an unexpected gift just to let that person know that you care can be more meaningful for both you and the recipient.

Selecting a gift

A gift is a free-will offering that expresses your affection and regard for another person. However, although the world may insist that it's the thought that counts, you have some rules to consider when it comes to selecting gifts. For example, you must give a gift that suits the recipient, not that you think should suit the recipient. You don't want to give your sister a copy of your favorite classical music CD when you know that she prefers country music.

A bit of research and thought can make the gift-selection process a whole lot easier. If you rush out at the last minute and grab the first thing you see, the gift usually reflects that haphazardness. (Did that jar of lavender bath salts really suit your Uncle Bill? I think not!)

When selecting a gift, consider the person's hobbies and interests. A person who loves to read may enjoy an anthology of short stories, for example. Someone who likes music may like a new pair of headphones or tickets to a concert.

Here are some other tips for selecting a gift that the recipient will love:

- **Plan ahead before you start gift shopping.** Shopping for gifts can be very stressful if you haven't put in some thought prior to hitting the malls. Especially during the busier holiday seasons, put together a list of gift ideas and roughly how much you want to spend. Nowadays, many stores are online, so you can search the Internet for ideas and prices before you go shopping, or you can always buy online.

- **When choosing gifts for children, gather information from their parents about what they like.** Your donation to a wildlife conservation fund on a child's behalf may not thrill him quite as much as a new baseball mitt would.

- **Be forewarned that clothing is a touchy area.** Unless you're absolutely sure of the person's tastes, purchase gift certificates in lieu of clothing. You may have perfectly good taste, but everyone's preferences differ, and a gift certificate to a favorite shop may save the recipient from having to return the gift.

- **Remember that some of the best gifts can't be purchased at any store.** Perhaps you have a skill or talent that you can use to create a painting, a handicraft item, or a piece of pottery that will have special meaning to the recipient. If cooking is your forte, consider giving a basket of home-made scones or jar of your peach jam. Remember, too, that you can often accomplish as much with a carefully selected greeting card and a handwritten message as you can with an expensive material item.

- **Shop now, save for later.** You always run the chance of finding the perfect gift for a close friend or family member, but having no current occasion to give it. Go ahead a buy it and put it away for later. So you don't forget, put a note on your calendar on this person's birthday or an upcoming holiday. You will be thankful to have the ideal gift when the date arrives and you don't have to go shopping!

Staying within your means is an important point to remember when selecting a gift. Don't cross the line between a gift and a sacrifice. Your cousin Sue who loves to travel will probably be just as pleased to receive a book about the country she is planning to visit this summer as she would be to get an expensive luggage piece. Make your selection according to your best judgment, wrap it nicely (see the next section), and don't worry about how much you did or didn't spend. See the section "Giving a Fitting Gift for the Occasion," later in this chapter, for more tips on choosing a great gift.

Global gift giving

Giving gifts to those with different customs or religions can be tricky. Research the gift recipient's background prior to giving any gifts. Here are some examples of cross-cultural protocols when gift giving:

✔ It is customary for Chinese to refuse a gift three times before accepting a gift. In turn, if you receive a gift, you should follow the same routine.

✔ In many Asian countries, especially Japan, gifts are to be offered with both hands. Yet in the Middle East, the gift should be given with only the right hand.

✔ In Singapore, the custom is to politely refuse the gift at least three times before accepting it. As for most South American countries, a gift would be immediately opened.

Wrapping your gift properly

Gift-wrapping is just as important as the gift you're giving. You should consider it as part of the gift, not an afterthought. Even the smallest, least expensive gift should be wrapped in eye-catching manner, which will truly put a smile on the recipient's face no matter what's inside the wrapping.

Wrapping a gift doesn't have to be with fancy wrapping paper, ribbon, and bows. Be creative! Use a new kitchen dish or tea towel to wrap a bottle of homemade vinegar; ask your local grocer for a piece of butcher paper and some twine to wrap a set of appetizer plates; buy a small paint can from a home repair shop and fill with cards, dice, and poker chips for a fun game set. Top your wrapped package with fresh flowers or herbs from your garden or small bag of chocolates for a final finishing touch. Whatever creative idea you come up with, keep the recipient in mind and make sure the wrapping is age appropriate, especially gifts for children!

Nothing is more embarrassing than having the recipient open your gift in front of you to find a price sticker on the bottom of the gift item! Before you or the retail shop person wraps the gift, check to make sure that all price tags and stickers are removed to avoid this very awkward situation.

Presenting your gift promptly

Always present your gifts no later than the day of the event. A late gift is better than no gift at all, but an on-time gift is far better.

Should you open a gift now or wait until later?

You should open gifts when they are given, except for wedding gifts or gifts at a large party, where opening many gifts would be impossible. Part of the fun for the giver is to see the recipient's reaction.

When you're opening gifts at parties and celebrations, etiquette insists that you behave in a way that puts everyone at ease. Be sensitive to the situation and show equal excitement and enthusiasm while opening all gifts.

If you see the person on the designated day, you can hand over your gift along with a handshake, hug, or kiss. If you live many miles from the recipient, make sure to send off the gift in plenty of time. (Mark the package with a Do Not Open Until label if you want him or her to open the gift on the exact date of the special occasion.) Remember to wrap fragile objects carefully.

Note: Wedding gifts call for special etiquette. See Chapter 18, which is all about the etiquette of weddings, for more information.

Giving a Fitting Gift for the Occasion

Different situations have unique "rules" when it comes to appropriate offerings. The following sections detail how to give appropriately for common occasions. (I discuss gifts for the birth of a child in Chapter 17, and wedding gifts in Chapter 18.)

Gifts within the family

The first place everyone learns about giving gifts is the family. Birthdays and holidays are often occasions for gift-giving — and, depending on the family, a dozen other potential gift-giving occasions may pop up during the year.

If you belong to a large family, gift-giving can become a financial burden, especially around holidays. One way to keep everyone happy is to draw names. This way, each adult family member gives one gift. My family has been doing this for years, although my mother has a hard time abiding by this rule and sneaks in small gifts for all of us!

The following items make wonderful family gifts:

- ✔ Photo album
- ✔ Diary or journal
- ✔ Cookbook
- ✔ Tickets to a sporting event, concert, or play
- ✔ How-to DVD or book for a new hobby
- ✔ Gift certificate for a facial or a day at a spa
- ✔ Book on CD
- ✔ Food gift basket

The family setting is a good place to teach children the etiquette of giving and receiving gifts. For example, you can take very young children to a shopping center, give them a modest allowance, and encourage them to select birthday and other-occasion gifts for their siblings. The shopping process is educational in a number of ways, not the least of which is beginning to understand the value of money by understanding how much a gift costs and what a child can or can't afford on a certain budget.

Children should be discouraged from giving items of significant material value to their parents. In families that have two or more siblings, this practice can rapidly escalate into a contest between children to see who can come up with a better gift. As a parent, you can suggest that Dad needs a new shirt and golf club head covers (which have a similar financial cost) and let the two children decide who wants to give Dad which gift.

Tailor gifts to senior family members to the occasion. More than anything, most seniors appreciate the gift of your time. For example, tickets to a concert, plus an invitation to dinner beforehand in a nice restaurant, with you (the gift giver) providing all the transportation, would be a nice gift.

Gifts to charities and other good causes

The world is full of good causes. Your own community has needs that only the gifts of generous donors can meet. Many law enforcement agencies conduct programs for disadvantaged children. Libraries are always seeking financial help from the community to expand collections, provide computer access, and improve their facilities. Just about every human illness has a research organization dedicated to seeking a cure or a support group to assist patients. The list of needy agencies and associations is endless, and these organizations widely publicize their appeals for assistance.

When you're faced with a gift-giving occasion for a person who has no need for material goods, a charitable gift in that person's honor is a fine alternative to yet another little household trinket. If you're aware of that person's favorite charity, send off a check to that organization, along with the name and address of the person you're honoring. Make sure to mention the occasion for the donation — the grateful organization will send a nice letter of acknowledgment to the honoree. If you don't know a person's preferred charity, select one of your own and make a contribution in your friend's name.

If you receive notice that a contribution has been made in your honor, a thank-you note is appropriate etiquette. In the note, you should use enthusiasm, reference the charity, and tell why it is meaningful to you such as in Figure 16-1. (See "Expressing Your Thanks for a Gift" later in this chapter for the scoop on writing thank-you notes.)

Figure 16-1:
Write a
thank-you
note when
someone
makes a
contribution
to a charity
in your
name.

> Dear Joan and Bill,
>
> I just received notification from the Marine Mammal Rescue Center of your generous contribution in memory of Louis. Thank you so much for helping one of Louis's favorite organizations carry on with its good work. Every time an unfortunate animal is nursed back to health and released into the sea, I'm sure that Louis's spirit will soar.
>
> Your thoughtfulness at this sad time is deeply appreciated.
>
> Love,
>
> Ellen

If you're a member of the congregation at a religious ceremony, such as a wedding, bar mitzvah, or confirmation, you usually find an envelope intended for offerings. If you insert a check or cash and indicate the honoree, your contribution will be mentioned in the next bulletin or newsletter. You can tailor this nice gesture to fit within your budget.

Here again, if someone makes a contribution in honor of you or a loved one, a simple note of appreciation is in order, like in Figure 16-2. In this note, be sure to be specific, adequately express your gratitude, and mention the name of the charity as well as the reasons why this is meaningful to you.

Dear Martin,

Thanks so much for your donation in honor of Christie's confirmation. Our congregation is always seeking funds for various good works, and all of us are grateful for your generosity.

Love,

Rhonda and Mike

Figure 16-2: A gift in honor of a religious ceremony deserves a thank-you note.

Anytime you contribute to a good cause, try to think of someone deserving of your kind thoughts. Dedicating your contributions to friends and relatives brings unexpected moments of pleasure to the honorees.

The gift of your time

Giving a material gift isn't the only way to give. The gift of your time for volunteer work or for helping out a friend or neighbor is also a form of giving — and one that may be appreciated more than a material item. Because many people think that they don't have enough time, a gift of time is one of the most valuable gifts you can give.

When I find it difficult to think of a useful gift for a friend or family member, I give that person a card stating, "This is good for one day of yard work." Imagine your elderly neighbor's delight if you offered to help her with yard work! Or, for no particular occasion, I'll make a date to take my mother to a nursery, let her select some plants, and then help her plant them.

Giving a gift of your time isn't meaningful unless you follow through on your promise. If your children give you a gift of time, such as a promise to mow the lawn for three months, as parents, you need to teach them that their word is good and be certain they follow through.

Expressing Your Thanks for a Gift

People give you gifts for all sorts of reasons — presents for your birthday, financial help when you're trying to pull together a down payment on a house, souvenirs from vacations, awards for professional work, and so on. Your success in communicating your gratitude helps you maintain your good relations with these generous individuals.

Always express your gratitude immediately upon receiving a gift. If the giver is there in person, say a sincere "Thank you" when you receive the package. If you open the gift on the spot, say something specific about the gift, other than just "Thank you." You can try something like, "Oh, Paula, I just love this little lamp. The color is perfect for the little table in my bedroom. This is going to be great for reading at night." If you receive a gift delivered by mail or an express delivery service, pick up the phone and let the faraway giver know that the gift arrived in good shape and that you adore it.

Even if you thanked Aunt Helen when she handed you a gift at your birthday party, you need to mind your manners by writing a well-constructed thank-you letter (no, an e-mail isn't acceptable!) as soon as possible. You may write your thank-you notes on your personal stationery — you don't have to use special thank-you cards. The letter should include as many of the following items as possible:

- ✔ A specific reference to the gift
- ✔ A sincere expression of gratitude
- ✔ Some indication of how you will use the gift
- ✔ An appropriate closing sentiment

Reviewing a few samples of proper thank-you notes may be useful; I provide several examples in the following sections. For more on how to select stationery and format a thank-you note, see Chapter 8.

It's never too late to send a thank-you note. And if you're writing a belated thank you, your intent should not be to make an excuse for being late. Apologize and thank the giver for the gift!

Birthday gifts

A well-written thank-you note for a birthday gift doesn't have to go on and on; however, always say something specific about the gift (the quality, color, or craftsmanship), mention why you like it, and how you plan to use it. Figure 16-3 is an example of a thank-you note that you may write to a friend to thank her for a birthday gift.

Monetary gifts

Thanking others for their gift of money can be tricky, but the best way to do this is to describe how you plan to use it. Acknowledge the gift giver's generosity, mention how you will use the money, and include a closing personal comment, such as, "I hope to see you soon." Figure 16-4 is a note that does so quite successfully.

Dear Paula,

I just rearranged my dresser top and found the perfect spot for the art deco lamp you gave me last week. Just as I expected, it's perfect for the room, and I love the way it lights up what used to be a dim corner.

Thanks so much for your thoughtful gift. I know that I'll think of your generosity every night.

Love,

Susan

Figure 16-3:
You can refer to a birthday gift specifically in a thank-you note.

Dear Aunt Jane,

You didn't have to send me money! I'm doing okay with my part-time job at the student union, and I've been able to stay within my budget. But because you were so generous, I was able to get a new set of tires for my car, and it felt much more steady on the road during last night's rainstorm.

Thanks again, and love,

Owen

Figure 16-4:
Honestly describe how you plan to use a monetary gift.

Your mother will always want to know what you do with the money she gives you, and she definitely doesn't want to hear that you hosted a beer bash for your entire dorm. Try to be considerate of the gift giver when deciding how to spend the money. Tires are good, a new coat is okay, and putting her gift into your savings account is best of all.

Thank-you notes for gifts of large sums of money for a wedding or college graduation are written in a similar manner as all thank-you notes. However, be sure to express your sincere gratitude with enthusiasm. You don't need to mention the amount of money, but write about your deep gratitude for the generous gift. Also, mention your plans for using the money — perhaps a down payment on a home, your honeymoon, or simply put in a savings account. Never make mention of using it on something that could be frivolous, such as buying a boat, a new car, or an item that isn't necessarily needed. Figure 16-5 shows how you can thank someone for a larger monetary gift.

Figure 16-5:
Larger monetary gifts deserve a sincere, heartfelt thank-you note.

> Dear Aunt Helen,
>
> William and I are overwhelmed by your generous check. Thanks to your thoughtfulness, we now have enough money to furnish our living room.
>
> We expect to be settled in another five weeks, and we look forward to welcoming you as one of our very first visitors.
>
> With love and gratitude,
>
> Sharon and William

Gifts for children

If your child has received a gift, encourage her to include some news about what's going on in her life in thank-you notes, especially when writing to close relatives who live far away. Figure 16-6 is a good example.

Figure 16-6:
Thank-you notes from children can include news about their lives.

> Dear Grandma,
>
> I was so excited when I opened your package and found the beautiful pen and pencil set you sent me. I'm writing this note with the pen! It writes as beautifully as it looks.
>
> I hope you can visit us this summer. I have a new pet gerbil and he's a friendly guy who will eat peanuts right out of your hand.
>
> Thanks again,
>
> Love,
>
> Sammy

Exchanging, Returning, or Refusing Gifts

Society is governed by laws and organizational rules regarding gifts. No matter how generous someone has been, you may find yourself in situations in which you simply can't accept a gift. In the following sections, you can find out how to exchange or return a gift without hurting the giver's feelings, and also how to gracefully refuse a gift that you can't accept.

Exchanging a gift

If you receive a gift and need to exchange it because of a valid reason, such as clothing that doesn't fit, be honest and tell the giver that you exchanged the item for something that that fit properly. If you receive a household item that you already have, you may want to let the giver know if they ask you about it. Most people are understanding about exchanges if a gift that they gave isn't quite right.

However, if you want to exchange a gift you simply don't like, be sure to express your thanks to the giver, but don't bring up your plans to exchange the gift unless she asks. In that case, politely say something like, "Thank you for the sweater! It's a perfect fit and just what I needed, though the color may not be that flattering for me. I thought I would exchange for another lighter shade; what do you think?"

Wedding gifts are normally exchanged only in case of duplication. Of course, you may receive something that you have no use for at all. In this case, you need to weigh your decision and decide whether exchanging the gift could cause hurt feelings. If you're comfortable re-gifting the item (to someone who will truly appreciate it), keep a record so the original gift giver doesn't know. When buying wedding gifts, remember to include the receipt without a price on it so that the couple knows where they can exchange it, if necessary. See Chapter 18 for full details on giving and receiving wedding gifts.

Taking a gift back to the store

Returning a gift for cash is considered rude. Most store policies allow only a return for credit or exchange. Deciding whether to let the giver know about your decision to return the gift depends on your relationship and the occasion. For example, if a close family member gave you something you want to return, you may want to let that person know. However, if you rarely see the gift giver, you may decide not to tell them and simply make the return.

If you do make a return, never include this detail in your thank-you note to the giver. If the subject comes up at a later time, and you feel comfortable, you can say you were delighted with the gift but that you received more than one, so you exchanged the gift.

Returning a gift to the gift giver

The only reason to return a gift to the gift giver is in the case that the occasion for the gift is cancelled or postponed indefinitely. This situation usually occurs when the gifts are sent before the event, like a wedding. When returning the gift to giver, always include a thank-you note and an explanation. However, you don't need to go into details or say anything derogatory about anyone else. Keeping an engraved gift is sometimes acceptable, but you must first check with the giver to see whether he can return the gift for credit. If this is the case, return the gift to the person that gave it to you.

Knowing whether it's ever right to re-gift

The ritual of re-gifting has been around for some time, however covertly. Most people are probably guilty of wrapping up an unwanted or duplicate gift and giving it to someone. I can think of few examples of gifts that I or someone I know has re-gifted: a bottle of Champagne, unopened cocktail napkins, picture frames, or unused golf balls.

Re-gifting can be proper etiquette if, and only if, you follow these rules:

- ✔ Give items that are new, recently received, and not used.

- ✔ Re-wrap the gift making sure no gift tags from the previous giver are still attached.

- ✔ Be upfront when giving the re-gifted item. For instance, when giving your Aunt Judy a set of candlesticks that were too modern for your home décor, state, "I just received these beautiful candlesticks, which I thought go perfectly on your contemporary dinning table."

- ✔ Stick to giving re-gifted gifts to close friends and family members.

- ✔ Know for certain that the gift would bring pleasure to the recipient and won't be thrown back into the re-gifting circle.

- ✔ Exercise the re-gift practice rarely.

If you're comfortable with re-gifting, keep a log of any gifts you want to re-gift along with the names of people who gave them to you, or you can tape this info to the gift itself. You never want to face the embarrassment of giving a gift to the person who gave it to you.

Politely turning down a gift

Believe it or not, some gifts are unwanted. Maybe you've broken off a relationship — be it a friendship or romance — and then you receive a bouquet of flowers from that person that you don't want as a reminder. Perhaps a gift is horrifically tacky or outrageously expensive — so much so that it makes you uncomfortable. How do you handle these awkward situations?

When you receive an expensive gift, you're perfectly justified in saying, "What a lovely gift, but you really shouldn't have gone to such an expense." Although expensive gifts are embarrassing, you can't do very much. If you need to reciprocate, don't worry about matching the gift financially; just buy what you can afford.

As a woman, if you receive an expensive gift from a man other than your husband, fiancé, or boyfriend, first ask the giver, "And what did I do to deserve such a nice gift?" If the answer is that you just brought in a huge piece of business for your advertising agency and the boss is showing his appreciation, you may feel perfectly comfortable accepting it. However, if the man has romantic intentions that you don't reciprocate, you shouldn't be afraid to refuse the gift. A simple explanation such as, "I'm sorry, but I simply can't accept this gift — we hardly know each other!" should suffice.

Some people, such as journalists and government employees, aren't allowed to accept gifts. In business, people who influence purchase decisions or issue purchase orders are frequently prohibited from accepting any sort of gift from a vendor. The rules are often so strict that these people can't even pick up a lunch tab for a buyer or an employee of a company that buys their goods or services.

If someone sends you a gift that violates the letter or spirit of such a rule, return the gift promptly along with a note that explains the situation and expresses your gratitude for the gesture. Or, if you did receive a nonreturnable gift such as a bouquet of flowers and can't accept the gift, you can pass the gift on to someone else instead of returning it, but be sure to explain yourself delicately in the note.

Writing a refusal letter is similar to writing an acceptance thank-you note. Your letter should be in your own words, as if you were talking with the person, and written with sincerity. Include a mention the gift you're refusing, provide a brief, clear explanation for why you can't accept the gift, and add a polite close. Figure 16-7 is a good example.

Figure 16-7:
Be direct about the reason why you can't accept a gift.

Dear Tom,

It breaks my heart to return such a lovely bottle of wine, especially one that comes from such a fine vineyard, but my company specifically forbids me from accepting any sort of gift.

I appreciate the thought, and I hope that you will not, in any way, take my conformance to company rules as a comment on our excellent relationship.

Sincerely,

Mary Smith

Part V
Making the Most of Special Situations

The 5th Wave   By Rich Tennant

"Remember, she had twins, so I go in first, and then you follow about 3 minutes later."

In this part . . .

The situations that you encounter less frequently often require you to remember a different set of etiquette rules. Special occasions such as weddings and funerals can put your manners to the test. Travel, whether it's within your own country or it brings you in contact with an entirely new culture, poses challenges as well. Interacting with people who have disabilities or illnesses may also take you into a new realm of etiquette in which you're unsure of the proper behavior. Look to this part of the book for help in these and other similar circumstances.

Chapter 17

Marking Life's Major Events

The human family forms a circle without end. Babies are born; children grow up, get married, and have children of their own; and eventually, life comes to an end. Every culture celebrates, honors, and mourns these milestones in its own ways, and many groups within a larger society have their own variants on those traditions. What draws all of us together is a common understanding and appreciation for the importance of these events and a willingness to share in some of the most meaningful and poignant events of our lives.

Life's major events are often a challenge: They call on you to stop what you're doing, take pause, and give of yourself to others — whether it's taking a weekend to travel to a high school graduation, spending time with your sister at home after the birth of her baby, or caretaking elderly parents. What counts most is that you're there for your friends and family and that you care. This chapter gives you the information you need to make it through life's big events with grace and style — and your composure intact.

Note: Because weddings necessitate an in-depth discussion of etiquette, I cover that rite of passage in its own separate chapter. See Chapter 18 for more information.

Celebrating the Birth of a Baby

Fortunately for the mother, giving birth to a baby isn't a social occasion to which you invite guests. However, as new parents, or as friends and family supporting the new parents, you should do a few thoughtful things before and after a little one comes into the world, as I explain in the following sections.

Holding a baby shower

Traditionally, a woman has a shower only with her first child. But times are changing, and I (and everyone else I know) don't see why the mom can't have a shower for every child who joins her family. This is especially true if the new baby is a different gender, or if multiples are expected. If the mom already has everything she needs for the baby and you just want to do something nice, a little get-together in her honor is a lovely idea. For example, you can host an afternoon tea and ask each guest to bring a small item related to tea or nurturing gifts for the mom-to-be such as luxury bath products and scented candles. In the following sections, I provide guidelines for successfully throwing a baby shower.

Adopted children should be welcomed as warmly as any other child, and a shower is great way to do so. If the adopted child is older, consider having a welcoming party, which is similar to a birthday party. When planning a shower for the adoption of an infant, make sure that the adoption is final before selecting a date for the shower. For this reason, many people wait until after the child is adopted to give a shower. If the shower is after the adoption, you may want to allow at least several weeks before hosting the shower for the new family to get adjusted. I discuss adoption in more detail later in this chapter.

Deciding who's invited

A good friend of the mom-to-be usually hosts the shower. In the past, it was considered inappropriate for a family member to give a shower, but today, having the mom-to-be's family help plan a shower isn't uncommon.

Traditionally, only women attend showers; however, many showers today include men as well. If you're going the traditional route, immediate female family members of both the mother and father-to-be's families should be invited, as well as close friends of the mother-to-be. The best route to go when making up the invitation list is to consult with the parents-to-be. If the shower is to be a surprise, make sure to check with the parents-to-be's families when making up your guest list.

Showers usually have between 6 and 25 guests. If the number of guests seems too large, consider having two showers — one for family and relatives and one for friends. Usually, a shower is held in the host's home, but it can also be held in a restaurant, a tearoom, a community room, or a church social hall. The shower should last about two hours.

Infertility and miscarriages can be emotionally painful issues. If you're inviting a guest who is having a difficult time conceiving or recently had a miscarriage, you may want to call her before sending an invitation. She may prefer not to attend, but it's best to let her know that you'd like her there and let her make the decision.

Picking a date and sending invitations

The shower is usually held two to three months before the baby's due date. This timing gives the mother a chance to evaluate what she's received at the shower and decide what she needs to purchase or borrow herself. It also provides some excitement in the last weeks of pregnancy (as if an expectant mother doesn't have enough excitement in her life!).

Be very wary of holding a shower within a month of the due date. You may find yourself with a new guest at the shower (baby, that is) if you cut it too close and the baby decides to arrive early!

Showers are usually held before the birth, but in certain circumstances (such as a difficult pregnancy), it may be wise to wait until after the baby is born. Waiting allows everyone to meet the new arrival and ensures that the occasion will be a joyous one. (If you're a mom-to-be concerned about the health of your baby and would rather wait until after the birth, throwing yourself a welcome-home party after the birth is absolutely fine.)

When inviting guests to a baby shower, include these components on the invitation:

- ✔ Guest of honor's name
- ✔ Shower date and time
- ✔ Host's name and phone number
- ✔ Address of shower
- ✔ Map of shower location (optional)
- ✔ RSVP date and phone number
- ✔ Shower theme information (if applicable)
- ✔ Gift registry information
- ✔ Sex of the baby (if known)

Mail the invitation to out-of-town guests about six weeks prior to the shower, and about four weeks prior for local guests. A good guideline for the RSVP deadline is two weeks before the shower.

Sending baby shower invitations via e-mail is fine. You can find many e-vite Web sites to help with the design and personalizing the invitation. The six-week rule also applies for sending an invitation by e-mail. (See Chapter 14 for more details about invitations.)

Dressing appropriately

Dress at a traditional baby shower held on a weekend afternoon is relaxed, but nice. A pantsuit, dress, or long skirt and sweater are all good choices. If the shower is themed, it may call for special dress. When in doubt, ask the host for advice. (Chapter 3 has information on dressing properly for any occasion.)

Giving gifts

As the host, you're responsible for guiding the guests to presents that are needed and will be appreciated. If possible, you may want to sit with the mom-to-be and make a list together. Things to discuss include whether or not she knows the gender of the baby, the style of the nursery, whether she plans to breast-feed, whether she'll be using cloth or disposable diapers, and whether she wants a breast pump. If she hasn't already done so, suggest that she register at one or two baby stores. You can then advise individual guests about her wish list. Occasionally, people host theme showers, such as nursery items (bedding, changing table, and so on), "for the outdoor baby" (mosquito netting for carrier, baby backpack), or "what little boys are made of" (boy clothes and toys).

As the host of a baby shower, you may want to present the guests with party favors. Favor ideas include small pots with flowering plants, decorative soaps, sample-size bath salts, nice chocolates, and sachets.

As an invitee to a baby shower, don't feel pressured into purchasing gifts from the gift registry only. The choice is completely up to you (the gift giver) to select whatever creative gift you would like to buy. Your thoughtfulness is all that is necessary.

Announcing the baby's birth

The first announcement of a baby's birth is usually a joyous phone call made by the new father or proud grandparents. The next step is for the parents to visit a stationer and select an announcement card to send to relatives and friends.

Birth announcements are normally decorative cards that announce a baby's birth and list the baby's vital statistics such as time of birth, weight, and length. Birth announcements aren't a solicitation for gifts. You can design your own card or do something as simple as having the child's name and date of birth and the parents' names and address printed on a card and attaching a pink or blue ribbon.

Asking family members or close friends for help in preparing and mailing the birth announcements is perfectly appropriate. When you're caring for a new baby, you have many pressing issues (other than stuffing envelopes!) to deal with.

You can tell the whole world about your new baby if you wish, but remember to address envelopes to out-of-town grandparents, aunts, and uncles first, followed by in-town grandparents, aunts and uncles, and then other relatives, close friends, long-lost college friends, colleagues, and bosses.

These days, sending an informal birth announcement via e-mail is acceptable, but only if you follow it with formal printed or handwritten cards that you send out through the regular mail. Ideally, the snail-mail announcements should be sent before the baby is 3-months-old.

Many new parents now share their baby's birth by creating a fun, personalized Web site so friends and family around the world can access the latest news, photos, and videos of their bundle of joy! You can find a number of sites that assist in the development, such as `www.babyjellybeans.com` and `www.babysites.com`.

When you receive a birth announcement, you should send a note of congratulations back to the parents. If you wish, you may send a gift to the parents at home or deliver it when you visit in person. If you're close to the new mother, you can send something along for her, too. Any bath or beauty product for the mom is a thoughtful addition to a baby gift.

Visiting the bundle of joy

Unless you're the baby's grandparent or another member of the immediate family, check with the mother before you visit the hospital. Today, the mother and child's stay at the hospital is very brief. In addition, getting used to motherhood is complicated business — sometimes further complicated by the mother's recovery from a long labor. Many new mothers would rather that you waited to visit until they're settled in at home.

After they're settled in at home, most new parents welcome visitors, because new parents love to show off their little one. Before you visit, telephone and ask for the best day and time to drop in. Bring a little gift for the baby if you want to, admire the child, be lavish with your compliments, and leave before you wear out your welcome. Don't expect to be served a meal — especially not during those very early days.

If the new baby has come into a family that includes other children, especially young children, you may want to bring a little gift for each sibling, too. You needn't spend a considerable sum on these gifts, but suddenly being overshadowed by a baby is hard for children to understand, and they appreciate the extra attention.

As a new parent or parent-to-be, a little planning can go a long way toward maintaining peace with eager well-wishers. You can make it clear exactly how long guests are expected to stay by working out a visiting schedule in advance of the birth, a schedule that will ensure equal visiting time for both sides of the family. Beyond the immediate family, asking other well-wishers to wait a few days or even weeks before visiting isn't impolite. You may also consider leaving a voice-mail message on your phone stating the upcoming schedule.

If you've created a Web site for your new arrival, post visiting hours and other guidelines along with the newborn photos. If you're worried about offending someone, try presenting the rules in a humorous way by writing captions for baby pictures: "I know I'm cute, but I still need my beauty sleep. Please stop by before 5:00 p.m."

Although visitors should never just drop by your house unannounced, some will. Turning away uninvited well-wishers can be tough, so be prepared. If an unannounced guest does show up wanting to see the new baby and mom, you can decline. Always invite the person in, but let her know that mom and baby are resting, and then suggest a better time for the guest to return. If you're the new mother, you may want to hand over the responsibility of handling guest visits to a family member or friend.

Giving and receiving baby gifts

If you wish to send a gift for the baby after the birth, by all means do so. However, a note of congratulations is all that is required. If you're a new parent, make sure to send a handwritten thank-you to everyone who sends a gift. It should be signed with the parents' names — not the baby's! Thank-you notes that come signed by Baby Emma are a bit too cute, and besides, everyone knows that Baby Emma can't write. For advice on wording thank-you notes, see Chapter 16.

Because so many aspects of etiquette involve the exchange of gifts, it bears repeating that no gift needs to exceed your means or your comfort level. Other people may be able to afford to give a prepaid college education or a large certificate of deposit (well, that may be extreme, but you get the point!), but if your budget limits you to the purchase of a small stuffed animal or a colorful rattle, do what you can and present your gift with love. Your thoughtfulness and prompt response are all that are necessary.

Dealing with challenging situations

In this day and age, you see more and more nontraditional families and births. Children are born to single mothers, and babies are adopted by single dads and gay couples. Whatever the situation, remember that the welcoming of a new baby is an occasion for joy, no matter how it happens, and your role as a friend or family member is to do your best to offer your warm congratulations and share the parent's (or parents') happiness. The following sections address a few of the more common situations that you may encounter.

When the baby isn't well

Every parent hopes for a healthy infant. Although medical care gets better every year, some babies come into the world with health problems, and the sad truth is that some don't survive. If you have a close relationship with parents who are facing such difficulties, lend as much support as you can (unless the parents clearly express that they want to be left alone). Ask what you can do to help. Parents with a hospitalized newborn spend a lot of time at the hospital, and you may be able to help by watching their other children at home, doing household chores, providing transportation, running errands to the grocery store or pharmacy, or doing whatever else needs to be done.

Sometimes parents of infants who aren't well don't want to talk. Sometimes they will, and when they're ready, your job is to be a good listener. Don't pry or ask too many questions. Simply listen to whatever the parents want to tell you, offer your sympathy, and continue to be present whenever they need your help.

When the baby has a disability

Parents suffer special anguish when their newborn is diagnosed with some sort of physical or mental abnormality. To deal with the challenge, the family needs a sense of community, and the baby needs love. The family will deeply appreciate your support in the form of a visit, a gift, an offer of assistance, or, above all, an ear. Don't worry about etiquette; just try to be a good friend.

For more information about interacting with people who have disabilities, see Chapter 20.

When a baby is adopted

Couples who adopt newborns are parents in exactly the same sense as those who give birth to their own, and they should be treated as such. The new families send announcements, receive gifts and notes of congratulation, entertain visitors, and observe all the other rituals of new parenthood.

An adoption announcement can read, "Mr. and Mrs. Russ Lewis are happy to announce the adoption of Sarah Beth, July seventeenth, 2006, age three months." Or you may use the phrase, "welcome into their home" in place of the phrase about adoption.

Making any reference to an adopted baby's birth mother (or either of the biological parents) is inappropriate. If the adoptive parents want to discuss the details of the adoption with you, by all means be a good listener, but don't press for details.

Discussing adoption with a child is the parents' responsibility. No matter how tempted you are, stay out of the conversation if you aren't the child's parent. It's not unusual for adopted children to develop a curiosity about their ancestry as they mature, and the responsibility is their parents' (sometimes with the help of professional counselors) to help them resolve those questions.

When a baby is given for adoption

If a female friend or family member gives her child for adoption, your best display of good manners is to stay in the background until the birth mother is up and around, and then resume normal social contact. In this situation, you can be a good listener if she brings up the subject; otherwise, don't initiate the discussion yourself.

The advice in this section also applies to voluntarily terminated pregnancies. Sometimes the best display of good manners is respectful silence.

Attending a baptism

Baptisms (also commonly called *christenings,* although the proper term is *baptism*) usually take place in a child's first six months. Catholic children are sometimes baptized very early, within the first six weeks of life. Protestant children are usually baptized during their first six months, although baptism can take place at any age.

Close family members attend the baptism, as well as the godparents, if there are any. Godparents should be intimate friends of the family, as their role is primarily a spiritual one. Godparents are meant to see that the child is given religious training and is confirmed at the proper time (I discuss confirmations later in this chapter). The godparent is also expected to take a special interest in the child, as a close relative would do. This responsibility includes sending Christmas presents and a gift on the child's birthday, until he becomes an adult. In the Catholic faith, godparents must also be Catholic. In certain Protestant religions, godparents aren't required.

Invitations to a baptism are usually issued over the telephone. Usually, the parents or grandparents have a small gathering afterward. Invitations to a baptism should be informal, such as, "Jill's baptism will take place at St. Luke's Church at three o'clock on Sunday, February 16th. Will you and Peter come to the ceremony and join us afterward for a reception at our house?" You should extend your invitation, either by mail or by phone, at least four weeks before the ceremony and five to six weeks in advance if out-of-town guests are invited.

Gifts are usually brought by the guests for the baby, as the guests are presumably very close relatives. For a girl, guests or godparents may give a small piece of jewelry to be worn when she's older. For both genders, guests may want to consider giving the child an engraved silver frame, small cup, or baby spoon. Other ideas include picture frames, a baby book, music box, or a gift certificate to a children's clothing store. A final tip: Dress for a baptism as you would for a religious service.

Attending a B'rith Milah

A circumcision and naming ceremony takes place eight days after a Jewish baby boy is born. The boy is also given godparents at this time. The ceremony can take place in the parents' home or in a special room in the hospital.

For a girl, a naming ceremony takes place on the first Sabbath after she is born, in a service at the temple. Her father is called up to the Torah, where he recites a short prayer and states his daughter's name. The rabbi then recites a special blessing. A reception is hosted afterward by the baby's mother.

Only a few family members and close relatives attend either ceremony, and invitations are usually issued over the telephone; however, formal invitations are becoming much more common. Gifts are sometimes presented for the baby on the occasion. Dress as you would for a religious service.

Becoming an Adult

Bar and bat mitzvahs, confirmations, quinceañeras, and graduations confer grownup status on the young people whom they honor. Your responsibility as a close friend or relative is to attend the ceremony, join in the celebration, and offer an appropriate gift that is within your means. The following sections cover the particulars of each of these ceremonies.

Virtually all rites of passage include refreshments following the service. Enjoy the food and fellowship as you would at any other party (see Chapter 15 for tips on being a gracious guest), and don't forget to bring a gift. If you're in doubt about an appropriate gift, remember that young people always appreciate cash gifts, regardless of the occasion. Chapter 16 has details on giving gifts with class.

Bar and bat mitzvahs

Jewish tradition celebrates the attainment of age 13 for boys (bar mitzvah) and age 12 for girls (bat mitzvah). At this milestone, the community considers the young person to be capable of participating in religious observances as an adult. To commemorate this event, families usually allow the celebrant (the boy or girl) to lead the congregation in a regular weekly prayer service, including the reading of a passage from the Torah in Hebrew.

After the ceremony, the immediate family may gather in a private room in the temple to greet members of the congregation who want to offer congratulations. Often, a lavish reception follows, which may be held in a temple reception room or a hotel or other public hall. The reception often includes a seated luncheon or dinner and may include dancing, flowers, and decorated tables.

Proud parents invite friends to participate in and witness the proceedings. Non-Jewish well-wishers may also be invited to sit among the congregation. All congregations welcome non-Jews and don't expect them to know the details of the ritual. What counts is your presence. Just make sure to stand when everyone else stands and sit when everyone else sits. After the ceremony is over, generously congratulate the celebrant and his or her parents.

If the reception is to be a large one, issue written invitations (see Chapter 14 for more instructions on how to do so). If it is a small affair with family and a very few friends, you can make your invitations by telephone or via e-mail. All invitations should be extended four weeks in advance, or six weeks prior to the event if you're inviting people from out of town.

In some congregations, men are asked to wear a small, symbolic head covering. In Orthodox congregations, women also cover their heads and sit apart from the men. Otherwise, wear whatever types of clothing you would normally wear to attend a religious service.

Gifts are very important on the occasion of a bar or bat mitzvah. Gifts shouldn't be brought to the temple or the reception, but sent to the child's home. Gifts are wonderful, but most children also appreciate checks. Gift ideas include a good book, a magazine subscription, or a gift certificate to a music store, video rental shop, or electronics store.

Quinceañeras

A quinceañera is full of pageantry, ritual, and Hispanic tradition that dates back to the Aztecs in 500 B.C. The quinceañera celebrates a 15-year-old girl's transition from childhood into young womanhood, and the ceremony is a reaffirmation of the baptismal vows. The celebration normally begins with a mass with special readings from family members, though customs vary from country to country. Printed programs are given to guests as they arrive for the church ceremony.

Invitations are normally sent from the parents, or both parents and daughter, at least six weeks in advance. The attire for the event is formal or semiformal, similar to a wedding, and guests are expected to bring gifts. A dinner and dance reception follows the religious ceremony. Quinceañera protocol calls for a formal written thank-you note from the young woman shortly after the celebration, thanking her guests for their presence, gifts, and blessings.

Confirmations

Confirmations are a rite of passage for Christians that means the confirmands are capable of participating in the religious life of their congregation as adults. The ceremony usually takes place when the child is in the seventh or eighth grade.

This event is usually a quiet family occasion, with only the godparents and close relatives present. If the family is holding a social gathering after the confirmation ceremony, bringing a small gift is appropriate — a book that is inspirational in some way would be a very fitting gift.

You should dress as you would to attend a service in a house of worship. The confirmand is usually dressed in his very best clothes.

Graduations

High-school and college graduations are some of the proudest occasions in a young person's life — and in the life of their proud parents. They mark completion of a stage of life, and the start of an exciting new life, whether that new phase is moving on to college or their first job. Friends and family who have supported the graduate throughout their schooling look forward to graduation day as a way of celebrating the graduate's accomplishments.

One tradition of graduation day is photos, and lots of them! It can be stressful for the graduate, who, in addition to the usual obligations of politeness and graciousness, must pose for photographs with assorted relatives and friends while clothed in cap and gown. Graduates should remember that no matter how awkward posing feels at the moment, doing so is an ordeal that all classmates share (and the photos will come in handy years later when your own children doubt that their parents know anything!).

In the following section I give you advice on how to smooth the way when sending or responding to graduation announcements and party invitations. I also list a few tips on just what to wear to these functions and on gift-giving ideas.

Distributing announcements and invitations

Graduation ceremony announcements and invitations are normally given out by the school, which means only immediate families are able to attend. Parents usually plan a party or afternoon reception after the graduation ceremony; the party can be elaborate or simple.

Depending on the nature of the party, invitations can be printed, handwritten, or telephoned. You should send written invitations at least two weeks before the event (sooner for any out-of-town guests). Again, the larger and more formal the party, the better it is to issue a written invitation. On the other hand, if the celebration is a backyard barbecue for family and a few neighbors and close friends, you may telephone the invitation. Often, graduates spend time at their own party, and late in the day begin circulating among their friends' houses to greet them and visit their graduation parties as well.

Parents often mail out announcements of a child's graduation, especially to out-of-town friends. This announcement differs from an invitation to attend a graduation ceremony or reception because you're simply sharing the good news, rather than inviting them to the event. You can send an announcement to the graduate's family, friends, and associates as a symbol of recognition and accomplishment. You should mail a graduation announcement two weeks prior to graduation. If you receive a graduation announcement, you aren't obligated to attend or send a gift. However, you should send a note of congratulations or a graduation card.

Figuring out who attends all the festivities

If you've attended a high school or college commencement recently, you know that seating is always limited and that parking can be a problem. Tickets to graduation exercises are rationed among the participants, so if you're invited to attend a graduation and you accept the invitation, go. Others are sitting at home pouting because there weren't enough tickets to go around. Usually, the graduate has just enough tickets for her parents and siblings and the grandparents. If you're allowed to invite more guests, other close relatives or family friends should be invited. If you can't invite everyone you'd like to the graduation ceremony, you should explain the reason to them. Most people will understand. However, everyone should be invited to a gathering honoring the graduate after the ceremony.

Dressing appropriately

A graduation ceremony and party are an opportunity to look your festive best. Suits and ties for the men and nice dresses or long skirt and matching tops for the women are in order. Graduates often wear a new outfit, often a suit or a special dress that they can then use in their new life at college or out in the working world.

Bringing gifts

Gifts are de rigeur at a graduation party. Even if you're unable to attend the party, as a close friend or relative, sending a gift to the graduate is the thoughtful thing to do. Depending on your preference and price range, gifts may include the following:

- ✔ Stereo equipment
- ✔ A book
- ✔ An atlas
- ✔ A dictionary
- ✔ An accessory for a bicycle
- ✔ A diary or journal
- ✔ A calculator
- ✔ Pair of tickets to a sporting event, rock concert, or play
- ✔ Gift certificate to an electronics store or clothing store
- ✔ A monetary gift in the form of cash, a check, or a cashier's check

Don't plan on handing a wrapped present to the graduate at the ceremony — it would only get lost in the confusion. Send your gift to the graduate's home or if the party is at the parents' home, bring it with you.

Dealing with a Loss

Most cultures and religions have some type of memorial when a person passes away. These services provide a sense of completion, a process for mourning, and comfort for the living. The outpouring of grief and support for the family enables them to eventually go on with their own lives. In the following sections, I describe proper etiquette in the event of a death.

Placing a notice

Notices should be placed in newspapers where family and friends of the deceased person live. The notice should be hand-delivered to the newspaper's editorial office. Notices can also be placed in cities where the departed previously lived, if family members and friends are there.

A notice can include the following information:

- Name and address of the person
- Date and place where he or she died
- Cause of death
- Name of spouse
- City of birth and date of birth
- Company where the person worked and her title
- Education, military service, or major awards or distinctions
- Names of survivors and their relationships to the deceased
- Information on the funeral or memorial service and whether it is private or for the public
- Where to send donations as memorials

Attending the events

In many cultures, the first event that follows a death is a visitation — a courtesy call at the funeral home prior to the funeral. The casket is present (open or closed), with flowers on display, and the family receives visitors who come to greet them and offer words of comfort and support. (This is a modern version of a very old custom that gave the family a day or two to socialize prior to the burial, to be absolutely certain that the deceased was truly dead and not just in a deep coma. Although no such uncertainty exists today, the custom persists.)

A funeral or memorial service may be a very public event, attended by family, friends, colleagues, neighbors, and even acquaintances. Funerals are often held in a chapel or a house of worship, and they may draw a very large congregation. Because the immediate family may be overwhelmed, you need only to greet the mourners and briefly offer condolences. Most important for the family is the knowledge of your presence. (If the service is private, those attending will be notified personally, usually by telephone.)

Burials usually follow funerals. Some cultures consider it a sign of respect to deposit a ceremonial shovel of earth into the grave. This ceremony is initiated by a member of the family and followed by others. If you were close to the deceased, you may take your turn.

You usually exchange expressions of support at the residence of the deceased, a reserved social hall, or a room at the house of worship immediately following the burial or memorial service. The gathering held after the event usually includes only family members, the minister or priest, ushers and pallbearers, close social and business friends, and anyone who came from out of town for the service. In almost all cultures, taking a meal in the company of friends and family is a symbol of the continuation of life and a moment of separation from the intense details of the death, funeral, and burial. Recalling fond memories of the deceased may inspire smiles and even laughter at this gathering — this behavior is perfectly acceptable.

In the days immediately following a funeral, custom calls for neighbors and close friends to visit the bereaved family on a daily basis. Bringing prepared foods that the mourners can eat and share with visitors is a nice gesture.

Expressing your condolences

Most people are at a loss for words when it comes to comforting someone who is grieving. If you don't know what to say, try by starting with these thoughts:

- You're so sorry to hear this sad news.
- The deceased will be sorely missed by friends and colleagues.
- How much you loved this person and how bereaved you feel.
- You know how much the deceased loved and cared for the people who are left behind.
- The grief you feel for the person who is left behind.
- What a wonderful person the deceased was.

Recounting anecdotes, warm remembrances, and stories about the deceased is a kind thing to do. Remembering the person's accomplishments and all that person meant to you and did for you, and sharing that with the family, is very important and much appreciated.

The etiquette of consoling a dear one is the etiquette of genuine affection. Do what you can to comfort and assist the survivors, and be alert for an indication that your attentions have been gratefully received and are no longer necessary. Sometimes people need to work things out for themselves.

Dressing properly

Black has long been the traditional color for mourning. However, wearing black isn't required any longer. Wearing a color other than black isn't a sign of disrespect, as long as the color isn't bright. Hats may be worn by women, and at Orthodox Jewish services, yarmulkes are worn by the men. Dark suits and ties for men and dresses or suits for women are appropriate.

Some religions impose strict standards of modesty on women. When in doubt, ask someone. If you don't know whom to ask, make sure that the only skin you display at a funeral is from the neck up and the knees down.

Sending flowers and making donations

During the mourning period before a funeral, you may send flowers to the funeral home. Donations may be made to the house of worship or made in the deceased person's name to a designated charity. Out-of-town friends and relatives who aren't able to attend the funeral may send flowers and messages of condolence to the funeral home, the place of worship, or the family's home.

When in doubt, go

Funerals can be difficult occasions. Many otherwise well-mannered people avoid funerals because they're sad and often emotional. The same goes for visiting a hospital patient who is seriously ill and may be connected to monitoring and life-support equipment.

As a general rule, you can assume that the more difficult the situation, the more the family will appreciate your presence and your words of support. Your willingness to go out of your way to say a word or two of comfort will be very much appreciated.

Chapter 18

I Do! Celebrating Engagements and Weddings

. . . .

. . . .

*B*ack in the dim reaches of history, a wedding was society's way of gathering together an audience to hear a man promise to take care of a woman. She, in turn, promised to obey him. You may hear faint echoes of those long-ago attitudes in the wedding vows that couples recite today, but the nature of a wedding has changed significantly over the years. People now have bachelorette parties in Las Vegas as opposed to a tea in medieval times — and the current trend for engaged couples is to develop Internet Web sites promoting their upcoming wedding.

Sure, you can still have a traditional ceremony, where the bride glides down the aisle of a huge cathedral on the arm of her tuxedoed father and meets the groom at the altar. But nowadays, a wedding can be as simple as filling out some paperwork at the county courthouse or running off to get married on the beach in Jamaica. Your wedding can take place in a shady glen with your favorite folk singer officiating, if that's the kind of ceremony you prefer. However you do it, your wedding allows you to declare your love for one another in the company of the people who are most important to you.

One of the little luxuries of the modern wedding is a wedding consultant (think Martin Short in *Father of the Bride*). This helpful person can handle everything from the announcements and invitations to the catering and flowers. However, many couples handle the details themselves. Some simply can't afford all the fancy touches. Others prefer to skip some — or even all — of the formalities. Divorced people who are giving marriage another chance face complications that the authorities on marriage often overlook. If you fall into any of these categories, you can find a lot of help in this chapter.

Note: Weddings are a complicated business. For more in-depth information about weddings and wedding etiquette, see *Wedding Planning For Dummies* and *Wedding Kit For Dummies,* both by Marcy Blum and Laura Fisher Kaiser (Wiley).

Getting Engaged

Getting engaged may be one of the most significant moments of your life. At the time, it may seem as though you and your beloved are the only two people on earth, but the reality of it is that a wedding is typically a uniting of families, not just a uniting of two people. Therefore, you need to know a few things about engagements to ensure that everyone involved feels nothing but joy for you and your spouse-to-be. The following sections tell you what you need to know about getting engaged.

In the past, a man would ask the woman's father for her hand in marriage. That custom has slowly passed into history, and many people now decide to get married without asking anyone's blessing. However, speaking with both sets of parents immediately upon engagement to share the joyous news is still a good idea (more on this subject later in the chapter).

Choosing an engagement ring

The diamond industry may insist otherwise, but an engagement doesn't require a diamond ring. Neither is the man required to have purchased a ring before asking the woman of his dreams to marry him. (These days, it's perfectly acceptable for the woman to propose!) In fact, it may be wiser to wait and shop for rings together, letting the bride-to-be select the ring that she likes best.

If you do want to present a ring when you pop the question, however, make sure to quiz your beloved on her engagement ring preferences and find out what she prefers in terms of size and shape of the stones, settings, and precious metals. This way, you're much more likely to choose a ring that she loves.

A brief history of the engagement ring

The wedding ring's origins go back to ancient times, when a groom would wrap braided grass around the bride's wrists and ankles to prevent her spirit from leaving her body. The grass later gave way to leather, carved stone, metal, and then silver and gold. The diamond engagement ring had its genesis in medieval Italy. The Italian custom called for a groom to give the bride's family precious stones as a sign that he was serious about marrying her.

The wedding ring is worn on the third finger of the left hand (the fourth finger, if you count the thumb), because centuries ago, people thought that a vein in that finger led directly to the heart.

If you receive an engagement ring that you're less-than-thrilled about, good manners require that you voice appreciation and admiration for the ring anyway. Many women have learned to love the rings their fiancés gave them. If you really would prefer something else, you can tell your fiancé a day or two later and go back to the store together to select something that better suits your tastes.

Financing an engagement ring under terms that require payments during the early months of a marriage, when you never seem to have enough money for your needs, is no favor to you as a couple. If you can't afford what you think is the ring of your bride's dreams, select a ring that you can afford and promise to add to it in later years, when fortune smiles upon you.

Announcing the engagement to family and friends

Congratulations! The two of you have agreed to marry and live happily ever after. What do you do next? Tell your parents as soon as possible. It's preferable, etiquette-wise, to tell the bride-to-be's parents first (if her parents are divorced, you should tell the mother of the bride-to-be first) and then the prospective groom's parents. Next, you tell your closest family members (grandparents, siblings, aunts, and uncles) and friends.

After you've announced your engagement, both sets of parents should get in touch by phone immediately to offer joint congratulations. It doesn't matter who phones whom, as long as they reach each other. This step is important in establishing cordial future family relations.

If you anticipate that the wedding will be small, you may want to mention this fact when calling family and friends. That way, you can avoid disappointing people if you aren't able to invite everyone.

What often follows an engagement is a formal or casual engagement party, which is traditionally hosted by the bride-to-be's family or a close family friend (more about engagement parties later in this chapter).

Proper etiquette forbids you to congratulate a woman on her engagement. To do so implies that she scored a remarkable achievement in snagging a man — a very outdated idea. Instead, merely wish her all the happiness in the world.

Putting the news in print

After you inform your families and friends, you may want to put an announcement of your engagement in the local newspaper, either right after you get engaged or closer to the wedding itself. Submit a nice photo of the bride-to-be or a portrait of you as a couple, along with a brief caption that identifies you, your parents, and other important information.

If you aren't sure what information to supply, call the newspaper and ask. Most newspapers send you a form to complete and then write the announcement for you based on the information you supply.

Your engagement notice should read something like this:

> The engagement of Laura Smith to Mr. William Rivera, a son of Mr. and Mrs. Harold Rivera of Los Angeles, has been announced by Dr. and Mrs. Gordon Smith of Highland Estates, parents of the bride-to-be. Ms. Smith is a graduate of Yale Law School and a member of the Jefferson County public defender's staff. Mr. Rivera is an airline pilot. The couple plan an autumn wedding.

If the bride or groom has been married before, or if the couple is living together, announcing the engagement formally by a printed announcement isn't necessary. It makes more sense for the couple to announce their intention to marry themselves.

Any bride or groom can also develop a personal Web site to announce their wedding and keep guests updated on details of your upcoming nuptials. A couple helpful wedding Web site developers include the following:

- ✔ www.ewedding.com
- ✔ www.wedshare.com

Breaking up

If you break off your engagement, call your family first and tell them. Then tell your friends. Keep your explanation brief, and remember to be fair to your ex. You wouldn't want that person saying awful things about you, so don't you say awful things about the person you previously thought you wanted to marry. Simply say that the decision to break off the engagement was mutual, even though that is rarely the case.

If the woman breaks the engagement, she should return the ring to the man. If the man breaks the engagement, she may keep the ring, although she often returns it because she doesn't want the reminder of the relationship. However, it may be possible for her to exchange the ring for a beautiful piece of jewelry.

If formal wedding invitations have been sent, you need to send a written cancellation to every invitee with words to this effect: "Mr. and Mrs. Gordon Schlessinger announce that the marriage of their daughter Angela to Rupert Harris will not take place."

The couple must return any engagement or wedding gifts they received. The easiest way to handle returning gifts is to mail them back (thus avoiding a personal visit and lengthy discussion of the breakup) and enclose a note expressing gratitude for the gift, but saying that it is being returned because the engagement has been cancelled.

Making Arrangements for the Big Day

After you get engaged, you're launched into a wondrous — and sometimes stressful — world of booking bands, selecting invitations, perusing menus, and trying on dress after dress after dress. Whether you enjoy this process or pull your hair out depends on your attitude. I hope that I can help keep you in a positive frame of mind with helpful information on the etiquette of handling the arrangements that contribute to a beautiful wedding.

Mapping out the financial details

First things first: Before any monetary deposits are placed, and before anyone writes a single check, both families should agree upon who is paying for what. Tradition calls for the bride's family to pay for the majority of expenses. The groom's family, traditionally, pays for the rehearsal dinner the night before the wedding, the purchase of the wedding license, the clergy fee, the bride's bouquet, the ushers' boutonnieres, the limousine service, and the honeymoon trip. The rest is left to the bride's family.

Today, with people getting married older and divorcing and remarrying more frequently, these traditions are often altered. Also, more families are taking each other's financial situations into account. For example, if the groom's family is wealthy and the bride's isn't, the groom's family often pays the majority of expenses, even though the invitations are sent out in the bride's family's name or oftentimes in both the bride's family's name and the groom's family's name. (I cover the wording of wedding invitations later in this chapter.)

In the case of a couple who are in their thirties and beyond, the bride and groom often pay a significant amount of the cost, depending on their parents' circumstances. In second marriages, the cost is often split between the bride and groom.

Whatever the case, writing down who agrees to cover what item is a good idea, and make a copy for both the bride's and groom's families to refer to throughout the wedding-planning process.

Deciding on the date and place

Do you have your heart set on a favorite hotel for the dinner reception you've dreamed of since you were 12 years old? If so, prepare to be a bit flexible when you try to set a date. Top hotels are booked long in advance, and you may find yourself going down a long list of possible places and dates before you find a site that can accommodate you, even ten months or more into the future. For many brides, the availability of a place for the ceremony and reception is the item that determines the time frame for the entire wedding.

The location of your wedding can be as personal or traditional as the wedding vows you choose, whichever is to the bride and groom's taste. If one of you prefers a religious ceremony in a church and the other wants a service in a secular setting — try to compromise by designing a ceremony that everyone can live with. Often, you can have a religious ceremony in a secular location with a minister or other religious officiate, or you can also hold a nonreligious ceremony in a nondenominational church.

The key is that you select a location that the two of you really want, a venue that reflects your style and personalities. You may want to consult with your parents or other family members, but your decision should be based on what feels right for the two of you. Remember, the wedding is for you first and then for your family and friends.

After you know where you want to have the wedding, etiquette calls for you to allow the following amount of time for completing these wedding planning tasks to enable everyone to do their jobs properly, so consider these factors before setting a date:

- ✔ **Selecting the bridal party:** Give your party the glad tidings at least four months before the ceremony if you're having a formal wedding. (See the next section for more information on choosing attendants.)

- ✔ **Outfitting the bride and bridal party:** To have a gown made and tuxedos ordered, allow at least four months' time.

- ✔ **Selecting, writing, and printing invitations:** Allow at least three weeks for printing after placing your order. (I cover invitations later in this chapter.)

- ✔ **Mailing invitations:** Drop the invitations in the mail six to eight weeks before the ceremony.

Of course, you can manage to put together a wedding in whatever amount of time you have. If you only have a month, given a willingness to make certain alterations to the traditional wedding expectations (for example, buying a wedding dress off the rack instead of ordering one and undergoing a series of fittings), you can certainly pull it off. For most weddings, though, you want to allow a minimum of five months to accomplish all the wedding details.

Selecting your wedding party

The etiquette of selecting a wedding party is very personal and subjective. Only you know, for example, that your sister Christina has been your closest ally since childhood and has been looking forward to your wedding day since age 3. On the other hand, a groom may have a very close group of male friends who have always assumed that they would take turns being best man at each other's weddings. Whatever your circumstances, think carefully about what you're asking of the people you invite to be in the wedding party.

Although being asked is a very special honor, being in a wedding involves many responsibilities and often a considerable financial cost. If you have your heart set on inviting someone who you think may have trouble meeting the costs, you would be kind to offer to cover the person's lodging or plane fare, for example.

Other questions you want to ask yourself when determining the wedding party include: Where is the wedding going to take place? Is the altar big enough to fit the number of people we want to involve in the ceremony?

Having the same number of bridesmaids as groomsmen isn't a rule you must follow. The bride and groom should each make a list of who they want in their party. If the number isn't even and you want it to be, you can assign other jobs to some of them, such as usher or reader.

You should give party members at least four months' notice, and understand that some of them may not be able to accept. Give yourself ample time to ask alternates, just in case.

Designing the ceremony

When you're deciding on the marriage ceremony, the first issue to decide is whether you want a religious or a secular wedding. I cover both options in the following sections.

Choose a style of music that reflects the surroundings. For example, if you're getting married in a cathedral in front of 200 guests, don't choose a folk guitarist. Likewise, if you're getting married in a hotel with a piano, you probably shouldn't invite the Mormon Tabernacle Choir to sing Handel's Hallelujah Chorus.

Religious ceremonies

If you opt for a religious ceremony and you don't belong to a house of worship, give yourself plenty of time to find the right place and the right officiant. Some congregations don't allow a guest officiant to perform a wedding or don't marry people who aren't members. Also, make sure to give yourself time to fulfill any premarital requirements of your house of worship. Some churches and temples require a program of premarital counseling or preparation, which can last from weeks to months.

Within the marriage ceremony, many shifts in etiquette have taken place. For example, the traditional question in Christian marriage vows of "Who gives this woman in marriage?" is rarely asked anymore. Today, when it comes to vows, the bride and groom are increasingly likely to make the same pledges. The traditional vow that the woman takes to "obey" is used very rarely, except in a conservative tradition.

When you meet the clergy member, that person directs you in the traditions of that place of worship and on the parts of the ceremony that you're able to decide, such as readings and hymns. Today, you can write your own vows and still retain the traditional readings and rituals of your faith in the ceremony. You're also able to select your own readings, often one from the scriptures and a poem, for example. And, from a selection given by the musicians, you can choose your own music.

Check with the church about the use of flower petals as well as the throwing of birdseed after the service; either practice may not be allowed. If you use floral decorations in the sanctuary, many places of worship appreciate the donation of some of the flower arrangements from your ceremony for use in their regular worship service.

Some places of worship have a cost attached to the use of the facilities for the wedding. If there is no such charge, you should make a donation to the work of the congregation. In addition to paying the clergy person's fee, it's appropriate and thoughtful to give a small gift and a note of thanks to your officiant, such as a gift certificate to a bookstore or restaurant.

Secular ceremonies

If you're in agreement on a nonreligious ceremony and a location other than a chapel, church, or a synagogue, combine your taste and interests and look into locations that are meaningful to you both. If you're born nature lovers, you can choose a venue outside — by the sea, on a mountain slope, at a ranch, on a sailboat or yacht, in a vineyard, or in a hot-air balloon! Are you the indoor type? Consider holding your service at a resort, a hotel, an old mansion, a museum, or an historical site; the choices are endless. If you have different interests, you can hold the wedding at one location and the reception at another.

When you research wedding locations, remember to ask lots of questions so you don't have any surprises. For example, ask questions about parking; is there enough space? Also ask whether there are any time limits on bands and the like. You'll find that many locations, whether they're in a neighborhood or a business district, have moratoriums on noise and traffic. There are no wrong questions, so ask away!

If you've selected an outdoor location for your wedding, make certain to have a bad weather back-up plan.

Selecting the right words for your wedding vows depends on the setting and the person that is officiating. As a couple, you should feel that you have some control over the ceremony to incorporate your own ideas, write your own vows, or add to the traditional vows. You can still have a minister or rabbi officiate, or you may feel more comfortable with a ceremony performed by a secular leader, such as a Justice of the Peace. Whatever you decide, always check references before meeting with your potential officiator, judge, rabbi, minister, or Justice of the Peace. When you meet the officiant, be sure to ask about that person's wedding ceremony experience, training, education, stance on wedding vow writing, and fees.

Planning the reception

Only you know the perfect way to celebrate your wedding. You may be able to use a church's social hall for an informal reception featuring hors d'oeuvres and nonalcoholic beverages; you can ask the whole gang back to your place for a barbecue; or you may invite guests to a cocktail party and a fancy sit-down banquet at the best hotel in town.

Time for a trip! Having a destination wedding

One increasingly popular trend is the destination wedding, where couples typically combine an ideal wedding destination with their honeymoon. A destination wedding can be like a vacation for the guests as well as the couple getting married. However, as with most event planning, doing your homework is important. When deciding on a destination wedding location, you need to keep the guest's needs and interests in mind. A ceremony in a humid remote rain forest may not be everyone's idea of fun!

A destination wedding can be far less expensive than the traditional wedding, but of course that depends on your destination location and the number of guests you invite. When it comes to covering the costs, normally the wedding couple is responsible for the cost of their travel, the ceremony, the reception, and the pre-wedding or rehearsal dinner. Destination wedding etiquette requires that the wedding party travel costs and other expenses be covered as a gesture only if the bride and groom can afford it. Otherwise, the responsibility is the wedding party's. When selecting your wedding party, be sure to let them know estimated cost and expenses. Invited guests pay for their own travel, all accommodation expenses, and any extra activities. On occasion, if the wedding couple or family can afford it, accommodations and airfare for some of their guests can be paid for as well.

The major disadvantage of a destination wedding is that they can take considerable planning and research when it comes to accommodations, transportation, photographs, flowers, music, an officiant, marriage license, and occasionally, the marriage laws. Especially if you've never been to your destination, you should consider hiring a wedding planning company that specializes in destination weddings, such as www.weddinglocation.com. Finding a company that does the grunt work for you may be the easiest and, in the end, even the least expensive option.

Don't forget about the folks that can't come! Some family and friends won't be able to travel for various reasons. Be sure to plan an after-wedding reception or party at home and let them know about it.

As far as the destination wedding invitation, the only difference from a traditional or "at-home" wedding is that you need to give the guests enough notice to make travel arrangements or to notify their employers. A save-the-date card should be sent out as soon as you have finalized wedding details, at least five to six months before the wedding date. (For the skinny on invitations, see the nearby section "Issuing Wedding Invitations.")

Be sure to check out *Destination Weddings For Dummies* by Susan Breslow (Wiley) for full details on planning a destination wedding.

Your family's ethnic traditions, your position within your community, your financial resources, and other factors all play a part in deciding how you celebrate your wedding. You have a virtually unlimited number of ways to share your happiness, but no matter how you celebrate, remember that your wedding reception planning is just as important as the ceremony itself. Here are some additional considerations:

✔ Try to create a memorable theme that truly represents you *and* your families, and then build your reception around that theme. You can do a lot to make your reception personal, such as setting out family photos, using personal monograms, or creating a signature cocktail. Take time to research the various options, and add a personal touch to the ambiance with the cuisine, flowers, lighting, music, and entertainment.

✔ If you're having a religious ceremony, when you're booking the reception location, make sure to coordinate the date with your house of worship. There's nothing like patting yourself on the back after grabbing the only free Saturday in June at your country club only to call your church to find out that they've already booked two weddings for that afternoon.

✔ You may discover soon enough that a catered reception in a nice setting is a very expensive proposition. You may want the entire world to share in your happiness, but when you're paying anywhere from $50 to $150 a person, you may need to limit the number of attendees.

Accounting for the time between the ceremony and the reception

Weddings are rare occasions when all family members are present and formally attired. Therefore, they're an excellent opportunity to capture the formal portraits and photographs that live forever in family albums.

Immediately after the ceremony and before everyone starts to wilt, an extended photography session often occurs. The bride and groom and their respective families seldom notice the time passing, but the assembled guests who are waiting to toast the new couple and kiss the bride may need some sort of activity to pass the time.

To help your guests with the wedding-to-reception transition, designate a person to round up the guests, escort them to the reception site, and encourage them to take some light refreshments in advance of the wedding party's arrival. A time lag of as much as an hour isn't uncommon.

Issuing Wedding Invitations

Designing the invitations for your wedding can be one of the more fun parts of the wedding-planning process. In the old days, you had one choice of wedding invitation: black type centered on the front of a folded card of white or ivory paper. Although you're certainly still free to opt for this traditional, formal invitation style, you're no longer limited to only one choice. Today, stationery companies offer hundreds of different styles, so you and your fiancé can choose an invitation that reflects your personalities and the style you've chosen for your wedding.

Your invitation is the first clue that your guests get to the style of your wedding. If you aren't having an ultra-formal wedding, you don't need an ultra-formal invitation. If your wedding has a theme or is more informal, you can go with something that reflects that taste.

The following sections give you some guidelines for designing, wording, and sending out your wedding invitations and all the elements they contain. I also give you a few tips on compiling your guest list and sending out wedding announcements after you're hitched. Have fun!

Because you need to mail the invitations six to eight weeks in advance, leave yourself plenty of time to check them over, have them reprinted if anything is incorrect, and then address them (or send them out to a calligrapher). Make sure to find out from the stationer in advance of ordering how long it will take for the invitations to be printed so that you can account for that time accordingly.

Making a guest list

In order to assure equanimity between the families, setting a maximum number of people and then dividing the amount evenly between the prospective bride and groom's families is wise. After each side completes their list, they should compare notes to check for duplicates (particularly if the prospective bride and groom are from the same hometown, for example).

Although you should plan on some people declining the invitation, don't assume that too many will. Nothing can bring people in from all corners of the globe like a wedding can!

Questions regarding the attendance of children at formal catered occasions have triggered legendary family feuds, so think about the implications of not including children on the guest list. Be aware, too, that a failure to invite the children may cause their parents to turn down the invitation. If you sense the possibility of bruised feelings, you may want to look into the availability of child care and try to ease the tension with a personal phone call with an offer of arranging a sitter (whom you know or who has sat for friends of yours, of course).

Often times, disagreements can arise between the bride and groom about certain guests. Remaining respectful of one another is important, and if inviting a certain someone would makes the bride or groom uncomfortable, then deciding not to invite that person is best.

Focusing on formal invitations

The most formal invitation is on ecru (cream) or white, heavy paper stock engraved with black or dark gray ink. The paper is folded in half, with the text of the invitation on the front, outside panel. A less formal invitation can be printed on an unfolded ecru or white card. Either of these papers may be plain or paneled.

The proper wording of a formal invitation is shown in Figure 18-1.

> *Mr. and Mrs. Peter Sun*
> *request the honour of your presence*
> *at the marriage of their daughter*
> *Lily Yuh*
> *to Mr. Terry Fischer*
> *on Saturday, the fifteenth of September*
> *two thousand seven*
> *at five o'clock*
> *Fourth Presbyterian Church*
> *Chicago, Illinois*

Figure 18-1: Follow this basic wording for a formal invitation.

If the wedding is to take place at a hotel or some other nonreligious place, word your invitation as shown in Figure 18-2.

If the reception will be held in the same place as the ceremony, word the invitation as shown in Figure 18-3.

Mr. and Mrs. Richard Kaufmann

request the pleasure of your company

at the marriage of their daughter

Denise Elizabeth

to

Mr. Albert Jay Friedman

on Saturday, the thirteenth of October

two thousand seven

at noon

Balmoral Hotel

500 North State Street

Omaha

Figure 18-2:
The wording
of an
invitation for
a secular
wedding.

Mr. and Mrs. Richard Kaufmann

request the pleasure of your company

at the marriage of their daughter

Denise Elizabeth

to

Mr. Albert Jay Friedman

on Saturday, the thirteenth of October

two thousand seven

at noon

and at a luncheon

immediately following the ceremony

Balmoral Hotel

500 North State Street

Omaha

Figure 18-3:
An invitation
for a
ceremony
and a
reception
held at the
same
location.

Looking at less traditional options

If you've decided that your wedding will be informal, you can take a less formal approach by customizing your invitation with more informal style and language. You can have your invitation printed rather than engraved or use an informal font or colored paper. You can also use an online invitation service, such as www.evite.com or www.sendomatic.com, which both offer many attractive and creative wedding e-invitations and e-announcements.

You can also choose to alter the wording of the invitation, as shown in Figure 18-4.

Figure 18-4:
A wedding invitation with less formal wording.

> Maria Anne Rosati
> and
> Ian Johnston
> request the pleasure of your company
> at their marriage
> Friday, December 14, 2007
> St. Peter's Lutheran Church
> New York, New York

Or, in another less traditional approach, the wedding may be hosted equally by the prospective bride and groom's families. In that case, you can word the invitation as in Figure 18-5.

Figure 18-5:
A wedding invitation naming both sets of parents.

> Mr. and Mrs. Samish Ali
> request the honor of your presence
> at the marriage of their daughter
> Gaiti
> to
> Rodger
> the son of
> Mr. and Mrs. Alexander Hill . . .

Another option for weddings hosted equally by the bride's and groom's families is shown in Figure 18-6.

Figure 18-6:
Another choice for a wedding hosted by both sets of parents.

> *Together with their parents*
> *Gaiti Ali*
> *and*
> *Rodger Hill*
> *request the pleasure of your company...*

Sorting out complicated family situations in the wording of invitations

How do you word the invitations when faced with circumstances like the following, in any combination: the bride's and/or groom's parents are divorced, some or all the parents have remarried, one (or more) of the mothers/stepmothers goes by her maiden name, some or all the parents/stepparents are hosting?

You may find it helpful to simplify the wording if you can exclude the groom's parents' names. If they aren't helping to host the wedding, you don't need to include them; in many cultures, the groom's parents aren't included in the wedding invitation in any case. Typically you list the parents who are paying for the wedding first, and then the rest of the parents follow.

If you want to include both sets of parents on the invitation and the bride's and/or the groom's parents are divorced, you don't need to include new spouses (but be sure to discuss this with your families first). However, if you want to include new spouses on the invitation, name the parents first, and then use the phrase *together with* to include the new spouses.

Including reception cards

If you're holding your reception at a different location than that of your wedding, you should include a reception card with your invitation. Doing so is helpful in the following ways:

✔ You don't have to crowd the text on your invitation.

✔ If you're inviting only some guests to the reception, you can easily add a reception card to the wedding invitations of those guests.

The card should include the name and address of the establishment with the words "Reception immediately following the ceremony" at the top of the card, as in Figure 18-7.

Figure 18-7:
The wording of a reception card.

Luncheon reception immediately following the ceremony
The Atrium at Swan Lake
4200 Lake Street
Oakville

Your invitations should tell your guests whether you're having a meal by indicating "Luncheon reception" or "Dinner reception," or, if you aren't planning a meal, by using wording such as "Cocktail reception."

Requesting RSVPs

Weddings are among the very oldest of social customs. People getting married naturally assume that everyone in the world wishes them happiness and wants to be on hand for the big event. Within families and circles of friends, hard feelings can arise from someone's absence, and a failure to show up may be misinterpreted as a negative comment on the marriage. To reduce the risk of hurt feelings, you may want to consider including a response card with your invitation.

As a guest, you simply check the "regret" or "accept" space on the reply card and return it in the envelope provided.

One word of caution here: Weddings can be complex events. Some folks may be invited to the ceremony but not to the luncheon or dinner reception. Study your invitation to make sure what is involved, and if you have any questions, telephone the person who issued the invitation and get things straight.

I can't overemphasize one rule of etiquette for guests: You must respond to the invitation promptly and as directed, and you must attend if you accept the invitation (unless you have an emergency, in which case you should notify the host by telephone). Caterers and hotels usually charge per table setting. If you say that you'll be there and then fail to show up, the bride's family may have to pay more than $100 for the meal you didn't eat and the drinks you didn't drink. Being a no-show after you've accepted the invitation is terribly rude.

Similarly, neglecting to send an RSVP and then appearing at a dinner is thoughtless. Yes, they'll seat you, because caterers always save the day, but you could've made the couple's life easier if you had signaled your intentions with an RSVP.

Assembling, addressing, and mailing your invitations

You've probably received a wedding invitation that seems to have envelope after envelope or stuffed full of information. In order for your guests to easily navigate your invitation, you need to assemble it in the right order.

If you choose to use tissue paper in your invitation, the tissue should be the first sheet of paper that covers the printed text of your invitation. The large sheet of tissue is for your invitation, the small one for your reply card and other small enclosures.

Place the items in the inner envelope in order of importance, beginning with the invitation, then the reply card tucked under the flap of the reply envelope, a reception card, and any other card (such as one for directions or accommodations). Don't seal the inner envelope, but be sure to write the guest's full name on the outside of it, including the names of any children and/or dates. (If you don't know the date's name, just write "and guest.") You can then place the unsealed inner envelope (guest's name face up) into the slightly larger outer envelope, which you can seal.

In addressing the outer envelopes, spell out all Avenues, Roads, Streets, Boulevards, and so on. Use the complete name of the guest: for example, Richard, not Rich. Write out numbers 1 to 20; larger numbers can be written numerically. Junior, Senior, and such should be stated on the outside envelope, but not the inner.

If you want kids to attend, you have a couple of options. Traditionally, you write "Mr. and Mrs. William Birkholtz and Family," or you can say "Mr. and Mrs. William Birkholz" on the outside envelope, and on the inside use "Mr. and Mrs. Birkholz, Susan, and Camille." In extremely formal situations, address boys as Master (if below age 8) and the girls as Miss. If a child is age 18 or older and you wish him or her to bring a guest, the child would receive a separate invitation.

Envelopes for formal invitations should always be handwritten. Never use labels! If you don't have neat handwriting, you can hire someone that provides calligraphy services or someone you know with nice handwriting.

Never assume that you know what the postage will be. Take a sample invitation to the post office and have it weighed so you know that you're using the proper amount of postage. Again, four to six weeks before the event is the general rule for mailing your invitations to ensure your guests receive their invitations and are able to respond in sufficient time. All invitations should be mailed at the same time to avoid potential hurt feelings (if your high school English teacher receives one and calls your Aunt Betty, who hasn't yet received hers, for example).

A good idea, especially for formal invitations, is to have your invitations hand stamped at the post office to avoid unwanted markings on the outside envelope from the postal machine.

Sending out wedding announcements

Some couples can't afford to invite everyone they know to their wedding. Many times, doing so would be impractical (with acquaintances who live far away, for example). In these cases, you can choose to send wedding announcements. An announcement simply tells the recipient when and, if you wish, where you got married. Typical wording is something like the wording in Figure 18-8 (follow the rules for wording invitations given earlier in this section).

Figure 18-8:
The wording of a wedding announcement.

> *Mr. and Mrs. Constance Avecilla*
> *have the honour of announcing*
> *the marriage of their daughter*
> *Michele May*
> *to*
> *Mr. Alfonso Natarelli*
> *on Sunday, the twenty-third of September*
> *two thousand seven*
> *Holy Trinity Cathedral*
> *Vail, Colorado*

Usually, you order announcements that look very similar to your wedding invitations. Arrange for someone to mail them on the day of the wedding. Recipients of announcements aren't expected to send gifts (as people who accept invitations are), although it's proper to send a note of congratulations.

Planning Other Wedding-Related Get-Togethers

The engagement process is easier to streamline than the actual wedding planning, where you're dealing with a bride, a groom, two sets of parents, and a lot of different opinions. Planning the wedding can get quite complicated and emotional, so you should try to make the prewedding parties and showers relaxing and fun! In order to pull this off, you should know the some of the rules of etiquette and protocol when it comes to hosting these parties and events, which I describe in the following sections.

Engagement parties

Most engagement parties are hosted by the bride's parents as a traditional way of announcing the engagement of their daughter, which is often left as a surprise for the group of guests. The family makes an excuse to host a party for relatives and friends, then during the party may drop subtle hints of an announcement to come.

When the time is right, the bride-to-be's parents call for order and express their great pleasure at their daughter's intentions to marry. Then they propose a toast to the couple's future happiness. The groom would then respond with a toast of his own, praising his future in-laws for the reception they have given him and saying how much he looks forward to becoming part of the family.

However, as times change, having other family members or friends host the engagement party is perfectly acceptable. The party can be held in the home of the bride or at a restaurant.

Normally, the family hosting the party sends the invitations, with the assistance of the future bride and groom. Invitations for the gathering are usually sent to close family and friends. Depending on the formality of the party, invitations can be extended via the mail, with a phone call, or through e-mail.

Be certain that you don't invite anyone to the engagement party who you don't plan to invite to the wedding. Also, you shouldn't register for gifts before the engagement party nor expect gifts from the guests who are attending. Engagement gifts from close family and friends can be accepted at another time.

No etiquette rule requires you to have an engagement party. The trend is somewhat dying out and nontraditional ways of announcing a marriage, such as e-announcements and wedding Web sites are becoming the norm. If you happen to live a long distance from your parents, a party may be difficult to arrange. In that case, you may choose to announce your engagement informally by telling friends and family members individually. (I explain how to announce an engagement to family and friends earlier in this chapter.)

Bridal showers

One tradition that has remained over the years is the bridal shower. Normally, bridal showers are given by the wedding attendants, usually the maid (or matron) of honor. A friend or family member who isn't an immediate relative of the bride or groom can also host the shower.

The invitees include the bride's closest friends, bridesmaids, and the bride and groom's relatives. If you host a shower, make sure that you discuss details with the bride beforehand. She can provide assistance with a convenient date, theme, and the guest list.

You can invite someone to more than one shower; however, a second gift isn't required, and etiquette dictates that those invited to the shower should also be invited to the wedding.

The type of shower that you plan can be anything from a dinner in a restaurant to a themed party in someone's home. It can also include the groom and his family and friends.

A themed bridal shower usually determines the type of gift that guests bring. These presents can be items such as linens or gifts for the kitchen, or even lingerie! My niece and her fiancé planned a destination wedding in Costa Rica, so their friends hosted a couple's shower with a Costa Rican theme; gifts included everything from a beautiful tropical oil painting to a canoe! Whatever theme you decide for the bridal shower, include details on the invitation so that guests bring along appropriate gifts and also mention whether the shower is formal or informal.

If you're planning a couple's shower, you may want to suggest to those invited to limit some of the more intimate gifts that could embarrass the bride, groom, or other guests.

Soon after the shower, the bride should give a gift to the hostess. And don't forget thank-you notes! These should be written promptly to all who attended, whether or not you received a gift. (I explain how to write thank-you notes for wedding gifts later in this chapter.)

Bachelor and bachelorette parties

Both bachelor and bachelorette parties historically were considered to be a rite of passage, from single life to marital life. Today, most people still consider these parties to be one last night of fun before the big day. Bachelor and bachelorette party trends vary from coast to coast and are changing fast in many social circles. Most every type of party is acceptable, from bachelorette sleepovers to joint bachelor-bachelorette parties where the entire bridal party spends an evening together!

Many of the social rules for a bachelorette or bachelor bash are the same, as you can see in the following questions and answers:

- ✔ **When should the party take place?** The date of the party is anywhere from a couple months to a week before the wedding. The date also depends on whether out-of-town guests are coming. For obvious reasons, you want to avoid having the party the night before the wedding.

- ✔ **Who's in charge?** The task of organizing a bachelor party is normally assigned to a male sibling of the bachelor or to the best man. However, any one of the prospective groom's friends can take on the responsibility. Oftentimes, the bachelorette-party planning becomes a joint effort between family and close girlfriends, or the maid of honor does the coordinating and planning.

- ✔ **Who pays?** For both the bachelor and bachelorette party, asking everyone invited to chip in to cover the bride and groom's expenses is perfectly fine. However, if travel expenses are involved, the bride and groom may want to cover their own costs. You should give the invitees a suggested contribution or cost per head for travel, meals, drinks, and entertainment. To avoid any misunderstandings, make certain in advance that each invited guest is clear about who pays for what.

Most people have heard about the bachelor and bachelorette parties that get out of control. These usually involve activities beyond the usual party, which include carousing, drinking an overabundance of alcohol, hiring a female or male stripper, or going to a strip club. Whatever style festivities are planned, risqué or chic, you need to use common sense. Don't let your party become a segment on tomorrow morning's news!

Rehearsal dinners

After the wedding rehearsal, treating the wedding party to dinner is customary. While traditionally the groom's parents host the rehearsal dinner, the expenses can be shared by both families. The dinner arrangements can be formal or informal and be held in either a restaurant or someone's home.

The bride must provide a list of names and addresses of people to be invited, which normally includes everyone who attended the wedding rehearsal — members of the wedding party, their spouses, and perhaps their children; clergy; the parents; and the grandparents. I also recommend inviting any out-of-town guest who arrived early for the wedding.

During the dinner, the best man should give a toast to the couple, and the couple should also give a toast to their parents. During this time, guests can feel free to say a word about the couple — perhaps a humorous story that relates to either the bride or groom or a toast to the couple's future. The rehearsal dinner is also the time that the bride and groom give their thanks to their families and the wedding party. Gifts are normally given to the wedding party during the rehearsal dinner.

Celebrating after the Ceremony

The ceremony has taken place, and now the time has come to celebrate! While you're having fun, don't forget your manners. To make it a wonderful celebration, I've outlined some traditional courtesies.

Saying the right thing in a receiving line

The receiving line is an opportunity for the bride, groom, and key members of the wedding party to meet and greet every guest on their way out of the ceremony. These days, most people do away with this ritual, which allows everyone to proceed to the reception that much quicker. As an alternative, some weddings have the receiving line in place as guests enter the reception.

If the couple has a receiving line, remember that the radiant bride and her adoring groom will be overjoyed and potentially overwhelmed by greeting dozens and dozens of guests. "Congratulations" or "I wish you happiness forever" is enough of a speech for a receiving line.

Making a toast

There is a very specific etiquette to toasting, and if you follow it, you will find that it brings warmth and humor to a wedding. Toasts give people at the wedding an opportunity to put their feelings into words and to express the collective feelings of everyone there. Toasts also allow a segue from the formal to the informal at the reception and allow the bride and the groom, and the friends and relatives who have contributed to the day's success, to relax and enjoy themselves.

You can no longer find any hard-and-fast rules as to what order the toasts are done. A general guideline to follow is that the best man toasts first, followed by the maid or matron of honor. Usually, the father of the bride then makes a toast, which is sometimes followed by a toast from the father of the groom. The bride and groom can also designate a good friend to make a toast, if they choose. The last toast should be from the groom, and the bride can also join the groom in a joint toast.

No matter what order the toasts fall, try to keep toasts to a minimum; otherwise, you risk opening a forum for other guests to speak and causing the toasts to drag on too long.

At larger, formal weddings, the first person to make the toast (normally the best man) should be sure everyone is seated and has a glass, but the tradition of getting everyone's attention by clinking a glass is sometimes seen as crass. The more appropriate way to gather everyone's attention is by using a microphone.

If you're responsible for presenting a toast, remember the following guidelines:

- ✔ **Be prepared.** Practice what you plan to say. Never try to wing it. A wedding toast should be both meaningful and memorable.

- ✔ **Don't make jokes.** Using some light humor or a small anecdote is fine, but no inside jokes or embarrassing comments about either the bride or groom.

- ✔ **Make it short.** Don't talk more than two to three minutes.

- ✔ **Keep it simple.** Use heartfelt and sincere expressions of love and hope for the bride and groom and close your toast with those sentiments.

Adhering to the Rules of Wedding Gifts

When it comes to weddings, the gift-giving process can seem complicated. Gifts are generally expected, but you may not know when to deliver your gift or how much to spend. The following sections cover the basic "rules" of wedding-gift giving and provide advice to the bride and groom on how to keep track of all those gifts and acknowledge them appropriately.

Giving wedding gifts

Although in the past bringing gifts to the wedding reception was common, today wedding gifts are more commonly sent to the bride's home. This practice frees members of the wedding party and family from the worry of transporting gifts (which may be breakable) during the reception, when they should be enjoying the party, or after the reception, when they will most likely be exhausted.

Different families have different wedding-gift customs, so you need to check with your relatives when a wedding in your extended family occurs. You may be expected to give a certain type of gift, or a gift of a certain value, so you want to know this ahead of time. Be alert for the family tradition that calls for cash gifts for the bride. The usual practice is to hand an envelope to the bride as you go through the receiving line after the ceremony. If the family expects this sort of giving, the bride designates a member of the wedding party to take the envelopes as they are given to her and to mark the envelopes with the name of the giver.

Make your wedding-gift purchases in time to have the gift delivered at the bride-to-be's residence before the wedding date. If the gift is delivered after the wedding, problems can occur if the couple is out of town traveling on their honeymoon. Also keep in mind that although the historical purpose of wedding gifts is to help the new bride set up a household, guests have up to one year to send a wedding gift.

Registering for gifts

Although you may think that registering for a large number of wedding gifts is a selfish act, doing so actually does your guests a great favor. Registering at large store chains helps well-wishers who otherwise wouldn't know what to give you for a wedding gift. It also ensures that you will like the gifts that they give you, so everyone ends up happy.

When making selections for your wedding registry, take care to include a wide range of items at a range of prices. Although some of your guests may want to give you lavish gifts, others can afford only gifts of modest value, and you want to accommodate all parties.

Many stores with wedding registries now have Web sites. Guests can click on the wedding registry, find the couple's name, pull up their list, and see what's already been purchased for them. You click on the item you want to purchase, denote who it's from, give your credit card information, and bingo! The wedding gift is shipped immediately. You never need to leave your home or office.

How did the cash gift tradition start?

Here's a bit of ancient legend about the way that guests figured out how much money to give the bride as a wedding present, in families where cash gifts are traditional.

In villages where nobody was extremely wealthy, the father of the bride would host a huge celebration with feasting for everyone, including wine, music, and dancing. Such a celebration used up all the financial resources of the father and prevented him from sending his own daughter off with a nest egg of her own. So the guests surveyed the party, made their best guess as to the cost on a per-person basis, and used that figure as the starting point for the value of their monetary gift. Often, they would add a little money as a gift for the bride.

Today, however, this method for figuring out how much to spend on a gift has gone by the wayside. Family members and friends should consider how close they are to the bride and groom, how much they have to spend, and how much help the couple needs in furnishing their household. Never overspend your limit on a wedding gift — remember that the truly meaningful part of the gift is the note you attach offering your congratulations, best wishes, and personal thoughts for the couple.

Telling someone where you're registered if they ask you what kind of gift you'd like is perfectly acceptable, but mentioning gifts in any way on your invitations is in very poor taste. I have received invitations to weddings in which a "We're registered at . . ." card was enclosed, which is an absolute no-no.

Some engaged couples set up Web site money registries or look for donations to assist them with the costs of the wedding. Others solicit cash for honeymoon expenses. My practical side says that asking for money to cover expenses isn't a bad idea — many cultures expect it. But my etiquette side says that it can come across as bad taste.

Keeping track of gifts and sending thank-you notes

Sending thank-you notes for gifts is a must after the wedding; you typically have up to one year to send notes, but I recommend that doing so sooner rather than later because everyone looks forward to hearing from the new bride and groom. The following sections detail the ins and outs of logging in gifts and sending thanks.

Logging in gifts

When you're planning a wedding, you have to take care of many, many details, so don't trust yourself to remember who gives you what. Instead, keep a gift log and write down what gifts you receive from whom and when. Also note when you send out the thank-you note to ensure that no gift gets overlooked.

You may want to designate someone other than yourself to receive and log in every gift that arrives. If the gifts are going to the bride's parent's house, then usually the bride's mother can keep track. Records of the gifts purchased from the couples gift registry are kept by the store, which makes record keeping a lot easier.

What do you do if you receive a gift that you either have a duplicate of or just plain don't like? You can certainly exchange duplicate gifts for something else, and the person who gave you a duplicate shouldn't take offense. However, the issue of returning a gift you don't like is a somewhat touchier subject. If a gift is given by a family member or close friend, you simply must keep it and display it when the person comes into your home. Returning or exchanging such a gift isn't worth the hurt feelings you may cause to someone who truly loves you. After a year or two, you can certainly "retire" the gift to the back of a cupboard or closet. Who knows? In 20 years, it may look quite chic!

Thanking gift givers

Writing and mailing thank-you notes as soon as the gifts arrive is perfectly acceptable — you don't need to wait until after the wedding to do so. You should send out your thank-yous within four to six weeks of receiving a gift. Remember, too, that written thanks are in order here. Even if you thank Aunt Enid on the phone for the lovely serving dish, you must follow up in writing.

No one expects you to offer lengthy, eloquent expressions of gratitude, but do mention the gift and its intended use in a note, like in Figure 18-9.

Traditionally, the bride always received the gifts and issued the thank-you notes. The practice of sending gifts only to the bride is a faint echo of the idea of a dowry, which gives a woman a few possessions with which to enter her marriage. Today, this practice no longer continues (because the bride may be a business professional who earns as much as her adoring husband does!). The bride and groom can share equally in the task of writing the thank-you notes and sign them as a couple.

Imprinted thank-you cards are a nice touch. They can carry the imprint of your first names, such as "Amy and Richard," which sidesteps the question of whether it's bad luck for the bride to use her husband's last name for any purpose before the wedding.

Presenting gifts to the wedding party

When a couple gets married, they don't just receive gifts; many times, they give them, too. It's customary for the bride to give a small gift to each of her bridesmaids and for the groom to give a gift to each of his groomsmen to thank them for participating in the wedding and for their continued friendship.

Dear Aunt Jean and Uncle Ned,

Thank you so much for the four place settings of our formal china. Jim and I look forward to welcoming you into our new home and serving you a meal on those beautiful dishes as soon as we are settled. We really appreciate your thoughtfulness.

Love,

Amy and Richard

Figure 18-9:
A thank-you note for a wedding gift.

You can give the maid or matron of honor and the best man a modestly more expensive gift, or you can give them the same gift that you give the other attendants — it's up to you. If you have a bridal shower, you can give the bridesmaids their gifts at that time; otherwise, present them at the rehearsal dinner. The same goes for the groomsmen.

Giving small gifts to flower girls and ring bearers is a nice gesture, and often-times couples give gifts to both sets of parents as a token of gratitude for paying for their wedding or just recognizing them for their unconditional love and support. Also, giving small gifts to ushers who aren't groomsmen and readers is a nice way to make them feel a part of the wedding party, or you may decide to give them a simple card saying how much you appreciate their involvement in your special day and their friendship.

The bride and groom may also choose to give gifts to each other. Customarily, each buys the other's wedding and engagement rings. Because the groom doesn't get an engagement ring in return, the bride may want to give him a gift to honor the engagement in order to even the score, so to speak. The couple may also give each other wedding gifts of their choosing to commemorate the occasion.

Dealing with Difficult or Unusual Circumstances

If you read the advice columns in your daily newspaper, you're sure to notice that weddings inspire many questions. What begins as a simple plan for a man and a woman to marry rapidly inspires some of life's most difficult controversies. You may need a little help standing up for your own thoughts. Some of the following discussions may serve that purpose.

Handling divorced parents

Your parents are divorced and now married to other spouses. Even if the bride's father is paying for the festivities, the bride's mother needs to be involved in planning the wedding day. However, say she is close to her daughter, but she feels shut out of the whole thing, and she really doesn't want to have anything to do with her ex-husband or his new wife.

If ever an ideal situation existed to hire a professional wedding consultant, this is it. As a disinterested third party, the consultant can determine the wishes and inputs of everyone involved and suggest compromises. Best of all, the consultant can keep everyone apart until the actual day of the wedding, when civilized behavior is the rule of the day.

In the absence of a wedding consultant, however, the best solution is for everyone to behave as adults. That means putting others' needs before their own desires. Both of the newer spouses should try to stay out of the fray and let the bride's and groom's mother and father run the show. The wedding day is for the bride and groom, and everyone needs to cooperate to bring off the wedding without conflict or strife.

If the bride and groom sense family discord that can't be set aside temporarily, getting married in a way that doesn't involve a lot of ceremony may not be a bad idea.

Dealing with a family who objects to the marriage

Yes, people fall in love and get married even when one of the families voices strong disapproval of the match. If a parent isn't happy with the news, he or she should keep the disappointment hidden until an opportunity arises to discuss the engagement privately with the son or daughter. Hopefully, with a good, open conversation, the son or daughter can bring the parent around without too much difficulty.

If the parent still disapproves, even after the best efforts of the son or daughter, it is the parent's duty to hold his or her peace and go along with the wedding. Allowing a child to make what you view as a mistake is better than creating a breach in the relationship that can alienate the child from the parent for a long time.

Saying "I do" after you already did

Proper etiquette dictates that a second marriage ceremony should be a small affair, including only your family and closest friends. The ceremony is followed by a reception, and that can include just about anybody and encompass any type of affair you want. The bride can certainly wear a white dress, although it's considered more appropriate to stay away from wearing a long, white bridal dress with a train and veil. The couple should also avoid having a large wedding party.

If the bride and groom are in their thirties or beyond, they usually extend the invitation to the ceremony themselves, either with a personal note or a telephone call. The written invitation to the reception would be worded as in Figure 18-10.

Figure 18-10:
An invitation
to a
reception
for folks
who are
marrying a
second
time.

> Barbara Lynne Brickson
> and
> Keith I. Johnston
> request the pleasure of your company
> at dinner
> following their wedding
> on Friday, June 8, 2007
> at six o'clock
> National Arts Club
> New York City

As far as gifts are concerned, most people who are remarrying are more established than first-timers, and you may consider putting a "No gifts, please" clause in the invitation. If it's the first time for one of you, however, or if you would appreciate some help starting your new life together, gifts are appropriate.

If you're having a religious ceremony for a second marriage, consult with the officiant to make sure that you fulfill any special requirements.

Chapter 19

On the Go: Travel Manners for Land, Sea, and Air

In This Chapter

▶ Planning ahead for personal comfort

▶ Arriving at your destination with ease

▶ Getting along on foreign turf

You can't find a tougher test of your manners than traveling. When you travel — whether your destination is the beach or the boardroom — you no doubt see other people displaying very bad manners and even unbelievable rudeness. Yes, travel can put people under tremendous stress. But being away from home doesn't give you permission to abandon politeness. On the contrary! Particularly when you're a guest in another state or another culture, you need to be extra mannerly.

Unfortunately, though, traveling can make you feel weary and out-of-sorts, and you may be tempted to do some teeth gnashing and fit throwing. That's where this chapter can help. Here, you can find ideas to help you keep your manners in good shape as you travel.

The rules of how people should act with others and how to behave in a polite and considerate manner out in the world are rules that have stood the test of time. And while some rules of etiquette have relaxed in this century, being rude or unkind will never be in style. And when in doubt, treat other people as you would want to be treated yourself.

Planning a Trip with Minimum Fuss

When you're considering a pleasure trip, take your travel personality into account and plan your itinerary accordingly. (Unfortunately, this doesn't apply to business trips, because you don't have much of a choice about where you're going or with whom you're traveling!)

What do you enjoy doing? Are you a beach and warm-weather person? Do you need lots of activity or just relaxation? What age group do you want to be around? (If you're over 30, you may not enjoy Cancun during spring break.) Do you like traveling alone or with a companion? Do you prefer big cities or small villages? What can your budget handle?

Taking all of these details into consideration is essential before you leave. What does that have to do with etiquette? The better prepared you are for a trip, the better you can cope with the effects of traveling, and the more likely you will be a kind and courteous tourist. Flexibility is key when you're traveling. Be as tolerant and adaptable as possible.

Choosing a travel companion, such as your significant other or a group of friends, is possibly more important than where you decide to go. After you decide where you'll be traveling, you should cover every detail of the itinerary, selecting specific activities you each enjoy. This way, you can set expectations and know what each person wants out of the trip. Making sure you both enjoy your getaway may also require that each person make a few small sacrifices. If one of you likes constant activity and the other lots of down time, make an agreement that you have a day or two to be do things separately. Be considerate of each other. It isn't always easy, but to ensure peace, always exercise patience and common courtesy.

Getting There Gracefully

Whatever your mode of transportation — be it plane, train, ship, car, bus, camel, bicycle, elephant, rickshaw, or space shuttle — the rules of travel are practically the same, and the most basic rule of travel etiquette, as with any other form of etiquette, is to respect others. In the often cramped and uncomfortable quarters that modes of transportation offer, etiquette infractions that may be slightly annoying in everyday life can escalate into tense situations while you're traveling.

Whatever you do, avoid provoking strangers. Generally, people who are traveling are under a lot of pressure and stress, and they may not respond as reasonably as they may otherwise.

To make your trip as safe and pleasant as possible, the following sections have some guidelines for getting to your destination with grace.

By any mode of transportation

Good travelers are ready for the unexpected. Although stress is inevitable when traveling, it doesn't have to make you miserable. The following helpful pointers can better prepare you for a smooth journey:

✔ **Double-check schedules.** Is it possible to wait at an airport gate for two solid hours, only to discover that your plane to Marseilles has been canceled due to a strike? Yes, it's possible. Moreover, it's not uncommon. The scene at any big-city airport or large train station is confusing enough when you speak the language, but it can be a nightmare if you're struggling to understand the various schedules and information displays.

✔ **Play it smart by using the services of a local travel agent.** If you're away from home and you don't know where to find a travel agent, ask the concierge at your hotel.

✔ **Make sure you have your travel documents in order.** Always bring proper identification and if traveling internationally, your passport and, if required, a visa and inoculation documents.

✔ **Don't be a target for thieves.** Leave your valuables at home in a safe. Purchase a slender wallet that hangs by a cord around your neck, under your shirt. Keep your passport, credit card, and large bank notes in that wallet, and go about your travels without worrying that someone may pick your pocket or steal your purse.

✔ **Allow plenty of time — then allow more.** The best way to minimize stress and anxiety while waiting to check in at an airport, railroad station, or bus terminal is to allow about twice as much time as your first impulse dictates. If you normally allow an hour at the airport, give yourself two hours. When traveling abroad, give yourself three hours. You can always use the extra time, if you have any, to shop or grab a snack.

Use that same expansion of time at the other end of your journey. It can take a lot of time to gather your belongings and leave an airplane or train station. If you're traveling internationally, clearing immigration and customs may take longer than you expect, and you may find yourself caught in unexpected rush-hour traffic.

✔ **Dress for a long journey.** If you're fated to spend many hours in the same outfit, wear casual, comfortable clothes that you can layer up and down as your environment gets warmer or cooler. You can look neat and well put-together while being practical about travel.

Women can try wearing knits, such as a long knit skirt or pants, plus a T-shirt and sweater. Carry a cozy wrap and an extra pair of socks in case the airplane or train is chilly. Men can wear loose, comfortable pants, such as khakis, and layers on top. Wear shoes that you can easily loosen or tighten, because feet tend to swell during long flights.

✔ **When traveling with children, do your best to keep them happy and occupied.** You must face it — you can't control your children's behavior at a young age. But, you can bring along enough distractions in the form of toys, books, crayons, games, stuffed animals, dolls, and the like to keep them busy. If the airline permits, snacks and drinks are also a good idea, because food service can be slow. Try to be considerate of passengers around you. Don't let your children run in the aisles, crawl around the row, kick the seat in front of them, or be careless with food and drink.

✔ **Mind your own business.** If your neighbor is reading or working on a laptop computer, don't intrude by asking, "What are you doing?" Don't talk if your neighbor is trying to rest. If you're talking with a neighbor and you receive one-word comments or answers, take the hint and end the conversation. Or if you aren't interested in talking, and your neighbor is, usually a polite, but succinct response to the talker is sufficient to pass the message that you aren't interested in conversation.

✔ **Be a conscientious sleeper.** If you're lucky enough to be able to sleep on the plane or train, try to sleep with one eye open (so to speak). Don't lean beyond the boundaries of your seat, and do your best not to drool or snore.

✔ **Use common courtesy when using personal electronic devices.** Don't play music so loud that the passengers around can hear the words or make out the song. If you're using a laptop computer, check with those next to you to see if they mind the keyboard noise. Women with long nails should be aware that the clicking on a keyboard could be disturbing. And remember that yelling into your cell phone isn't necessary.

✔ **Make accommodations for special needs.** If you or your travel companion has any special needs, be sure to provide details to the airlines, hotels, or cruise ship before traveling.

By air

Airline travel has never been so convenient in theory or more hectic in practice. The increasing numbers of people traveling by air has caused airports and airlines to work beyond capacity — causing stress for airline staff, crew, pilots, and passengers that can translates into rudeness and anxiety. The following pointers can help you cope with planes and airports and survive the stress of airline travel:

✔ **When checking in your bags at an airport skycap, make sure to tip a minimum of a $1 to $2 per bag.** You want to make sure your luggage gets onto the airplane, right? Besides, these people work hard, rain or shine, to make it easier for you to get to your flight.

✔ **Use the facilities before you leave the airline terminal.** You may be parked on the tarmac for quite a while with the plane restroom off limits.

✔ **When boarding or exiting the aircraft, be considerate of the people you're passing.** Walk through the aisle carefully, keeping your baggage either directly in front of you or holding it behind you. If you happen to bump or stumble into another passenger, apologize and smile. And don't fight your way through the line to get to your seat first — or, in the case of unassigned seats, to get a better seat.

✔ **After you're seated, share the armrests.** Each passenger should have one.

✔ **Avoid moving about the plane as much as possible.** Doesn't it seem that the people sitting in the window seats always need to get up the most? If you have that tendency, please book an aisle seat! Have your books, snacks, or papers that you need easily accessible — this way, you won't have to get up to rummage through the overhead compartments or disturb your neighbors.

✔ **Be aware of the airline's rules when it comes to baggage.** If you're uncertain, call ahead. Don't wait until you're at the airport to discover that you won't be able to check in two suitcases, a golf bag, and four huge boxes. Preparing your luggage ahead of time can also help you get through security with more ease.

  If you have carry-on baggage, be considerate of the other passengers when placing it overhead or under your seat. You should try to limit yourself to one carry-on — two if you must and if it's allowed. And, keeping your carry-on under the seat in front of you or in the overhead bin directly above your row is best. Try to assist those who may not be able to reach the overhead bins.

✔ **Give the passenger behind you a warning before you recline your seat.** Nothing is more annoying than the seat in front of you flying back when you aren't prepared. Always glance behind you first to make sure the passenger's tray doesn't have food, a hot cup of coffee, or a laptop computer on it. When the food cart first comes through, put your seat up. Leave it up at least until the flight attendants have taken away the food trays. And, reclining your seat all the way back to rest or take a snooze isn't necessary.

✔ **Please don't grab the seat in front of you!** This can be so incredibly annoying to the passenger in front of you, especially if she's sleeping, eating, or drinking. If possible, lift yourself out of the seat with the armrests. If you have to use the seat back in front of you, alert the passenger, excuse yourself, and apologize. And, be extra careful not to pull the hair of the unsuspecting passenger while grabbing the seat back.

✔ **Avoid calling the flight attendants, if possible.** Their job is to make every passenger happy and comfortable while on the plane — not an easy task with a couple hundred anxious individuals onboard.

After you've finally made it to your destination, show your gratitude for a good flight by smiling and thanking the flight attendants and pilots as you leave. When retrieving your luggage in baggage claim, help others if they need assistance, and always make room for others to reach their luggage while you're standing at the conveyor belt waiting for your own.

By sea

A cruise is unlike any other vacation. The cruise ship is like a large floating city, and the fact that you will be living with hundreds or thousands of other people makes it important that you understand basic cruising etiquette. Here are just a few common-sense rules you should follow while you're cruising:

- **The skipper or captain is boss.** No matter the size or type of vessel, he is responsible for all those aboard the ship and for any accidents that occur, which is why you must always follow instructions. Abiding by the rules is a matter of respect as well as safety.

- **Get to know the ship.** Prior to leaving the dock, know where safety equipment is located and memorize some common nautical terms, such as the difference between starboard (right) and port (left). All ships, boats, and yachts are always referred to in the feminine tense. Always call a ship a ship and not a boat.

- **Tipping varies on each cruise line.** Most cruise lines automatically charge you for tips and gratuity at the start of the cruise; the amount can range from $10 to $20 per staff member per day. On some ships, leaving money in an envelope in your room at the end of the cruise is customary. Check with your travel agent or the company that booked your cruise to find out what's expected.

- **Adhere to the shipboard dress code.** Most cruise lines distribute onboard newsletters listing the day's activities and events. Dressing accordingly to what has been published and at the appropriate times is important.

Casual doesn't mean wearing a pair of jeans and a T-shirt, or warm-ups. Casual by day attire would be resort wear, such as slacks, skirts, and blouses for women and slacks and a shirt or sweater for men. Casual at night requires a man wear a jacket and tie and women cocktail dresses or dressy pantsuits. For a formal evening, gentlemen should wear a dark suit or tuxedo, and ladies should don cocktail dresses or formal gowns.

- **Don't overindulge, especially if you don't have your sea legs!** If you're feeling a little seasick, don't stuff yourself at the all-you-can-eat seafood buffet. Be mindful about alcohol intake and always drink responsibly.

- **Bring soft luggage.** Duffle bags and soft luggage are easier to handle and store aboard ship, where you rarely find full-size closets.

- **Keep the noise level down in your cabin and shut doors quietly.** Be considerate of your fellow passengers in nearby staterooms by following the ship's policy on noise. Take notice you late-night revelers: Don't talk, yell, or laugh too loudly while walking to your cabin. And after you're inside, keep your voice and the TV volume down. Keep in mind that the walls between cabins on some ships can be thin.

✔ **Never waste fresh water.** Always be mindful of your use of water while aboard ship. Remember you're on a floating city so you need to respect the regulations regarding the use of fresh water.

✔ **Smoke in designated areas only and always use ashtrays.** Never throw a cigarette (or any item) overboard.

✔ **Don't be a chaise-lounge hog or slather yourself in suntan oil and then sit on upholstered furniture or cushions.** Rushing out early in the morning to reserve deck chairs by placing personal items on them and then letting the chairs sit empty for a couple hours is rude. The rule is a first-come, first-serve basis only after you're sitting in the chair.

For more onboard etiquette, refer to *Cruise Vacations For Dummies* by Heidi Sarna and Matt Hannafin and *Sailing For Dummies,* 2nd Edition, by JJ Isler and Peter Isler (both published by Wiley).

Reaching Your Destination and Enjoying Your Stay

Congratulations! You've survived the journey and successfully reached your destination. Now the time has come for the real fun to begin. What follows are some general suggestions for gracefully enjoying the sights and sounds of your travel destination.

Arriving at your hotel

You may take a hotel shuttle, a taxi, a bus, or train to your accommodations. If you're taking anything but a public form of transportation, make sure to tip the driver between 15 and 20 percent (see Chapter 22 for more in-depth information about tipping). If you're renting a car and take a rental car company shuttle to your vehicle, tip the driver $1 per bag if he assists you. When you arrive at the hotel and the doorman assists you in getting into the hotel lobby, you should tip $1 to $2.

When you arrive, a bellhop might assist you with your bags. She should be tipped $3, or if you have a lot of bags, $5 to $10. If you decide to handle your own bags, make sure you can do so with ease. If you're struggling with a large suitcase or several smaller bags and refuse a bellhop's assistance, you may look cheap.

The one exception to this rule is when you're leaving the hotel: If you're late for a train or airplane and think that the bellhop would only slow you down, then you're excused from asking for assistance!

In many countries, the hotel must report foreign guests to the authorities. If the hotel clerk asks you to leave your passport at the front desk when you check in, don't worry. You aren't surrendering your passport. An hour or so later, after taking care of the paperwork, the clerk will return your passport to you.

Visiting tourist attractions

Even if you're enjoying a slow-paced, relaxed vacation, you need to do some planning of your itinerary. Museums, cathedrals, and other tourist attractions operate on schedules that may frustrate you. Call ahead to inquire or check with your hotel concierge on the hours of admission of the attractions you want to visit.

When you head for a specific destination, write out the name and address of the place on a small card, or ask the hotel clerk to write it for you. You can then show the card to your taxi driver or to a helpful passerby on the street for help in heading in the right direction.

Long lines are a fact of life if you travel to a popular destination in high tourist season. Arriving early is the key to reducing your time in line. Show up about 15 minutes before the official opening time to be among the first visitors in line. Don't be surprised to find two lines — one for you and your fellow independent tourists, and one for organized groups under the leadership of an official guide. Guided tours are always admitted ahead of ordinary individuals.

Photography is a major etiquette issue in many museums. Generally, taking flash photographs isn't allowed, so you may want to leave your camera back at your hotel. In many cases, you can purchase photos in the museum gift shop that may be far better than anything you could produce on your own.

When in Rome: Navigating Your Way through International Cultures

These days, tourists and businesspeople alike think nothing of jumping on an airplane to do business around the globe. The ease and speed of international travel, the ability to communicate instantly through satellite and computer, the interlocking and overlapping business interests in the Americas, Europe, Africa, and Asia mean that people are in touch with the world as never before. If you're one of those travelers, you need to know that the moment you set foot on foreign soil, the rules of etiquette change. Even if you're well on your way to bona fide expertise in American etiquette, practices that pass as polite in San Francisco may be deemed downright rude in Seoul or Sevilla.

When you travel to a foreign country, you can offend people through ignorance as easily as you can through bad intentions. Before your trip, take time to get to know the cultures you're going to visit. Although the following sections are a good start, you may want to consult a reputable guidebook for the country or countries you'll be visiting to discover more specific rules of conduct.

Behaving with extra courtesy

You may be familiar with the golden rule: "Do unto others as you would have them do unto you." International travel puts a slight twist on that golden rule: "Do unto others as they would have you do unto them." When you step onto foreign ground, you can no longer assume that you know what behavior is acceptable. Your "normal" behavior may look completely different through the eyes of someone from another culture! When you're on foreign turf, try to see situations through the natives' eyes and respond accordingly.

Human nature being what it is, tourists are often judged by whether they behave like natives. But many customs are deeply rooted in history, culture, and temperament — something a recently arrived traveler couldn't possibly understand. Be unfailingly courteous and considerate while traveling. You should also be patient, practice good listening skills, and remain flexible. Good manners go far in creating good feelings and making new friends. If you happen to make an etiquette faux pas, don't panic. Most local residents are impressed by travelers who are as interested in their outlook and way of life as they are in their monuments and museums.

Perhaps most important, keep your sense of humor. If you can laugh at yourself in an awkward situation or alleviate a fellow traveler's embarrassment at making a mistake, people appreciate it. Keeping your sense of humor is important at any time in life, of course, but even more so in international travel, when stress levels may be high and you may feel like a fish out of water.

Dressing appropriately

Clothing fashions change rapidly, and what's suitable one year may be hopelessly obsolete the next. However, you can utilize a few general guidelines when you pack for a trip and select your outfit for each day of travel activities:

✔ **Less flash is better when it comes to travel clothing.** Lean toward the inconspicuous instead of standing out in garish garb. Although college students on a backpacking tour can get away with more casual clothing, you should make an effort to look neat and well put together.

✔ **Your clothes should be natural to the surroundings you're visiting.** In other words, no sarongs and bikini tops on the streets of London, and no stiletto heels or black pantsuits at a Caribbean beach!

✔ **Skin can be a sin.** Religious establishments, in particular, impose strict modesty rules, especially for female visitors. Depending on the religion and the place, women may be required to cover their shoulders, arms, heads, legs, and/or feet. In general, dress rules aren't strictly enforced for tourists, but you show your good manners when you show less of yourself.

✔ **Casual business dress doesn't translate.** Corporate officers may put in a productive day in California while wearing blue jeans, running shoes, and open-neck shirts, but the rest of the world hasn't quite caught up with casual business attire. When conducting business abroad, dress conventionally, conservatively, and appropriately.

✔ **Baubles inspire bandits.** You know how to avoid trouble when you're at home, but you may have no idea how criminals operate in other countries. Play it safe by leaving your precious jewelry locked up at home, and make do with costume jewelry and timepieces that you can bear to lose.

Communicating with the locals

The first thing you may notice upon arriving at your international destination, depending on the country, is that you can't understand a word of what people around you are saying. The language barrier is the biggest potential pitfall of etiquette-conscious travelers.

You can't be courteous if you can't communicate. If you plan to travel to — or through — a country where the language isn't your own, learn a few of the most polite phrases in the local language. At a bare minimum, you need to know how to say hello, goodbye, please, thank you, yes and no, and how to ask where . . . ?, how . . . ?, when . . . ?, and how much . . . ? Every large bookstore sells small, pocket-sized phrasebooks and audio tapes in just about every language you'll ever need. You can learn at least a dozen words on the airplane as you fly toward your destination.

English is taught as a second language in many countries, and you may find your verbal exchanges easier if you begin a new contact by asking, "Do you speak English?" More often than not, the answer will be, "A little."

The following sections explain the particulars of various aspects of communication in a foreign country.

Remembering that English isn't a secret code

You're thousands of miles away from home, surrounded by natives who speak a language that you don't understand. You may be tempted to use your native language, English, as a secret code to exchange private comments with your travel companion. However, this is almost always a mistake. Even when the people around you are conducting their conversations in Italian, French, or Hindi, you can bet that they know at least a few words of English.

Never say anything in English to your companion that you wouldn't want others around you to overhear. Your inability to speak the language of your host country is no excuse to abandon everyday good manners.

Fitting in by using polite expressions

You'll be welcomed into a country more easily if you learn a few commonly used expressions. This is particularly important because many cultures rely more heavily on these words than Americans do. "Good morning," "Good evening," "Please," and "Thank you," when spoken in the native language of the country you're visiting, go far in making you appear to be a polite and courteous traveler. However, if you don't know them, say the words in English.

Europeans punctuate their conversations with "Thank you" and "Please" far more frequently than Americans do. Scandinavians, for example, are particularly effusive with polite expressions. During a meal, they give thanks each time a course is served, and they thank the host for the entire meal when they rise from the table. Scandinavians also exchange a round of thank yous again before they leave. As a visitor, you're expected to follow suit.

Conversing about proper topics

What is considered a polite topic of conversation differs from country to country. For example, most people in other countries find it strange when Americans speak freely about income and family matters — subjects they consider too private to share. Although Americans find it perfectly acceptable to ask what people do for a living and whether they're married, citizens of other countries often consider these questions rude.

Unless you're speaking to a close friend of many years from another country, remember these rules when conversing with a person from another culture:

- Don't ask personal questions.
- Don't criticize the person's country or city.
- Don't compare the person's country to the United States.

✔ Don't mistakenly denigrate the country or city you're visiting by saying that it's cute, quaint, or old-fashioned.

✔ Don't discuss politics, local royalty, religion, or customs (although you should be prepared to discuss American crime, freedom of the press, political scandals, and the like).

✔ Don't tell jokes (they often don't translate well).

✔ Do pay compliments on the culture, beauty, and achievements of the country or city you're visiting.

If your conversation begins to lag, food, the arts, and sports are generally good, safe topics to introduce to revive talk.

Gesturing appropriately

Contrary to what you may think, gestures don't have universal meanings. For example:

✔ In many parts of the world, a thumbs-up is an obscene gesture.

✔ People outside the United States, especially people from Asian countries, consider pointing the index finger rude.

✔ The American bye-bye gesture means "come here" to people from Southeast Asia.

✔ In Brazil and Portugal, the "okay" gesture that you make with your index finger and thumb is considered obscene.

✔ In Germany, you start counting on your fingers with your thumb, not your pointer finger, so if you hold up your pointer finger to indicate that you want one item, you may end up with two.

Make sure to study a guidebook for the country or countries you're visiting to find out which gestures and body language to avoid while you're there.

Making physical contact

Your body language can say as much about you as the words that come out of your mouth. In addition to gestures, which I describe in the preceding section, the appropriate level of physical contact varies greatly from culture to culture. The following are some examples:

✔ Japanese people don't approve of public body contact and thus have developed a complex system of bowing to express relationships. Touching a member of the opposite sex is particularly repugnant to Japanese sensitivities; consequently, they also consider kissing or any other form of body contact in public disgraceful.

✔ Many Asians believe that the head houses the soul. Therefore, if another person touches their heads, that action places them in jeopardy. As an outsider, avoid touching an Asian person's head and upper torso. Also avoid direct eye contact.

✔ Same-sex handholding between Asians, Middle Easterners, Latinos, and those from the Mediterranean countries is a sign of friendship. Walking with arms on each other's shoulders or with hands or arms linked also equates with camaraderie.

Keeping your distance (or not)

The need for some personal space is innate, but differences in how much space people from different cultures need can create uncomfortable situations. An American's personal space is much greater than that of an Arab or a Russian, but much smaller than that of someone from Great Britain.

Good manners dictate that whatever the social attitudes of the place you're visiting may be, you must try to follow them, even if they make you a bit uncomfortable or seem overly formal to you. Backing off when someone enters your personal space can send a negative message, just as stepping into someone's personal space can. Be wary of touching other people, too — even an arm on the shoulder or a pat on the back can violate someone's personal space.

Displaying emotion

Every culture has its own rules for how to show various emotions. Some cultures frown upon public expressions of sorrow or joy, and others encourage it. When you travel, understand what is acceptable by observing the natives. For example, the Japanese rarely express affection in public; the Chinese feel that emotional candor is rude; and showing your impatience is considered bad manners in the Middle East. On the other hand, people are very demonstrative in Italy, Spain, and some Latin American countries, for example. You don't need to change who you are when you're traveling, but accept others' manners while you're among them and blend in.

Meeting and greeting

As they say, you get only one chance to make a first impression. Therefore, you want to behave properly when you meet someone for the first time; I give you some guidelines in the following sections.

Every culture follows its own particulars when it comes to meeting and greeting, so it's wise to consult a guidebook for specific advice.

Checking out different gestures of greeting

A good greeting goes a long way. Following are some common forms of greeting that you may experience:

- ✔ The Japanese bow and smile when they greet others; handshakes are rare. The deeper and more numerous the bows, the greater the respect demonstrated.

- ✔ Indians and people from Buddhist countries lightly press their hands together as if praying and incline their heads at the same time.

    As a Westerner, you aren't expected to either bow or press your hands together. A Japanese or Indian person who knows Western ways may hold out his hand for you to shake instead, but waiting for that lead before offering your hand is best.

- ✔ The Chinese usually bow or nod their heads in greeting. If a Chinese person offers his hand, giving an American-style handshake is okay, but don't judge the person by the handshake, because it may not be as firm as a handshake that you'd expect from a fellow American.

- ✔ Europeans, Latin Americans, and people who have been educated in Western countries customarily shake hands when they're introduced, each time they meet, and when they part. Even children follow this custom, and not shaking hands is considered rude.

- ✔ In many European and Middle Eastern countries, friends kiss each other on the cheeks when they meet. Business associates most likely shake hands.

- ✔ In Austria, Germany, France, Italy, and Spain, a man may bow over the back of a woman's hand and make a gesture of kissing it — although these days, men shake women's hands more often than they kiss them. Because you never know which gesture a man may prefer, hold out your hand and prepare for either. If you're wearing gloves, don't bother to take them off, because the man doesn't actually kiss your hand, but instead raises it to within an inch or so of his lips.

Using names correctly

The American frontier left a strong tradition of being free and easy — including a casual use of names. Depending on where abroad you go, however, you may find that you have to make quick adjustments to the habit of automatically calling someone by her first name. Here are some points to remember about names:

- ✔ In Australia, Canada, and South Africa, the use of names (and titles, which are discussed in the following section) is similar to that in the United States. Although the rule against using first names isn't as strict in these countries as it is in Europe or South America, proceed slowly and wait for permission before you use a first name.

- In Europe and South America, you should never automatically call someone by his first name. Use the person's title and last name unless you're invited to do otherwise.

- In the Asian tradition, the order of first and last names is reversed.

- In some cultures, people avoid using names entirely and describe their social relationships instead. People in many cultures believe that addressing someone by her first name is disrespectful. Younger people in particular must take special care to address older people by their titles (or as custom dictates).

To avoid offending someone, asking which name(s) a person prefers is always safer. If a name is difficult to pronounce, admit that you're having difficulty and ask the person to help you say it correctly.

Addressing locals by their titles

People are rather sparing with the use of titles in the United States. This isn't the case in other countries. In the U.S., physicians, dentists, and ministers are almost always addressed with their title, but you address almost everyone else as plain Mr., Mrs., Miss, or Ms. When traveling abroad, however, you may find that people normally address each other with a variety of elaborate and often descriptive titles.

It may seem daunting, but using titles is one of the things that makes travel a learning experience. Keep in mind that titles are either hereditary or professional, which I describe in the following:

- Titles in the hereditary category are Prince, Duke, Marquis, Earl, Count, Viscount, Baron, Princess, Duchess, Countess, and so on. If you expect to meet titled people, you would be wise to study the correct use of hereditary titles.

- In the professional category, titles include Doctor, Professor, or the name of a specific profession, such as Architect, Engineer, or Lawyer.

When in doubt, try to follow the lead of others. Don't panic even though you may be confused. Most people don't expect visitors to know all the intricacies of names and titles. If you make a mistake and are corrected, politely apologize and repeat the name correctly.

Eating and drinking

When the phrase *when in Rome* was coined, it not only meant to embrace the customs and culture, but it also included trying the food and drink! If you're adventurous, food can be one of the best parts of traveling.

Although you may love to try new foods and experience new flavors, you may long for the tastes of home after a few days away. And if you travel to a time zone that's many hours earlier or later your own, your body clock may be so thrown off that you don't even know when to be hungry. Then you have to factor in the differences in table manners and eating habits from culture to culture: How do you know what to do? The following sections can help steer you around the gastronomical glitches that often trip up international travelers.

Adapting to local foods and mealtimes

Jet lag may have thrown you for a loop, but try to adjust to the eating habits and cuisines of the culture you're visiting. Here are some points to keep in mind about adapting to the local ways of eating:

- Although it may come as a shock to Americans who were taught that breakfast is the most important meal of the day, the American idea of a hearty breakfast is virtually unknown in most foreign countries. Europeans tend to drink a glass of fruit juice, eat a croissant or roll with butter and jelly, and follow it with a cup of strong coffee. Some people even skip the bread. In most countries, you're unlikely to find fried eggs and bacon, pancakes with maple syrup, and hash-browned potatoes. You may want to try carrying a piece of fruit as a midmorning snack on your first few days to get you to lunch.

- In some countries, all the retail stores close a few minutes before noon and don't reopen until midafternoon. Therefore, if you want to have an impulsive picnic, you must put your plans into action by 11:00 or 11:30 a.m. at the latest.

- In many countries, restaurants use the same menu for lunch and dinner; they have no such thing as a luncheon menu. Especially in warm climates, the fashion is to eat a hearty lunch, take a nap, and then resume activity in midafternoon. In such societies, dinner is eaten quite late — 9 or 10 p.m. — by North American standards.

In order to acclimate yourself to unusual meal hours, carry snacks and use them to tide you over to the next meal. Crackers, trail mix, and high-energy bars are all easy to carry and are lifesavers when you're running low on fuel.

You may occasionally face foods that repel you in taste, smell, or appearance. Try your best to grit your teeth, swallow, and smile. Depending on the country you're visiting, you may or may not offend your host if you leave something on your plate because it disagrees with you, so do some research a head of time for what is appropriate. No matter what culture and custom, you most likely *will* offend your host if you don't try the food because it's strange to you. Do your best to be a good sport, and you'll be fine.

Adjusting your table manners

If you follow proper American dining etiquette, you can do passably in most countries. However, you should note a few exceptions:

- In China, eating is communal; you use chopsticks to serve yourself from a large platter. Don't cross chopsticks — leave them on the chopstick rest or place them parallel across the top of a bowl. If you have problems managing chopsticks, you may lift your rice bowl to your mouth to scoop with your chopsticks or ask for a knife and fork. (For more on using chopsticks, see Chapter 12.)

- Asian restaurants provide toothpicks for you to use frequently and casually at the table. Just remember to shield your mouth with your other hand.

- In Europe, you find a slightly different table setting from the one that's common in the United States. For example, in France, the forks and spoons are placed upside down, the tines of the fork are down, and spoons turned over. Europeans eat their salad course last, so the salad fork is the one nearest the plate.

- The European method of using a knife and fork differs from the American way. But both systems are correct, so you don't have to change your method if you don't want to.

  If you don't want to stand out as an American, the first tip-off is your style of dining. If you're traveling in Europe, learn the Continental style (see Chapter 12), and you can blend right in. And when traveling in an Asian culture, learn the proper way to use chopsticks.

- In France, you rarely touch food with your fingers. French diners use their forks and knives in creative ways to manipulate and eat various foods that Americans pick up with their fingers.

- Some people in Middle Eastern countries and parts of India eat with the first three fingers of the right hand — never the left. Until you know the rules, keep your hands in your lap and watch the natives. After you get a sense of how things are done, you can give it a try yourself. However, your host may be able to provide you with Western utensils if you ask.

Many other subtle differences in table manners exist. Ask your host what to do if you're uncertain.

However you eat it, remember that leaving food on your plate or refusing a second helping at a meal in a private home may be considered impolite. You don't want to imply that you don't enjoy the food that was set before you. In the Middle East, refusing cups of tea or coffee, which are offered endlessly in homes, shops, and offices, is also insulting to the host.

Smoking in foreign lands

Although Americans have cut down on smoking and have outlawed it in many public places, the same rules don't necessarily apply in the rest of the world. Be prepared to find smokers in public, in private, and in transit. Smokers in public places in many foreign countries are within their legal rights, so you should either move away or put up with it. If you're highly sensitive to smoke, you should avoid bars and café areas that are frequented by smokers.

Playing it safe with beverages

When you eat, you drink, and in many countries, the drink you're served with lunch or dinner may well be alcoholic. Wherever your travels take you, being intoxicated isn't good manners. In many places, intoxication is considered a sign of bad breeding. Be careful with beer as well as wine. Beer in other countries is much stronger than American beer, and a bottle or two can pack a punch that you may not expect.

Tipping

Tipping after a meal varies from country to country and is custom-tailored to each culture. In the Far East, tipping is done very discreetly, whereas in Arab countries, it may be done with great fanfare. You leave a small tip at a café in France, but you don't leave a tip at many Italian espresso bars. Even in countries where service is included in the bill, leaving a small, additional tip is customary.

Restaurants often add on a certain percentage of the tab for service. If the restaurant at which you're dining engages in this practice, you can see the charge itemized on your bill. When the tip is built in, you can leave a small extra amount (somewhere between the foreign equivalent of $3 and $6) on the table.

Chapter 20

Being Sensitive about Disabilities and Illnesses

More than 54 million Americans have serious disabilities — vision, hearing, speech, mobility, and developmental impairments. Millions more have hidden disabilities, such as heart disease or AIDS. These individuals come from every ethnic group, religion, economic class, and age bracket. They also pursue every hobby, profession, and dream you can think of.

At times, communicating with those who are ill or have a disability can be awkward and uncomfortable. Usually, these barriers are created by a lack of awareness and thoughtlessness. The first key to sincere and thoughtful communication is to remember that the *person* isn't the *condition*. Avoid attitudes and language that could cause the person with the disability or illness feelings of isolation or an object of pity.

In this chapter, I give you guidance on behaving appropriately around people who have disabilities and illnesses.

Using People-First Terminology

If you care enough about social politeness to have purchased this book, you surely understand that certain expressions — such as "crip" — aren't respectful or acceptable. On the other hand, don't resort to euphemisms, either. Many disability groups consider terms such as *physically challenged* and *differently abled* patronizing.

A good general rule: Acknowledge the disability but place the person first. Simple as it may sound, if you use the term *person with a disability* rather than *disabled person,* you're off to a good start.

Here are some further guidelines:

- ✔ Individuals and conditions aren't synonymous; don't label a person with her disability or illness. Saying "a woman who has epilepsy" places the individual first; calling her "an epileptic" is judgmental.

- ✔ Refer to people without disabilities as *nondisabled* rather than able bodied or healthy. Many people with disabilities are in excellent health.

- ✔ The preferred term for a person who can't talk is *without speech* — not mute and certainly not dumb.

- ✔ Don't tie yourself in knots over the literal meaning of common expressions. It's okay to say "Do you see what I mean?" to a woman who is blind or to invite a man in a wheelchair to join you for a walk.

- ✔ Avoid the words *handicapped* and *crippled.* The more respectful choice is *disabled.*

- ✔ Don't refer to someone as "wheelchair-bound" or "confined to a wheelchair." The chair, in fact, is a freedom machine, affording independence and mobility.

- ✔ The word *invalid* implies a lack of validity. The terms *victim, afflicted with,* and *suffering from* carry negative — and often inaccurate — connotations. Even *courageous* and *inspirational* can seem patronizing to a person engaged in a normal, busy life — would you say "You're so courageous" to a person wearing glasses to correct poor eyesight? Try to focus on the interests and accomplishments of people with disabilities or illnesses, distinct from their challenges.

- ✔ Avoid asking a person with an illness (as well as the nurses and the doctors) about the person's prognosis or when he may be going home. Refrain from asking, "How are you?" Keep in mind that most people prefer not to discuss their illnesses. Show your sincerity by saying something along the lines of, "I've been thinking about you."

- ✔ Never make comments on how a person with an illness looks, whether frail or strong. Instead, ask if you can do anything for her or bring something to her.

Understanding the Rules of Disability Etiquette

Fear of the unknown and lack of knowledge about how to act can cause nervousness when meeting a person who has a disability. Certain rules of disability etiquette — such as never feeding a guide dog — are hard and fast. Others are more fluid, because the individuals involved don't always agree on what is offensive or correct.

In most encounters with a person with a disability, you behave exactly as you would with anyone else. Don't stare. Don't look away as if he doesn't exist. Talk to the person, not to the companion pushing the wheelchair, acting as interpreter, or sitting in the adjacent seat on the plane.

Offering to help a person with a disability is never wrong, but if the person declines your assistance, never insist. If she accepts, ask for specific instructions and follow them. Talk about the person's disability if the subject comes up naturally, but don't pry.

The guidelines in the following sections can help you behave graciously toward people with a range of disabilities. But the most important rule is this: If you ever have a question — what to do, how to do it, how to say it — the person with the disability is always your first and best resource.

Mobility impairment

Despite that universal sign of disability, not everyone with a mobility impairment uses a wheelchair. A man with rheumatoid arthritis in his hands has limited mobility. So does a woman weakened by a stroke.

Ideally, your behavior toward people with mobility impairments affirms their dignity. Here are some guidelines:

✔ Shake the hand that's extended to you. If you're offered the person's prosthesis or hook, shake that hand. If you're offered the left hand, you can shake it with your right. If shaking hands isn't an option, touch the person on the shoulder or arm as a sign of greeting and acknowledgment.

- When greeting a person in a motorized wheelchair, wait until he shuts off the power before shaking hands. You don't want to activate the controls inadvertently.

- Never move mobility aids, such as crutches, out of a person's reach.

- Don't push a wheelchair without offering first. If your offer is accepted, respect your limitations. If you don't think that you're strong enough to push the chair up a ramp or over a curb, let the person know.

- A wheelchair is part of its user's personal space. Never lean or hang on it.

- When speaking with a person in a wheelchair for more than a few minutes, place yourself at her eye level. Doing so is not only more respectful, but it's also easier on the person's neck. If you can pull up a chair, great — you'll both be more comfortable. You can also try squatting or kneeling if you have sturdy knees.

- Some illnesses hinder one's ability to do some tasks. For example, someone with arthritis may have difficulty opening a jar. If you notice someone struggling, you can politely offer to help.

Vision impairment

Not all people with visual impairments live in a world of total darkness. Those individuals with tunnel vision can look into your eyes when they speak with you but see nothing in the periphery. Peripheral vision — the loss of central vision — is the reverse. Other people experience spotted, blurred, or double vision in the entire visual field.

Whatever the degree of disability, use common sense and empathy when you deal with people who have vision impairments, as I describe in the following sections.

Using words rather than gestures

People with vision impairments often can't see your face well enough to identify you. They aren't aware that you've extended your hand for a handshake, and they can't perceive when you shrug your shoulders, nod your head, or raise your eyebrows in surprise. Remember to use words instead, such as in the following examples:

- Introduce yourself and anyone with you when you first approach. "Hi, Mr. Eliot. It's Daphne Jones. And I have Maria Perez here with me, to your left. Shall we shake hands?"

✔ Never leave without saying that you're leaving. The person may think that there was simply a pause in the conversation and start talking to thin air. Even if you only move from one end of the couch to the other, let the person know.

✔ Particularly in business settings or large groups, use names with every exchange so that the person with vision impairment knows who's talking to whom. "Valerie? John here. Can you give us the latest on the Mitchell account?" In a small group of friends, though, the person is more likely to recognize voices.

✔ Offer to read written material out loud. For example, "This box has lots of instructions. Shall I read them to you?"

✔ If you see a person with a visual impairment in a potentially dangerous situation, voice your concerns calmly and concisely.

Offering help politely

People with vision impairments use many tools to navigate smoothly in the world. Some carry canes. Others are accompanied by guide dogs (I discuss these marvelous animals later in this chapter). It's always appropriate to offer to help someone with a visual impairment. Do so politely, and don't be offended if your offer is refused.

Here are some types of help that you may want to offer:

✔ If you're asked to act as a guide, offer your elbow rather than grabbing the person's arm. He will probably walk slightly behind you to follow the motion of your body. Describe the route as you walk: "We have three steps coming up." Pause before the steps, but don't stop.

✔ When walking with a vision-impaired companion, describe your surroundings, not only to alert the person to obstacles but also to share the scene. Describe the layout of a room, the view out a window, and so on.

Give your descriptive powers free rein. A person of few words isn't a good companion to a person who is visually impaired.

✔ If you lead a person to a seat, place her hand on the back of the chair. If you leave her standing in unfamiliar surroundings, make sure that she can touch something — a wall or a table, for example — so that she isn't left uncomfortably isolated.

✔ When giving directions, be as specific as you can: "You'll go 200 yards and then make a 90-degree turn to the left around the corner of the building." Detail any obstacles along the route.

✔ Leave doors and cupboards either all the way open or all the way closed.

✔ At a meal, relate where dishes and utensils are placed on the table. Use the face of a clock to describe the food on a plate: "You've got potatoes at 1 o'clock, Brussels sprouts at 4 o'clock, and turkey at 9 o'clock. Do you need some help cutting the turkey?"

✔ Describe any item exchanging hands. If you're handing over several objects, describe their relationship to one another so that the person doesn't take hold of one item and drop the others: "Here's your costume for the play. The robe's on the bottom, and then the shoes, and the crown's on top."

✔ When exchanging money, separate the bills into denominations and hand over the stacks one at a time: "Here's four fives and two ones." You don't need to separate the coins, which are easy to identify by feel: "And 62 cents in change."

✔ If a person with a visual impairment needs to sign a document, guide his hand to the signature line and offer a straight edge — a ruler or a card — for alignment.

A final reminder: Never move items in the home or workplace of a person with impaired sight. Yes, that vase may look nicer on the mantle, but moving it is the equivalent of hiding it from a person who can see. And moving furniture can be downright hazardous.

Hearing impairment

Hearing impairment can range from complete deafness to mild hearing loss, and unless you notice a hearing aid, the disability tends to be hidden. Be alert to the possibility of deafness when a person doesn't respond to audible cues.

To get the attention of someone with a hearing disability, tap her lightly on the shoulder or give a visual signal, such as a wave. Establish how you plan to communicate. Some people who are deaf can speak, and others can't. Not everyone with a hearing impairment can read lips; even those who lip-read catch maybe four out of ten words and rely heavily on facial expressions and body language.

In the following sections, I provide guidance on two methods of communication you can use with folks who have hearing impairments: lip reading and American Sign Language.

Never shout at a person with a hearing impairment. If the person is deaf, shouting won't do a bit of good. If the person is hard of hearing — especially if he uses a hearing aid — shouting distorts the sound and can even be painful or dangerous.

Lip reading

Even the best hearing aids can't keep the hearing impaired from having trouble understanding speech. Lip reading is a skill that those individuals with hearing difficulties must learn, but isn't considered a substitute for hearing. *Lip reading* trains one's eyes to recognize movements of the lips when pronouncing words. The term *speech reading* also includes watching movements of the face and body.

To facilitate lip reading or speech reading, do the following:

✔ Position yourself so that you're facing both the light source and the person you're speaking to. Don't walk around while you converse.

✔ Speak clearly, slowly, naturally, and expressively. Never over enunciate or exaggerate your lip movements; doing so makes lip reading more difficult, plus you'll look very silly.

✔ Don't eat, chew gum, or smoke while you're talking. Gesture with your hands with abandon, but don't block your face. If you have a mustache, try brushing it away from your upper lip.

✔ Rather than repeating a sentence, try rewording it. "I'll scoop you up at six" may be hard to lip-read; "Wait for me after your meeting" may be fine.

✔ If necessary, write notes, but don't talk and write at the same time.

American Sign Language

Many people in the United States use American Sign Language to communicate. ASL isn't a universal language, although some signs are similar worldwide. If you know even minimal sign language, try using it. If an interpreter is present, observe the following etiquette:

✔ The interpreter should sit or stand next to you, facing the person who is deaf or hard of hearing.

✔ Maintain eye contact with the person with the hearing disability, even though that person will be looking between the interpreter and you.

✔ The interpreter may lag a few words behind you, especially when finger spelling. Pause occasionally so that she can catch up.

✔ In a business situation, never consult the interpreter — he's present only to facilitate communication. In a social situation, include the interpreter in a friendly manner, but remember to maintain eye contact with whomever you're addressing.

Speech impairment

A person whose speech is impaired due to cerebral palsy may pronounce each word with difficulty. Another person may speak flawlessly for phrases at a time and then block or stutter. Whatever the cause, and whatever the manifestation, the etiquette toward people with speech impairments remains the same, as you can see in the following:

✔ Give the person speaking your full, relaxed attention. Be patient and encouraging.

✔ Speak normally, without raising your voice. Most people with speech impairments have no problem hearing.

✔ Never supply a word unless you're asked to do so. Always allow the person to finish what she's trying to say. Your impulse may be to help, especially when you see how much effort the person is putting into the attempt, but be patient.

✔ Keep your questions simple. If possible, ask questions that the person can answer with short responses or with a shake or nod of the head.

✔ Never pretend that you understand if you don't. Repeating what you think you heard to make sure that you heard correctly is okay: "You'll be catching a 6:00 flight and need to be at the airport by 5:00. Is that right?"

✔ Pen and paper are wonderful inventions. Offer them to the person with a speech impairment in an encouraging manner — never as an act of impatience.

Guide and service animals

A guide dog leading a blind person is a familiar image in our culture. But did you know that carefully bred and trained dogs serve as partners to individuals with a range of disabilities? Service dogs can conduct business transactions for people in wheelchairs, passing money to cashiers and accepting change and packages. They turn lights on and off, help their partners get in and out of bed, and even pick up the laundry — although, like many humans, they have to be told to do so.

A person who is deaf may wake up in the morning to a Corgi or Labrador jumping on his bed. His "hearing dog" will alert him with a gentle paw prod when he hears certain sounds — a smoke alarm, a doorbell, or even his handler's name spoken in the workplace — and then go sit by the sound.

Guide and service dogs make constant decisions that impact the welfare of their human companions. They have an important job to do, and frequently a hazardous one. Never distract them. Your actions toward these dedicated animals aren't just a question of politeness, but also of safety.

Here are some additional points to remember:

- Never touch guide or service animals unless the handler gives you permission to do so, particularly while it's doing its job in public. The rules may be more relaxed at home; still, always ask.

- Never call a dog's name or try to get its attention.

- Traffic presents particular hazards to guide dogs and their handlers. Streets are busier and wider than ever, and cars are quieter. You may think that honking your horn or calling out that the road is clear would be helpful, but it would only be distracting, so please refrain from doing so.

- Never, ever feed working dogs. Don't even offer them water without asking first. These animals have feeding schedules and relieving schedules, and disturbing their routine can be, at best, an inconvenience. If you sneak a guide dog a snack and the dog becomes ill, you could put the dog's handler in danger.

- Puppies in training, like their working counterparts, can go many places where pets can't, accompanied by their nondisabled trainers. They usually wear identifying jackets. Treat puppies in training the way you would treat fully trained guide or service dogs so that they can learn their job.

- You may be tempted to ooh and ahh when you see a scene as endearing as a service dog carefully placing a package in its handler's lap. Go ahead and express yourself, as long as you don't distract the dog, but first make eye contact with the handler. As always, the first rule of etiquette toward people with disabilities is to put the person first — before the disability, before the wheelchair, and before the dog.

Dealing with Disability Issues in the Workplace

Whether you work with someone who has a disability or a chronic illness or you interact with them as clients, you're likely to be in contact with people with disabilities in the workplace. If you combine the business etiquette pointers from Chapter 11 with the guidelines in this chapter and throw in a healthy dose of common sense, you'll do fine. Here, however, are a few additional thoughts:

- ✔ Familiarize yourself with the location of accessible elevators, restrooms, and drinking fountains in your workplace.

- ✔ Learn about the assistive technologies (such as the following) that your co-workers use, and adapt your presentations and communications to accommodate them:

  - High-tech devices of all kinds are available to individuals with limited mobility.

  - People with vision impairments use scanners to move text from page to computer and screen-reading software to synthesize the words on the screen.

  - People with hearing impairments use telecommunications devices for the deaf (TDDs) or similar tools.

For more info on assistive computer technologies, you can check out Apple Computer's accessibility Web site at www.apple.com/ accessibility (for Mac users). For additional computer and software resources and new technologies, visit www.makoa.org/ computers.htm.

- ✔ If you own a business, make every effort to hire workers with disabilities and to implement Americans with Disabilities Act (ADA) requirements. You may be surprised how little it costs to fully accommodate a worker with a disability, and what a tremendous contribution that worker can make to your company.

- ✔ Make the effort to court clients who are disabled as well; doing so makes good business sense.

- ✔ Consider creating a text-only version of your Web site. Complex formatting and graphics are difficult for screen readers to translate. Nondisabled individuals with slower computers will appreciate the version, too.

The National Organization on Disability (NOD) is a great place to start if you want to discover more about disability issues. On its Web site (www.nod. org), you can find Frequently Asked Questions, a summary of the Americans with Disabilities Act (ADA), links to other sites, and more. Or contact the organization for information: National Organization on Disability, 910 16th St. NW, Suite 600, Washington, DC 20006.

Doing the Right Thing When Someone Has an Illness or Serious Injury

Patients, families, and caregivers dealing with life-threatening illnesses face many challenges. A diagnosis of an illness or severe injury of any kind can be devastating and can bring a multitude of emotions from fear to resentment, or denial. Not everyone diagnosed wants to talk about the illness and many may not want to let family members or friends know about it.

The following list provides some guidelines on what to say and do when you someone you know has been seriously injured or diagnosed with an illness:

- When you want to know what to say, you can't really find one right answer or any magic words. Most patients appreciate your thoughtfulness when you just say, "I'm sorry."

- Offering advice on a particular form of treatment or diet or talking about other's experiences *isn't* the best choice. Many times, the conversation can depend on the mood of the patient; she may want you to talk about everything except her illness or not to say a word. If and when appropriate, you can remind a person with an illness that many people survive the same diagnosis and live to a ripe old age.

- Avoid saying something like, "I understand your situation." The person has many different decisions to make, and many times you don't know what you would do.

- You can provide support by being a good listener. Normally, what you say isn't what matters most, but how you listen. More than anything, newly diagnosed patients need to express their feelings, whether the emotion is anger, fear, or helplessness. You can help by encouraging the person to talk about his feelings.

- Just spending time with the person and providing encouragement can make a difference. You can ask what you can do to help with practical things, such as accompanying her to doctor's appointments, running errands, housecleaning, or preparing meals.

- The best way to support a friend or relative who is ill is to remember to take care of *you*. You can do this by joining a support group that provides you with education and help when you're feeling helpless or overwhelmed. To find information on support groups and organizations near you, contact your city or county offices, your local hospital, or a hospice care organization.

Visiting the Sick in the Hospital and at Home

Visiting a sick relative or friend in the hospital can be an uncomfortable experience. This task is often difficult because most people have no training in this field and find it hard to know what to say, how to act, and when to end the visit. Try to keep the important part in mind — that you're visiting not just because it is the polite thing to do, or to meet your own needs, but to meet the needs of the ill person. Besides cheering someone up, you make him feel cared for.

Here are a few guidelines you can follow when visiting the sick:

- ✔ Close friends and relatives should visit before casual acquaintances.

- ✔ Don't just show up at the hospital; always check visiting hours, and if possible, call first to see whether the patient can have visitors.

- ✔ Ask ahead whether flowers or food items are allowed. Many times scents and strong fragrances can be bothersome to the patient.

- ✔ Always call ahead before going to someone's home. Ask for a convenient time to visit or if you can relieve the caretaker so she can run errands.

- ✔ Offer to run errands for a caretaker.

- ✔ Always remember to wash your hands before and after a visit.

- ✔ Be certain to knock before entering the patient's room.

- ✔ Never sit on the patient's bed unless you ask first. Stand or sit in a chair so he can easily see you and hear you.

- ✔ Speak softly so you don't bother other patients. Do your best to keep conversations upbeat by not bringing up negative topics, gossip, or talk about your own or other's health problems.

- ✔ If the patient brings up an emotional subject or speaks of being afraid, don't change the subject; this is the time to listen compassionately. What you say to a person who is sick isn't what matters most to her, but instead, how you listen.

- ✔ If you're at a loss for words, you can ask whether you can do anything. If you're comfortable, offer to read to the patient or ask if you can say a prayer.

- ✔ Talking isn't always necessary; sometimes just having company quietly sitting in the room can bring much comfort.

✔ Don't be in a rush to leave or stay too long. Fifteen to 20 minutes is appropriate.

✔ If visiting someone in the hospital, say hello, smile, and be friendly to the other patients. It could be an opportunity to make new friends or cheer up someone who may be afraid or lonely.

Talking to Your Children about People with Disabilities and Illnesses

Many children already know a person with a disability or a chronic illness, perhaps a grandparent who has arthritis or uses a walker, or a classmate at school. Use these experiences as a springboard for discussion. Explain that people of all ages have disabilities and why: an accident, an illness, or simply the way the person was born. Let your children know that having a disability or an illness is okay, a fact of life, and that these people can still do many things.

Some children, if given inadvertent free rein, will walk up to a person with a disability, tug on her sleeve, and say, "You look funny." The proclamation isn't a so much a judgment as a statement of fact, a manifestation of the child's curiosity about the world. Make sure that your child knows that saying or doing anything that can hurt a person's feelings is never okay. At the same time, don't discourage the child's natural curiosity. The worst thing you can tell a child — unless you first explain why — is not to stare. Doing so is as good as saying, "Let's pretend the person with crutches doesn't exist."

If your child is curious about a person's wheelchair — or her white cane, or his life — explain that asking questions is okay, but that it's also okay if the person doesn't really want to talk. If possible, make eye contact with the person who has the disability or illness. If he seems receptive to your child, approach, let the child say, "Could I ask you a question?" and see what happens. Many people with disabilities or illnesses are very willing to respond to children's questions, especially because a child's reaction to the answer is likely to be, "Oh, neat." No discomfort, no fear.

However, some children may have unexpressed fears, and talking through the issues and answering their questions can help them overcome these obstacles. Before talking to your children about people with differing disabilities or illnesses, you need to dispel misconceptions. When discussing the topic, be sensitive, positive, and candid. Teach children the appropriate terms to be used; for example, don't say "the autistic child," but rather, "the child with autism." Remind children the importance of being accepting of others with differing abilities, that everyone requires the same needs in life, to be treated with respect, friendship, and love.

If children today feel at ease around people with disabilities, adults tomorrow will feel the same way. Everyone wants their children to be polite. If they happen to grow up to make the world a better place, that's okay, too.

Part VI
The Part of Tens

The 5th Wave   By Rich Tennant

"What did you mean when you said you were 'covering your bases' when meeting people here in Japan?"

In this part . . .

1f you're just looking for a quick etiquette lesson or two, this part is for you. Here, you can find ten etiquette points to teach your children and teenagers and ten tipping situations and how to handle them.

Chapter 21

Ten Etiquette Tips for Children and Teens

In This Chapter

▶ Modeling respectful behavior

▶ Practicing etiquette with your children and praising your children's efforts

As you're probably aware, social graces at home and within the classroom aren't what they should be today. Parents and teachers are constantly bombarded with rudeness from their children and students. And all too often, the students and children aren't even aware that they're being rude!

Although etiquette should be taught in the home, the sad reality is that it often isn't, creating a difficult situation within the home and classroom: How do you teach "the basics" when the students can't even behave in a way that is conducive to learning?

When it comes to teaching manners to kids, the phrase "monkey see, monkey do" says it all. Children learn by example. As an adult, the way you behave around kids speaks volumes. This rule goes double for the youngest children, who may not yet understand verbal instructions — but believe me, they watch every move you make!

Inevitably, your child will ask, "Why do I have to learn about etiquette?" You can respond by explaining that you show who you are by how you behave and appear to others. Behavior and appearance refer to the way you look, the way you talk, and the way you walk and sit and stand — just about everything you do!

Children can begin learning manners beginning at age 2 and continue learning through their teenage years. This chapter outlines the ten most important lessons to teach children regarding good manners.

Be Respectful

The rules of etiquette were created as a way to show respect for yourself as well as for others. Living your life in a respectful way is the best way to teach your children respect. Children watch their parents closely and begin learning from them at a very young age, so be gracious and courteous in the way you treat your spouse, your neighbors, and even strangers, such as the checkout person at the grocery store. In this way, you demonstrate how your children should treat others. Make sure to include elders, people of other religions and cultures, and people with disabilities when you teach your children about respect. (See Chapter 2 for more details about becoming a model of good manners.)

Children learn to respect others when they're respected as individuals. Make a conscious effort to respect your children's privacy and time. For example, don't just barge in unannounced if your child's bedroom door is closed — knock first! Show your child that you respect the need to have time alone.

Speak and Listen Courteously

The fastest way to show your good manners is to say "Please," "Thank you," "Excuse me," and "I'm sorry." (This rule applies to both children and adults.) You can begin teaching your children these simple words when they're toddlers.

Although what you say is important, the way you say it is just as important. Again, teaching by example is best. Don't allow yourself to scream and yell around the house. Don't argue with your spouse in front of your children. Settle disputes quietly. If you find yourself in an argument with your children, have them go to their rooms to take a timeout before the argument gets too heated.

Nip your children's poor conversation and listening habits in the bud. Bad listening habits include appearing impatient, completing other people's sentences, failing to respond, changing the subject, interrupting, neglecting to make eye contact, making wisecracks, talking back, and walking away during a conversation. The appropriate way to address your child's poor listening and conversation habits is to step in and correct the situation as it happens. For example, if Susie just jumped in and began talking over her younger brother, who was telling a story, you can say, "Susie, I believe Sam was in the middle of a story. Why don't we let him finish? When Sam's done, you can tell us all about your science teacher."

Share and Share Alike

One manners mantra is to treat people the way you want others to treat you. What better rationale exists for sharing? Opportunities for teaching your children to share include sharing toys with friends and siblings and taking turns in the bathroom. These lessons can begin when they're toddlers (although they often take years to fully sink in!). Remember, the more patient you are, the more progress they ultimately make. As your children get older, you can take sharing to another level by showing them how to share their time and talents with others.

Look Good and Feel Good

What's the use of having good manners if you have dirty fingernails, bad breath, or a shirt with holes in it? You can teach children that grooming and dressing properly show the world that you care about yourself.

Children need to learn to take care of themselves on a daily basis. Teaching your children to get enough sleep, exercise, shower or bathe, comb their hair, brush their teeth, and eat right gives them a sense of independence and responsibility that nurtures their self-respect. These consistent activities can become rituals, which provide a sense of security for children.

As kids get older, they sometimes experiment with hairstyles. Don't let your children's hairstyles alarm you — sometimes you have to let children have some freedom. Even if a child's hair is purple, you can still insist that it be clean. This same principle applies to clothing. Children, especially as they become young adults, like to push the envelope by wearing outfits that adults may consider over the top. When it comes to school, though, children need to understand that dressing appropriately means wearing clothes that aren't too short, too long, too tight, too big, or too see-through. Children don't have to look dowdy or hide their bodies in sacks, but their appearances doesn't need to embarrass anyone or make others feel uncomfortable. Whatever your children wear, teach them that the most important thing is that their clothes are clean and neat. (Head to Chapter 3 for full details on presenting yourself properly.)

When children are young, you may want to try to set boundaries about dress that respects the views of both the parent and child. This stops you from constantly saying, "You're not really going out of the house like that, are you?"

Help Around the House

Performing chores with patience and a light heart (in a happy mood, so to speak) is one of the biggest etiquette lessons that you can teach children. I always told my children that being grumpy doesn't make the chores go away; it just makes you feel bad while you do them. Doing chores with energy, on the other hand, makes you feel good — the work gets done quickly, and you can then enjoy other parts of your life.

Having your children perform jobs around the house teaches them to do things for themselves. Giving children tasks, such as setting the table, taking out the garbage, keeping their rooms clean, and feeding pets, gives them a sense of responsibility. Even at the age of 3 or 4, children can have chores, such as picking up toys when they're done playing or putting their clothes in the laundry hamper. As your children grow, give them slightly more complicated tasks and more responsibilities. Always praise them when the chores are completed.

By keeping your home tidy, you show your children that keeping their own space clean is important, too. Tell your children that having a neat, uncluttered home shows others that you respect yourself and your living space. (It also enables you to be ready to invite guests into your home at any time without embarrassment!) Nagging, threatening, or issuing ultimatums about housework rarely works. After a while, leading by example makes your message clear. The more they practice doing chores and taking care of other responsibilities, the more they can enjoy all the parts of their lives. Chapter 4 has more information on maintaining household harmony.

Meet and Greet with Manners

Remember the awkwardness you felt as a kid when you met adults? Even though meeting people seems routine to adults, kids wonder what they should say to someone they don't know. How do you find out who the person you're meeting is?

I teach kids that the best thing to do is to make it easy for the other person by talking about yourself. Tell your children to smile and then say in a clear voice, "Hello [or Hi], my name is _____, and I'm _____." For example, your child may say, "I'm a senior at Westmore High," or "I'm a freshman at Stanford this year," or "I live across the street." Kids should take their time, relax, and talk in their normal voice when they introduce themselves — tell them not to mumble!

As for the ever-so-scary handshake, tell your kids to extend their right hand in greeting and then shake hands with the other person while introducing themselves. Hold the person's entire hand, fingers, and palm to where the thumbs meet and cross over each other. Then squeeze firmly (not too hard!) and shake three times, being sure to look at the other person's eyes when introducing themselves.

Check out Chapter 7 for more details about making proper introductions.

Practice Table Manners

As with any performance, practicing before a big event, such as going out to a restaurant, is a good idea. I know of people who dress their kids up, sit them down at the family dining room table, and hand out homemade menus to practice eating out!

Even if you don't do a full dress rehearsal before you go to a restaurant, teach your children the proper way to act at the table. No matter how rushed your schedule is, don't have pizza in front of the television all the time. A couple of times a week, make the effort to have a sit-down dinner so that your children can learn table manners. Start with the basics: Don't eat until everyone sits down, don't talk about unpleasant subjects, and don't grab for food — wait for dishes to be passed around the table. (See Chapter 12 for much more on table manners.)

Be a Good Guest (And a Good Host)

Being a good guest is something that you can teach your children early. Kids can learn the importance of RSVPing promptly, bringing a gift to a party, and writing thank-you notes, for example. If the neighbor's 8-year-old son invites your 8-year-old son to his birthday party, for example, you can have your child call his friend to accept the invitation. He can then help you select a birthday present. With a little prodding, you may get him to write a thank-you note, too! See Chapter 15 for more on being a gracious guest.

Teaching kids how to be gracious hosts is also a good idea. You can allow your own children to greet your guests, answer the door, take coats, and so on to teach them proper party etiquette. Head to Chapter 14 for details on being a good host.

Respect All Cultures

You and your children live in a multicultural world, which creates the need for many new rules of etiquette. As an adult, you set an example for your children when you pay attention to your behavior and comments about others, especially when it comes to people of a different race or religion whose customs and cultures are unfamiliar to you.

I find that sitting down with children to explain child-rearing differences in various cultures is helpful. For example, some cultures give priority to family loyalty; therefore, their children may miss school to help support their families. Likewise, other children may celebrate holidays and practice customs that yours may not. For example, other children may have been raised to remove their shoes when entering a home. Tell your kids that if they notice shoes outside a friend's front door, they should remove their own shoes as well. (This goes for all types of customs — you should follow suit when you're in someone else's home.)

See Chapter 19 for more information about multicultural etiquette.

Focus on the Positive

Remember to stay consistent and correct your children's behavior without accusing, berating, or talking down to them. The point of teaching children manners is to build self-esteem and self-confidence. Explain to them that these rules are important because they're really acts of kindness and consideration for others.

When a child does something correctly — such as holding a door for someone — make sure that you acknowledge the kind deed. However, if your child gets confused and makes a mistake, it's not the end of the world. I used to tell my boys that mistakes happen — life isn't perfect, and neither are we!

Let your kids continue through life, and correct their behavior and praise them when the opportunity presents itself. When children behave well, parents should acknowledge their good deeds, which reinforces good behavior. Tell your children often that you love them and that you appreciate their courteous behavior.

Chapter 22

Ten (Or So) Tips for Tipping Appropriately

The word *tip* comes from an old innkeeper's sign, "To Insure Promptness." When patrons deposited a few coins, they received their drinks faster. Today, you give a tip to someone who performs a service for you. Figuring out how to tip (and especially how to figure the tip gracefully without involving others at the table) is an important skill. This chapter discusses ten (or so) situations in which tips are expected and helps you figure out how much to tip which people.

In general, you can tip less than is suggested in this chapter if the person providing the service performs that service in a substandard manner. You're justified in forgoing a tip if the person is hostile or rude.

Having a Drink at a Bar

If you sit at a bar and have a drink, tip the bartender 10 to 15 percent of the tab. If you sit at a table in a cocktail lounge, tip the cocktail server 15 to 20 percent, depending on the quality of service.

Receiving Assistance in Selecting a Bottle of Wine

Give the wine steward or sommelier a tip that equals up to 15 percent of the cost of the wine. Give this tip in addition to the normal tip to your server of 15 to 20 percent of the cost of the meal, including wine.

If you can't discreetly hand the sommelier a cash tip, you can simply include the amount on the bill as part of the entire tip. (Today, the standard for excellent service in an upscale restaurant is edging toward 20 percent before sales tax. But if you aren't in a big city or a fine restaurant, you can get away with 15 percent.) In most fine restaurants, the server shares the tips with the others who serve the table.

Being Attended to in a Restroom

Give a men's or ladies' room attendant 50 cents to $1 for providing a hand towel, which is a standard service. Tip another $1 for any additional service that the attendant provides, such as helping you remove a stain or providing hairspray or cologne.

Checking Your Coat with a Cloakroom Attendant

Tip a cloakroom attendant $1 per coat that you check. If you hang two coats on one hanger, add another $1 for the additional coat.

Dining in a Sit-Down Restaurant

Tipping today is more of a payment for the service than a generous impulse on the behalf of the customer. At most restaurants, you should tip between 17 and 20 percent of the before-tax amount of the bill. Usually, you can use the sales tax as a guide by simply doubling the amount of tax, which gives you about a 16.5 percent tip. When in doubt, leave a little extra. Over tip only if it is well deserved.

If you happen to receive good service but a not-so-good meal, you still tip for the service. But you can discreetly mention your disappointment in the meal to the manager or owner. Giving a tip of less than 17 percent in a restaurant should only be done if the service is poor.

If you frequent the same restaurant often, you may want to leave a higher tip so you are remembered when you return and hopefully receive better service.

Eating at a Lunch Counter or Buffet

If you eat at a lunch counter, tip 15 percent of the bill. If you eat a meal at a buffet-style restaurant, a 10 percent tip for the person who services your table is appropriate.

Ordering Takeout Delivery

Tip food delivery people a minimum of $2. If you ordered a large quantity of food, such as two large bags of takeout food or enough pizzas for a large party, tip $5. If the weather is inclement, please be more generous — add another $1 or $2 to the tip.

Hiring a Babysitter

Depending on where you live, a babysitter customarily receives anywhere from no tip to a 20 percent tip on the total amount you paid.

If you're unsure of what your sitter expects, check with other local mothers or ask the sitter what she normally receives.

Giving gifts as tips

Although people who expect a tip generally prefer to receive cash, on a few occasions you may give a small gift to express your appreciation instead. You may want to give a gift to the housekeeper or maid if you stay in someone's private home, for example. Giving a gift as a tip to the owners of a bed and breakfast, a hotel manager, or an official who has gone out of the way to assist you is also acceptable. An appropriate gift is a gift certificate to a nearby restaurant or shop, a flowering plant, or an engraved item, such as a pen or business card holder.

Having an Appointment at a Hair Salon or Spa

Give your barber or hairstylist a 15 to 20 percent tip if you're having a cut, color, or perm. If you have a separate colorist and stylist, each person should receive 15 to 20 percent of the cost of the particular service that he or she provided. If you're having your hair set or washed and blow-dried, a 20 percent tip is sufficient.

If other people in the salon help you (for example, if a junior assistant washes your hair), tip each of them a few dollars for their services. If you have a manicure or pedicure, tip the manicurist a minimum of $3 or 15 percent of the cost of the manicure or pedicure.

Taking a Taxi

A taxi driver who operates on a meter system should receive a 15 percent tip (with $1 as the minimum tip). For a $5 ride, tip $1. If the ride is a long one, pay 20 percent in tips.

In cities in which a zone system is in place, you tip for shorter rides by rounding up to the nearest dollar. For example, if your bill is $4.60, pay the driver $5. If the bill is much higher, again, tip 20 percent of the total fare.

You may alter your tip accordingly, depending on the circumstances. For example, if the driver takes the long route and runs up the fare, you can omit the tip. On the other hand, if you're caught in a traffic jam, you should pay slightly more than normal, because a driver loses money during the waiting period. If, say, you're stuck in traffic for ten minutes and the meter reads $10.50 when you reach your destination, you may want to raise your usual $2 tip to $3. If the driver gives you assistance with your luggage an extra tip of $1 to $2 dollars is expected.

Utilizing a Bellhop's or Skycap's Services

Tip bellhops and skycaps a minimum of $1 per bag. If you have a lot of luggage, you may want to add more. For three bags, for example, it would be courteous to give $5.

Every time a bellhop brings something to your room, tip $2. If the bellhop runs a special errand for you — to pick up a particular newspaper, for example — tip $5.

Index

• D •

• *G* •

• Z •

BUSINESS, CAREERS & PERSONAL FINANCE

0-7645-9847-3   0-7645-2431-3

Also available:
- Business Plans Kit For Dummies 0-7645-9794-9
- Economics For Dummies 0-7645-5726-2
- Grant Writing For Dummies 0-7645-8416-2
- Home Buying For Dummies 0-7645-5331-3
- Managing For Dummies 0-7645-1771-6
- Marketing For Dummies 0-7645-5600-2
- Personal Finance For Dummies 0-7645-2590-5*
- Resumes For Dummies 0-7645-5471-9
- Selling For Dummies 0-7645-5363-1
- Six Sigma For Dummies 0-7645-6798-5
- Small Business Kit For Dummies 0-7645-5984-2
- Starting an eBay Business For Dummies 0-7645-6924-4
- Your Dream Career For Dummies 0-7645-9795-7

HOME & BUSINESS COMPUTER BASICS

0-470-05432-8   0-471-75421-8

Also available:
- Cleaning Windows Vista For Dummies 0-471-78293-9
- Excel 2007 For Dummies 0-470-03737-7
- Mac OS X Tiger For Dummies 0-7645-7675-5
- MacBook For Dummies 0-470-04859-X
- Macs For Dummies 0-470-04849-2
- Office 2007 For Dummies 0-470-00923-3
- Outlook 2007 For Dummies 0-470-03830-6
- PCs For Dummies 0-7645-8958-X
- Salesforce.com For Dummies 0-470-04893-X
- Upgrading & Fixing Laptops For Dummies 0-7645-8959-8
- Word 2007 For Dummies 0-470-03658-3
- Quicken 2007 For Dummies 0-470-04600-7

FOOD, HOME, GARDEN, HOBBIES, MUSIC & PETS

0-7645-8404-9   0-7645-9904-6

Also available:
- Candy Making For Dummies 0-7645-9734-5
- Card Games For Dummies 0-7645-9910-0
- Crocheting For Dummies 0-7645-4151-X
- Dog Training For Dummies 0-7645-8418-9
- Healthy Carb Cookbook For Dummies 0-7645-8476-6
- Home Maintenance For Dummies 0-7645-5215-5
- Horses For Dummies 0-7645-9797-3
- Jewelry Making & Beading For Dummies 0-7645-2571-9
- Orchids For Dummies 0-7645-6759-4
- Puppies For Dummies 0-7645-5255-4
- Rock Guitar For Dummies 0-7645-5356-9
- Sewing For Dummies 0-7645-6847-7
- Singing For Dummies 0-7645-2475-5

INTERNET & DIGITAL MEDIA

0-470-04529-9   0-470-04894-8

Also available:
- Blogging For Dummies 0-471-77084-1
- Digital Photography For Dummies 0-7645-9802-3
- Digital Photography All-in-One Desk Reference For Dummies 0-470-03743-1
- Digital SLR Cameras and Photography For Dummies 0-7645-9803-1
- eBay Business All-in-One Desk Reference For Dummies 0-7645-8438-3
- HDTV For Dummies 0-470-09673-X
- Home Entertainment PCs For Dummies 0-470-05523-5
- MySpace For Dummies 0-470-09529-6
- Search Engine Optimization For Dummies 0-471-97998-8
- Skype For Dummies 0-470-04891-3
- The Internet For Dummies 0-7645-8996-2
- Wiring Your Digital Home For Dummies 0-471-91830-X

* Separate Canadian edition also available
† Separate U.K. edition also available

Available wherever books are sold. For more information or to order direct: U.S. customers visit www.dummies.com or call 1-877-762-2974.
U.K. customers visit www.wileyeurope.com or call 0800 243407. Canadian customers visit www.wiley.ca or call 1-800-567-4797.

 WILEY

SPORTS, FITNESS, PARENTING, RELIGION & SPIRITUALITY

0-471-76871-5

0-7645-7841-3

Also available:
- Catholicism For Dummies
  0-7645-5391-7
- Exercise Balls For Dummies
  0-7645-5623-1
- Fitness For Dummies
  0-7645-7851-0
- Football For Dummies
  0-7645-3936-1
- Judaism For Dummies
  0-7645-5299-6
- Potty Training For Dummies
  0-7645-5417-4
- Buddhism For Dummies
  0-7645-5359-3

- Pregnancy For Dummies
  0-7645-4483-7 †
- Ten Minute Tone-Ups For Dummies
  0-7645-7207-5
- NASCAR For Dummies
  0-7645-7681-X
- Religion For Dummies
  0-7645-5264-3
- Soccer For Dummies
  0-7645-5229-5
- Women in the Bible For Dummies
  0-7645-8475-8

TRAVEL

0-7645-7749-2

0-7645-6945-7

Also available:
- Alaska For Dummies
  0-7645-7746-8
- Cruise Vacations For Dummies
  0-7645-6941-4
- England For Dummies
  0-7645-4276-1
- Europe For Dummies
  0-7645-7529-5
- Germany For Dummies
  0-7645-7823-5
- Hawaii For Dummies
  0-7645-7402-7

- Italy For Dummies
  0-7645-7386-1
- Las Vegas For Dummies
  0-7645-7382-9
- London For Dummies
  0-7645-4277-X
- Paris For Dummies
  0-7645-7630-5
- RV Vacations For Dummies
  0-7645-4442-X
- Walt Disney World & Orlando
  For Dummies
  0-7645-9660-8

GRAPHICS, DESIGN & WEB DEVELOPMENT

0-7645-8815-X

0-7645-9571-7

Also available:
- 3D Game Animation For Dummies
  0-7645-8789-7
- AutoCAD 2006 For Dummies
  0-7645-8925-3
- Building a Web Site For Dummies
  0-7645-7144-3
- Creating Web Pages For Dummies
  0-470-08030-2
- Creating Web Pages All-in-One Desk
  Reference For Dummies
  0-7645-4345-8
- Dreamweaver 8 For Dummies
  0-7645-9649-7

- InDesign CS2 For Dummies
  0-7645-9572-5
- Macromedia Flash 8 For Dummies
  0-7645-9691-8
- Photoshop CS2 and Digital
  Photography For Dummies
  0-7645-9580-6
- Photoshop Elements 4 For Dummies
  0-471-77483-9
- Syndicating Web Sites with RSS Feeds
  For Dummies
  0-7645-8848-6
- Yahoo! SiteBuilder For Dummies
  0-7645-9800-7

NETWORKING, SECURITY, PROGRAMMING & DATABASES

0-7645-7728-X

0-471-74940-0

Also available:
- Access 2007 For Dummies
  0-470-04612-0
- ASP.NET 2 For Dummies
  0-7645-7907-X
- C# 2005 For Dummies
  0-7645-9704-3
- Hacking For Dummies
  0-470-05235-X
- Hacking Wireless Networks
  For Dummies
  0-7645-9730-2
- Java For Dummies
  0-470-08716-1

- Microsoft SQL Server 2005 For Dummies
  0-7645-7755-7
- Networking All-in-One Desk Reference
  For Dummies
  0-7645-9939-9
- Preventing Identity Theft For Dummies
  0-7645-7336-5
- Telecom For Dummies
  0-471-77085-X
- Visual Studio 2005 All-in-One Desk
  Reference For Dummies
  0-7645-9775-2
- XML For Dummies
  0-7645-8845-1

Printed in the United States of America
ED-11-07-12